Caroline M. Kirkland

Patriotic Eloquence

Being selections from one hundred years of national literature

Caroline M. Kirkland

Patriotic Eloquence
Being selections from one hundred years of national literature

ISBN/EAN: 9783337308759

Printed in Europe, USA, Canada, Australia, Japan

Cover: Foto ©ninafisch / pixelio.de

More available books at **www.hansebooks.com**

PATRIOTIC ELOQUENCE:

BEING

Selections from One Hundred Years of National Literature.

COMPILED FOR THE USE OF SCHOOLS IN READING
AND SPEAKING.

BY
MRS. C. M. KIRKLAND.

NEW YORK:
CHARLES SCRIBNER & CO., 654 BROADWAY.
INGHAM & BRAGG, CLEVELAND, OHIO.
1866.

INTRODUCTION.

In Dr. Young's Night-Thought Days, the public was supposed to be so little informed on the claims of "great heirs of fame" of other times, that the learned and courtly Doctor thought it necessary, on mentioning the name of Demosthenes, to subjoin an explanatory note setting forth that the said Demosthenes was "a great Grecian orator."

We would not be suspected of entertaining a similar idea respecting the interest felt, here and now, in the noble speakers who contributed to enlighten and inspire the popular mind, from the moment of the first "glorious discontent" to the crowning hour when the UNION was celebrated in undying words by a consummate orator of our own day. The happy and generous prescience of the earlier advocates of Freedom, and the splendid enthusiasm of him who celebrated its triumph are universally recognized and honored among us, and the Anglo-Saxon tongue affords no new epithet with which to enhance our praise of the eloquent fathers and sons of American Liberty.

Yet in the haste of our new American life it is not quite certain that the thoughts and feelings which have become part of the very texture of life with us, will, without care on our part, be equally precious to our children. Intrinsic value is not always enough to secure regard. Family jewels must be new set for the gay young bride, and grandpapa's buckles made into "three seal rings" for the dashing heir. The humble citizen who undertakes these mechanical works must catch the fashion of the day and make the gems portable and attractive, or juvenile impatience and fastidiousness will condemn to the casket what ought to be worn on the breast and finger. The good Book says of guiding thoughts—" Thou shalt *teach them diligently to thy children*, and shalt talk of them when thou sittest in thine house, and when thou walkest by the way, and when thou liest down, and when thou risest up. And thou shalt bind them for a sign upon thy hand, and they shall be as frontlets between thine eyes."

So let it be with the grand inspiring sentiments of our own times. Let them be an ever-present shield against degeneracy.

This little book pretends to no completeness as a repository of American oratory. Its aim is simply patriotic. I wish to recall the noble spirit of our fathers as an example and inspiration to the young people who owe them so much. The prosperity and happiness they won for us seem but too likely to make us forget their services. The grand results of their protest against oppression are so satisfying, that we sometimes forget to recur to the principles on which they acted, and in defence of which they perilled all. Reverence for them and their doings needs to be kept alive in the minds of our children by every possible means. Particularly in the course of their education should we be careful to store their memories with the thoughts and expressions once so potent as watchwords of freedom, lest the excitements of a life hurried and enterprising as that which our unexampled condition opens for them, should make them sordid and unreflecting, intent on gain and pleasure, rather than on nobleness and devotion to duty.

As specimens of artistic eloquence, these extracts do not profess to claim the highest place. More sounding periods, more labored sentences, more showy and fascinating declamation might easily be found. But this early American eloquence came warm from the heart; its argumentative part was inspired by reason, experience, high principle and manly courage. Its charm is its truth and sincerity; its power lies in its confident appeal to conscience, honor and common sense; the materials of its pathos were real sufferings and impending ruin. Its relations with our present daily life are close and important; its relations to our future well-being perhaps even more so. It has the double value of simplicity and a sublime earnestness—qualities which we may well desire to see perpetuated in our American public speaking. It offers a dignified manly protest against the flashy tone too popular in our day, by the contrast it exhibits between the pithy things men say when great interests and high principles are at stake, and the floods of talk they pour forth when inspired only by the desire to display their powers or gain some petty object.

In making my selections, I found I could not do justice to the spirit of the time, or give a faithful picture of the state of things, without adding a few specimens of the Parliamentary speeches of that excited period. There were noble souls on both sides of the water, and men who spoke for Liberty and in our favor at the foot of the throne whose occupant was determined on our humiliation. They deserve our gratitude and our remembrance; for their passionate appeals for justice to us at once advanced our cause there and inspired the hearts of our patriots at home. They are to be honored as disinterested friends who adopted our cause and became our advocates, from a sense of justice and right, and with no motive of personal interest or mere partiality.

The plain Saxon English of most of the speeches is also, in my view, no slight recommendation to them as exercises in speaking and reading. Fashion infringes too much upon this; and although the best writers of our language are now trying by precept and example to return to the simplicity and purity of elder times, the popular tendency is in an opposite direction. It has become really hard, in our country, to write and speak plain, pure English, such foothold has a mixed and ambitious diction obtained. I would gladly habituate the ears of our young people to the language of Dryden, Pope, Addison, Goldsmith, as used by Fisher Ames, Patrick Henry, Franklin, Hamilton, and Washington.

In order to give some slight historic value to the extracts, I have thought it well to arrange them in the order of time, and to add, occasionally, a few words explanatory of the circumstances and feeling of the hour. History is made more interesting, and learned more easily in proportion as we can make it personal instead of abstract. The men who act are more engaging than the deeds they accomplish; stirring speeches make more impression upon fresh young minds than the grand results which those speeches helped to bring forth. As a companion to the study of history, this slight aid may prove useful.

With a similar idea, I have interspersed the extracts with some of the more popular songs of our early and struggling days, and with other verses breathing a kindred spirit. The old songs have no great poetic value; some of them are even uncouth in their versification, and all have an old-fashioned jingle which does not accord very well with the music of Tennyson, or the stately elegance of Bryant. Yet there is a soul in them, and they have a right to live. Our children should not forget or despise them, but keep them sacredly, as we do the quaint old china of our grandmothers, or the centipedal tables which bear the aroma, if they never graced the narrow cabin, of the May Flower. I have never yet happened to find a school-boy or girl who knows anything about "Adams and Liberty," or "Liberty Tree," or who could repeat Hail Columbia from beginning to end.

Let us not so worship the dress of things, that we undervalue the Spirit, which is life.   C. M. K.

NEW YORK, *July*, 1860.

NOTE.—This work not having been brought by Mrs. Kirkland beyond the beginning of the Rebellion, it has been thought best to give additional value to the collection by introducing some specimens of the oratory and poetry which have been called forth by the events of the past four years. It is proper also to mention that the notes, which formed a part of the compiler's original plan, have been added by another hand.

NEW YORK, *November*, 1865.

CONTENTS.

Ex.			PAGE
I.	Ministry vs. the People	John Dickinson.	1
II.	Protest against Injustice	Col. Isaac Barré.	2
III.	Eloquence of James Otis	Mrs. Child.	4
IV.	The Liberty Tree		5
V.	Colonial Resistance Defended	Lord Chatham.	6
VI.	A Plea for Representation	Lord Camden.	9
VII.	The Glory of Liberty	Jonathan Mayhew.	10
VIII.	The Way to obtain Supplies from America	Thomas Pownall.	12
IX.	Exhortation to Self-Defence	Josiah Quincy.	13
X.	A Song to the tune of "Hearts of Oak,"	John Dickinson.	14
XI.	Timely Warnings	Thomas Pownall.	16
XII.	Rebuke of the British Ministers	Col. Barré.	18
XIII.	First Anniversary of the "Boston Massacre,"	James Lovell.	20
XIV.	The Contrast	Earl of Chatham.	22
XV.	Anniversary Oration	Dr. Joseph Warren.	23
XVI.	Rules for Reducing a Great Empire to a Small One, Gentleman's Magazine.		25
XVII.	Protest against British Aggression	Sons of Liberty.	27
XVIII.	King George's Tea-Party		28
XIX.	An Old Man's Advice	Earl of Chatham.	30
XX.	Abandonment of Taxation	Bishop of St. Asaph's.	31
XXI.	True and False Dignity	Edmund Burke.	33
XXII.	Great Britain's Right to Tax America	Edmund Burke.	35
XXIII.	Address to the People of Great Britain, Sept. 1774		36
XXIV.	Gen. Gage and the Ministry	Edmund Burke.	38
XXV.	Inexpediency of Maintaining Troops in Boston	Earl of Chatham.	39
XXVI.	Tribute to the Continental Congress	Earl of Chatham.	41
XXVII.	Attitude of America towards Great Britain	James Wilson.	42
XXVIII.	The Call to Arms		44
XXIX.	Difference between Rebellion and Revolution	John Wilkes.	45
XXX.	Opinions of an English Traveller in America	Temple Luttrell.	47
XXXI.	Anniversary Oration	Dr. Joseph Warren.	49
XXXII.	Useless Toil	Lord Camden.	50
XXXIII.	The Revenue Question	Edmund Burke.	52
XXXIV.	Spirit of Enterprise in New England	Edmund Burke.	54

CONTENTS.

Ex.		Page
XXXV.	Lexington....................................*Oliver Wendell Holmes.*	56
XXXVI.	Address of the Congress of Massachusetts Bay to the Inhabitants of Great Britain...	58
XXXVII.	War Inevitable..............................*Patrick Henry.*	60
XXXVIII.	Conflict of Duty and Inclination..............*Earl of Effingham.*	62
XXXIX.	Warren's Address before the Battle of Bunker Hill....*J. Pierpont.*	64
XL.	Eulogium on Gen. Joseph Warren, who fell at the Battle of Bunker Hill, June 17, 1775..	65
XLI.	Bunker Hill..............................*Alfred B. Street.*	66
XLII.	Declaration of Rights by the Continental Congress...............	68
XLIII.	Parliamentary Levity Reproved..............*Earl of Shelburne.*	70
XLIV.	Effects of the Policy of England....................*John Wilkes.*	71
XLV.	Song, 1776...	73
XLVI.	The Duties of Patriots..........................*John Rutledge.*	74
XLVII.	Funeral Oration..............................*Dr. Morton.*	76
XLVIII.	Instructions to Mr. Ezra Sargent, a Delegate to the Continental Congress, by the Inhabitants of the Town of Malden, Mass...	78
XLIX.	Song...	79
L.	Assertion of the Rights of America..........*Richard Henry Lee.*	80
LI.	Declaration of Independence, by the United States of America in Congress Assembled......................*Thomas Jefferson.*	82
LII.	Supposed Speech of John Adams, in favor of the Declaration of Independence..............................*Daniel Webster.*	86
LIII.	War and Washington................*Jonathan Mitchel Sewall.*	89
LIV.	Address to the American Troops before the Battle of Long Island, August 27, 1776...........................*Gen. Washington.*	90
LV.	Charge to the Grand Jury of South Carolina.......*Judge Drayton.*	91
LVI.	Song of Marion's Men....................*William Cullen Bryant.*	93
LVII.	Expostulation with Parliament....................*Edmund Burke.*	95
LVIII.	Proclamation................................*Gen. Burgoyne.*	97
LIX.	Answer to Burgoyne's Proclamation............................	99
LX.	A Camp Ballad............................*Francis Hopkinson.*	101
LXI.	Charge to the Grand Jury of New York..................*John Jay.*	102
LXII.	Barbarity of Employing Indians in War........*Earl of Chatham.*	104
LXIII.	Protest against Ministerial Misconduct..........*Earl of Chatham.*	106
LXIV.	Folly of Attempting to Conquer America........*Earl of Chatham.*	107
LXV.	A Hymn....................................*William Billings.*	109
LXVI.	On the Choice of a War with America or with France, *Charles James Fox.*	110
LXVII.	America Lost to Great Britain......................*John Wilkes.*	111
LXVIII.	Address to the States, by the Continental Congress, May 26, 1779..	113
LXIX.	Eulogium on those who have Fallen in the Contest with Great Britain, delivered July 5, 1779......*Hugh Henry Brackenridge.*	114

CONTENTS.

Ex.		Page
LXX.	Hymn at the Consecration of Pulaski's Banner, 1779, *H. W. Longfellow.*	116
LXXI.	Answer to Inquiries as to the Condition of America, Paris, 1780 *John Adams.*	117
LXXII.	Anniversary Oration, delivered March 5, 1781......*Thomas Dawes.*	119
LXXIII.	Address from the Legislature of the State of New York to their Constituents, March 13, 1781................................	120
LXXIV.	An Englishman's Opinion of the American War.....*William Pitt.*	123
LXXV.	The Attack on Fort Griswold.........................*T. K. Potter.*	124
LXXVI.	In Memoriam.......................................*Philip Freneau.*	125
LXXVII.	Circular Letter from Congress to the States, December 17, 1781....	126
LXXVIII.	Return of British Fugitives Advocated............*Patrick Henry.*	127
LXXIX.	Election Sermon...*Dr. Stiles.*	129
LXXX.	Address..*Gen. Washington.*	131
LXXXI.	On Disbanding the Army......................*David Humphreys.*	132
LXXXII.	National Dependence upon God..............*Benjamin Franklin.*	133
LXXXIII.	The Federal Constitution........................*James Wilson.*	134
LXXXIV.	" " ....*Benjamin Franklin.*	136
LXXXV.	" " ....*Edmund Randolph.*	137
LXXXVI.	" " ....*Patrick Henry.*	139
LXXXVII.	" " ....*Patrick Henry.*	140
LXXXVIII.	" " ....*Edmund Randolph.*	142
LXXXIX.	Definition of Government............?........*Wm. Gilmore Simms.*	144
XC.	Inaugural Address to both Houses of Congress, April 30, 1789, *Washington.*	145
XCI.	Washington as President.....................*Charles James Fox.*	147
XCII.	The Toast......................................*Francis Hopkinson.*	149
XCIII.	On the Danger of Violating our Treaties.............*Fisher Ames.*	149
XCIV.	Shall we break our Faith...........................*Fisher Ames.*	151
XCV.	Hail Columbia...............................*Samuel Hopkinson.*	153
XCVI.	Farewell Address.................................*Washington.*	154
XCVII.	" " continued.............................. "	156
XCVIII.	" " " .... "	158
XCIX.	" " " .... "	159
C.	Adams and Liberty.......................................	161
CI.	Necessity for Preparation for a War with France. *Robert Goodloe Harper.*	163
CII.	Injustice of the Alien and Sedition Laws.........*John Randolph.*	164
CIII.	Eulogy on Washington.............................*Fisher Ames.*	166
CIX.	Washington a Model for the Formation of Character...*Wm. Wirt.*	168
CV.	Washington..*Eliza Cook.*	170
CVI.	Eulogium on Washington.........................*C. Phillips.*	171
CVII.	Genius of Washington.........................*Edwin P. Whipple.*	172

CONTENTS.

Ex.		Page
CVIII.	Inaugural Address.............................*Thomas Jefferson*.	174
CIX.	Against the Repeal of the Judiciary Act.......*Gouverneur Morris*.	175
CX.	Necessity of Avoiding a War with France.........*De Witt Clinton*.	177
CXI.	Necessity of Preparing for a War with France..*Gouverneur Morris*.	178
CXII.	Song...	180
CXIII.	Jefferson's Purchase of the Louisiana Territory..*Henry S. Randall*.	181
CXIV.	War Discountenanced.............................*John Randolph*.	182
CXV.	Justice Demanded for the Soldiers of the Revolution..*P. Sprague*.	184
CXVI.	Pensioners' Muster, Aug. 3, 1807...............................	185
CXVII.	Remonstrance against the War of 1812-15......*John Randolph*.	186
CXVIII.	Reasons for Prosecuting the War...............*John C. Calhoun*.	188
CXIX.	The Star-Spangled Banner.....................*Francis Scott Key*.	190
CXX.	On the Conduct of the War of 1812-15..............*Henry Clay*.	191
CXXI.	Right of Opposition............................*Daniel Webster*.	193
CXXII.	Song......................................*James Gates Percival*.	194
CXXIII.	Address to the army at New Orleans, Dec. 18, 1814, *Andrew Jackson*.	195
CXXIV.	Retrospective View of the War of 1812-15............*Henry Clay*.	196
CXXV.	The American Flag.......................*Joseph Rodman Drake*.	198
CXXVI.	The Missouri Compromise.....................*James Tallmadge*.	199
CXXVII.	Our Country............................*William Jewell Pabodie*.	202
CXXVIII.	Liberty and Greatness........................*Hugh S. Legaré*.	203
CXXIX.	The American Revolution...................*John Quincy Adams*.	205
CXXX.	Ode composed after listening to the Oration of which the above forms a part...................................*William Cutter*.	206
CXXXI.	The Example of America.......................*Francis Jeffrey*.	207
CXXXII.	The Ship of State..........................*H. W. Longfellow*.	208
CXXXIII.	Bunker Hill Monument........................*Daniel Webster*.	209
CXXXIV.	Ode for the Fourth of July....................*Charles Sprague*.	211
CXXXV.	Parting Address to La Fayette, Sept. 7th, 1825..*John Quincy Adams*.	211
CXXXVI.	Reply to President Adams.........................*La Fayette*.	213
CXXXVII.	New England and the Union.....................*S. S. Prentiss*.	214
CXXXVIII.	New England's Dead..........................*Isaac McLellan*.	215
CXXXIX.	Appeal to the Republic............................*Joseph Story*.	217
CXL.	National Recollections the Foundation of National Character. *Edward Everett*.	219
CXLI.	The Young American......................*Alexander H. Everett*.	220
CXLII.	The Sword and the Staff...................*John Quincy Adams*.	221
CXLIII.	Consequences of American Independence..........*Virgil Maxcy*.	223
CXLIV.	Devotion to Country.........................*Alfred B. Street*.	224
CXLV.	American History.........................*Gulian C. Verplanck*.	225
CXLVI.	Ennobling Recollections of the Revolution......*Robert Y. Hayne*.	227
CXLVII.	Ode..*Anne C. Lynch*.	228

Ex.		Page
CXLVIII.	Bond of Union between North and South..........*Daniel Webster.*	229
CXLIX.	The Union Must be preserved........................ " "	231
CL.	Union and Liberty.............................*Thomas S. Grimke.*	232
CLI.	Appeal to the People of South Carolina..........*Andrew Jackson.*	233
CLII.	Indian's Farewell Speech..........................*Black Hawk.*	236
CLIII.	Farewell Address to the People of the United States, 1837. *Andrew Jackson.*	237
CLIV.	The United States Flag....................*William Ross Wallace.*	238
CLV.	Secession Doctrines Combated....................*Daniel Webster.*	240
CLVI.	The Birth-Day of Washington....................*Rufus Choate.*	242
CLVII.	"E Pluribus Unum"..........................*John Pierpont.*	243
CLVIII.	Remonstrance against the War with Mexico, 1847....*Thos. Corwin.*	244
CLIX.	Injustice of the War against Mexico............*John M. Berrien.*	246
CLX.	Civil War Deprecated..............................*Henry Clay.*	247
CLXI.	Impossibility of Peaceable Secession.............*Daniel Webster.*	249
CLXII.	On the Admission of California into the Union...*Wm. H. Seward.*	250
CLXIII.	Liberty Triumphant............................*Daniel Webster.*	252
CLXIV.	A Fourth of July Address on Secession............*Francis Lieber.*	253
CLXV.	Elegy.................................*Thomas Buchanan Read.*	256
CLXVI.	The American Sailor............................*R. F. Stockton.*	257
CLXVII.	Old Ironsides............................*Oliver Wendell Holmes.*	258
CLXVIII.	Eighty Years Ago..............................*Charles Sprague.*	259
CLXIX.	Reasons for Celebrating the Fourth of July.....*Abraham Lincoln.*	260
CLXX.	The Fourth of July................................*J. Pierpont.*	261
CLXXI.	The Crisis...............................*John Greenleaf Whittier.*	262
CLXXII.	Secession as viewed by a Virginian.................*Joseph Segar.*	263
CLXXIII.	False Prophets..............................*Emeline S. Smith.*	264
CLXXIV.	Shall we give up the Union..................*Daniel S. Dickinson.*	265
CLXXV.	A Song on our Country and her Flag.............*Francis Lieber.*	266
CLXXVI.	Never, or Now..........................*Oliver Wendell Holmes.*	268
CLXXVII.	Appeal to Secessionists.....................*Daniel S. Dickinson.*	269
CLXXVIII.	Unseen Spirits...	270
CLXXIX.	"All of Them."..	271
CLXXX.	Stand by the Flag................................*Joseph Holt.*	273
CLXXXI.	Kentucky....................................*Sophia H. Oliver.*	275
CLXXXII.	Consequences of Secession......................*Edward Everett.*	276
CLXXXIII.	The Massachusetts Volunteers......................*W. S. Newall.*	277
CLXXXIV.	Marching On................................*George W. Bungay.*	279
CLXXXV.	Secession of Louisiana Considered...............*Edward Everett.*	279
CLXXXVI.	Sword and Plough.......................*Charles Dawson Shanley.*	281
CLXXXVII.	The Southern Confederacy, if recognized, becomes a Foreign Power, *Edward Everett.*	282
CLXXXVIII.	The whole Story told in Rhyme.................................	283

CONTENTS.

Ex.		Page
CLXXXIX.	Army Hymn............*Oliver Wendell Holmes.*	285
CXC.	A War Hymn............*Theodore Tilton.*	285
CXCI.	On Board the Cumberland, March 7th, 1862......*George H. Boker.*	286
CXCII.	The Varuna............*George H. Boker.*	289
CXCIII.	Thanksgiving-Eve, 1862............	290
CXCIV.	The Picket Guard............	291
CXCV.	No Party Now—All for our Country............*Francis Lieber.*	293
CXCVI.	The Fulfillment of Destiny............*Roscoe Conkling.*	295
CXCVII.	The Heart of the War............*Dr. J. G. Holland.*	297
CXCVIII.	Address at the Consecration of the Soldiers' Cemetery, at Gettysburg, November, 1863............*Abraham Lincoln.*	300
CXCIX.	Dirge for a Soldier............*George H. Boker.*	301
CC.	After the Battle............	302
CCI.	A Thanksgiving Hymn............*Park Benjamin.*	303
CCII.	I have a Country............	304
CCIII.	Second Inaugural Address of President Lincoln, March 4, 1865.....	305
CCIV.	Restoration of the Flag to Fort Sumter, April 14, 1865, *Henry Ward Beecher.*	307
CCV.	Abraham Lincoln............*Rev. J. P. Thompson.*	308
CCVI.	Abraham Lincoln............*W. C. Bryant.*	310
CCVII.	Commemorative Address on the Death of President Lincoln, *Parke Godwin.*	310
CCVIII.	Abraham Lincoln............	312
CCIX.	Future of the Freedmen............*Andrew Johnson.*	313
CCX.	Nature and Destiny of our Government.......... " "	316
CCXI.	Dialogue—The Old Continental............	318
CCXII.	Dialogue—The Yankee Marksman............*William Bentley Fowle.*	321
CCXIII.	Dialogue—Impressment of an American Seaman....*Epes Sargent.*	323
CCXIV.	Dialogue—John Bull and Son............*William Bentley Fowle.*	329
CCXV.	Dialogue between Mr. Dole, Indian Commissioner, and Opothleyoholo and Lagarash, Indian Chiefs, 1862......*Rebellion Record.*	331
CCXVI.	Indian Names............*Lydia Huntley Sigourney.*	333

PATRIOTIC ELOQUENCE.

EXERCISE I.—*MINISTRY* vs. *THE PEOPLE.*

Speech delivered in the Assembly of Pennsylvania, May, 1764, on the Occasion of a Petition from that Body, praying the King for a Change of Government.

JOHN DICKINSON.*

WE are not the subjects of ministers, and therefore it is not to be wondered at if they do not feel that tenderness for us that a good king will always feel for his people. Men are not born ministers. Their ambition raises them to authority; and when possessed of it, one established principle with them seems to be, "never to deviate from a precedent of power."

Indeed, Sir, it is vain to expect that where the spirit of liberty is maintained among a people, public contests should not also be maintained. Those who govern and those who are governed, seldom think that they can gain too much on one another. Power is like the ocean, not easily admitting limits to be fixed to it. It must be in motion. Storms, indeed, are not desirable, but a long, dead calm is not to be looked for; perhaps not even to be wished for. Let us not, then, in expectation of smooth seas and an undisturbed course, too rashly venture our little vessel, that hath sailed round our own well-known shores, upon the midst of the un-

---

* Gov. Dickinson, at this time a member of the Pennsylvania Assembly, was several times afterward a member of the general Congress, and lost some popularity by opposing the Declaration of Independence, on the ground that we were not strong enough, as a people, to take such a hazardous step without more certain assurance of foreign assistance. He vindicated his patriotism, however, by being, as he himself said when attacked on the subject, the only member of Congress who marched, immediately after the Declaration, to meet the enemy!

tried deep, without first being fully convinced that her make is strong enough to bear the weather she may meet with, and that she is well provided for so long and dangerous a voyage.

No man, Sir, among us, has denied, or will deny that this province must stake on the event of the present attempt, liberties founded on the acknowledged rights of human nature, liberties that ought to be immortal! The inhabitants of remote countries, impelled by that love of liberty which an all-wise Providence has planted in the human heart, deserting their native soil, committed themselves with their helpless families to the mercy of winds and waves, and braved all the terrors of an unknown wilderness, in the hope of enjoying in these woods the exercise of those invaluable rights, which some unhappy circumstance had denied to mankind in every other part of the earth.

Thus, Sir, the people of Pennsylvania may be said to have purchased an inheritance in its constitution, at a prodigious price; they have not hitherto been disappointed in their wishes; they have obtained the blessings they sought for; and I can not believe, unless the strongest evidence be offered, that they are now willing to part with that which has cost them so much toil and expense.

Ex. II.—*PROTEST AGAINST INJUSTICE.*

Speech delivered in the British Parliament, 1765.

COL. ISAAC BARRÉ.[*]

SIR:—I have listened to the honorable member who spoke last, with astonishment. Has he forgotten the history of the colonies?—"Will these Americans, children planted by our care, nourished by our indulgence, protected by our arms, refuse their mite?"

[*] Col. Barré, a person of considerable distinction in the British Parliament, was a stanch friend of America throughout our Revolutionary struggle. His claim to a superior knowledge of this country was not unfounded, he having been with General Wolfe during the campaign in Canada, and fought by his side at the siege of Quebec. It was in consequence of a severe wound received in this battle that Col. Barré, after an interval of thirty years, lost his sight, and remained blind for twelve years before his death, retaining, however, the cheerfulness and vivacity which had always characterized him, to the last.

They planted by *your* care! No; your oppression planted them in America. They fled from your tyranny, to a then uncultivated and inhospitable country, where they exposed themselves to almost all the hardships to which human nature is liable; and among others, to the cruelty of a savage foe, the most subtle, and, I will take upon me to say, the most formidable of any people upon the face of the earth; and yet, actuated by principles of true English liberty, they met all hardships with pleasure, compared with those they suffered in their own country, from the hands of those who should have been their friends.

They nourished up by *your* indulgence! They grew by your neglect of them. As soon as you began to care about them, that care was exercised in sending persons to rule them, in one department or another, who were, perhaps, the deputies of deputies to some members of this house, sent to spy out their liberties, to misrepresent their actions, and to prey upon them; men whose behavior, on many occasions, has caused the blood of those sons of liberty to recoil within them; men promoted to the highest seat of justice; some, who, to my knowledge, were glad, by going to a foreign country, to escape being brought to the bar of a court of justice, in their own.

They protected by *your* arms! They have nobly taken up arms in your defence; have exerted a valor, amidst their constant and laborious industry, for the defence of a country whose frontier was drenched in blood, while its interior parts yielded all its little savings to your emoluments.

And, believe me; remember I this day told you so, that the same spirit of freedom which actuated that people at first, will accompany them still. But prudence forbids me to explain myself further. Heaven knows, I do not at this time speak from motives of party heat; what I deliver are the genuine sentiments of my heart.

However superior to me in general knowledge and experience the respectable body of this House may be, yet I claim to know more of America than most of you, having seen and been conversant in that country. The people, I believe, are as truly loyal as any subjects the king has, but a people jealous of their liberties, and who will vindicate them if ever they should be violated. But the subject is too delicate; I will say no more.

Ex. III.—*ELOQUENCE OF JAMES OTIS.**

(Supposed Speech in Congress, 1765.)

MRS. CHILD.

ENGLAND may as well dam up the waters of the Nile with bulrushes, as to fetter the step of freedom, more proud and firm in this youthful land, than where she treads the sequestered glens of Scotland, or couches herself among the magnificent mountains of Switzerland. Arbitrary principles, like those against which we now contend, have cost one king of England his life, another his crown—and they may yet cost a third his most flourishing colonies.

We are two millions—one-fifth fighting men. We are bold and vigorous, and we call no man master. To the nation from whom we are proud to derive our origin, we ever were, and ever will be, ready to yield unforced assistance; but it is not, and it never can be, extorted.

Some have sneeringly asked, "Are the Americans too poor to pay a few pounds on stamped paper?" No! America, thanks to God and herself, is rich. But the right to take ten pounds implies the right to take a thousand; and what must be the wealth that avarice, aided by power, can not exhaust? True, the spectre is now small; but the shadow he casts before him is huge enough to darken all this fair land. Others, in sentimental style, talk of the immense debt of gratitude which we owe to England. And what is the amount of this debt? Why, truly, it is the same that the young lion owes to the dam, which has brought it forth on the solitude of the mountain, or left it amid the winds and storms of the desert.

We plunged into the wave, with the great charter of freedom in our teeth, because the faggot and torch were behind us. We have waked this new world from its savage lethargy, forests have been prostrated in our path, towns and cities have grown up as suddenly as the flowers of the tropics, and the fires in our autumnal woods are scarcely more rapid than the increase of our wealth and population. And

---

* This spirited composition, although the production of an author of our own times, is inserted here as a successful imitation of the style of Mr. Otis, who was among the most vigorous and eloquent speakers of his day. He was a man of commanding character and versatile talents, and a leader of the popular party in its earlier development. He did not live to take part in the Revolution proper, but was killed by a stroke of lightning in May, 1772.

do we owe all this to the kind succor of the mother country? No! we owe it to the tyranny that drove us from her—to the pelting storms which invigorated our helpless infancy.

But perhaps others will say, "We ask no money from your gratitude—we only demand that you should pay your own expenses." And who, I pray, is to judge of their necessity? Why, the king—(and with all due reverence to his sacred majesty, he understands the real wants of his distant subjects as little as he does the language of the Choctaws.) Who is to judge concerning the frequency of these demands? The ministry. Who is to judge whether the money is properly expended? The cabinet behind the throne. In every instance, those who take are to judge for those who pay; if this system is suffered to go into operation, we shall have reason to esteem it a great privilege, that rain and dew do not depend upon parliament, otherwise they would soon be taxed and dried.

But, thanks to God! there is freedom enough left upon earth to resist such monstrous injustice. The flame of liberty is extinguished in Greece and Rome, but the light of its glowing embers is still bright and strong on the shores of America. Actuated by its sacred influence, we will resist unto death. But we will not countenance anarchy and misrule. The wrongs that a desperate community have heaped upon their enemies, shall be amply and speedily repaired. Still, it may be well for some proud men to remember, that a fire is lighted in these colonies, which one breath of their king may kindle into such fury that all the blood of all England can not extinguish it.

Ex. IV.—*THE LIBERTY TREE.**

In a chariot of light from the regions of day,
  The goddess of Liberty came;
Ten thousand celestials directed the way,
  And hither conducted the dame.

---

* The "Liberty Tree" was a great elm in Boston, under which the opponents of the Stamp Act were accustomed to assemble. Persons supposed to be in favor of this detested act, were hung in effigy on the branches of this tree.

A fair budding branch from the gardens above,
　　Where millions with millions agree,
She brought in her hand, as a pledge of her love,
　　And the plant she named Liberty Tree.

The celestial exotic struck deep in the ground,
　　Like a native it flourished and bore;
The fame of its fruit drew the nations around,
　　To seek out this peaceable shore.
Unmindful of names or distinctions they came,
　　For freemen like brothers agree;
With one spirit endued, they one friendship pursued,
　　And their temple was Liberty Tree.

Beneath this fair tree, like the patriarchs of old,
　　Their bread in contentment they ate,
Unvexed with the troubles of silver and gold,
　　The cares of the grand and the great.
With timber and tar they old England supplied,
　　And supported her power on the sea;
Her battles they fought without getting a groat,
　　For the honor of Liberty Tree.

But hear, oh ye swains, ('tis a tale most profane,)
　　How all the tyrannical powers,
King, commons and lords, are uniting amain,
　　To cut down this guardian of ours.
From the east to the west blow the trumpet to arms!
　　Through the land let the sound of it flee;
Let the far and the near, all unite with a cheer,
　　In defence of our Liberty Tree.

Ex. V.—*COLONIAL RESISTANCE DEFENDED.*

Speech in Parliament, 1766.

LORD CHATHAM.*

SIR, I rejoice that America has resisted. Three millions of people, so dead to all the feelings of liberty, as voluntarily

---

* William Pitt, Earl of Chatham, was one of the greatest of British statesmen and orators. From the time of his earliest remonstrance against the Stamp Act, to the day when he fell in a fit in the House of Lords, and was

to submit to be slaves, would have been fit instruments to make slaves of the rest. With the enemy at their back, with our bayonets at their breasts, perhaps the Americans would have submitted to the imposition; but it would have been taking an ungenerous, an unjust advantage. I am no courtier of America—I stand up for this kingdom. I maintain that the parliament has a right to bind, to restrain America. Our legislative power over the colonies is sovereign and supreme. When it ceases to be so, I would advise every gentleman to sell his lands, if he can, and embark for that country. When two countries are connected together, like England and her colonies, without being incorporated, the one must necessarily govern; the greater must rule the less, but so rule it, as not to contradict the fundamental principles that are common to both.

If the gentleman does not understand the difference between internal and external taxes, I can not help it; but there is a plain distinction between taxes levied for the purpose of raising a revenue, and duties imposed for the regulation of trade, for the accommodation of the subject, although, in the consequences, some revenue might incidentally arise from the latter.

The gentleman asks, when were the colonies emancipated? I desire to know when they were made slaves? But I dwell not upon words. When I had the honor of serving his majesty, I availed myself of the means of information which I derived from my office; I speak, therefore, from knowledge. My materials were good: I was at pains to collect, to digest, to consider them, and I will be bold to affirm, that the profits to Great Britain from the trade of the colonies through all its branches, is two millions a year. This is the fund that carried you triumphantly through the last war. This is the price that America pays you for her protection. And shall a miserable financier come with a boast, that he can fetch a pepper-corn into the exchequer, to the loss of millions to the nation! I dare not say how much

carried out, never to return, his constant theme was the injustice offered to the American Colonies, the folly of attempting to coerce them, and the certain loss of them which would ensue to the Crown if their reasonable demands were not met. But the monarch whose interest he wished to serve, was blind and deaf to every thing save his own passions and prejudices; and Chatham's subsequent prediction that the Stamp Act would be repealed, was fulfilled only to have the obnoxious measure replaced by others equally odious to the country, whose allegiance, instead of being strengthened by such means, was soon to be cast off altogether.

higher these profits might be augmented. I am convinced that the whole commercial system might be altered to advantage. You have prohibited where you ought to have encouraged; and you have encouraged where you ought to have prohibited. Much is wrong, much may be amended for the general good of the whole.

A great deal has been said without doors, of the power, of the strength, of America. It is a topic that ought to be cautiously meddled with. In a good cause, the force of this country can crush America to atoms. I know the valor of your troops, I know the skill of your officers. But on this ground, on the Stamp Act, when so many here will think it a crying injustice, I am one who will lift up my hands against it.

In such a cause, even your success would be hazardous. America, if she fell, would fall like a strong man; she would embrace the pillars of the State, and pull down the constitution along with her. Is this your boasted peace? Not to sheathe the sword in its scabbard, but to sheathe it in the hearts of your countrymen? Will you quarrel with yourselves, now the whole House of Bourbon is united against you? True, the Americans have not acted in all things with prudence and temper. They have been wronged, they have been driven to madness by injustice. Will you punish them for the madness you have occasioned? Rather let prudence and temper come first from this side. I will undertake for America that she will follow the example. There are two lines in a ballad of Prior's, of a man's behavior to his wife, so applicable to you and your colonies, that I cannot help repeating them:

"Be to her faults a little blind,
Be to her virtues very kind."

Upon the whole, I will tell the House what is really my opinion. It is that the Stamp Act be repealed absolutely, totally and immediately. That the reason for the repeal be assigned, because it was founded on an erroneous principle. At the same time, let the sovereign authority of this country over the colonies be asserted in as strong terms as can be devised, and be made to extend to every point of legislation whatsoever; that we may bind their trade, confine their manufactures, and exercise every power whatsoever, except that of taking their money out of their pockets without their consent.

Ex. VI.—*A PLEA FOR REPRESENTATION.*

Speech in Parliament, 1766.

LORD CAMDEN.*

My Lords:—When I spoke last on this subject, I was indeed replied to, but not answered. In the mean time, I took the strictest review of my arguments; I re-examined all my authorities; fully determined, if I found myself mistaken, publicly to own my mistake, and give up my opinion; but my researches have more and more convinced me, that the British Parliament have no right to tax the Americans.

My position is this—I repeat it, I will maintain it to my last hour—taxation and representation are inseparable; this position is founded on the laws of nature; it is more—it is itself an eternal law of nature; for whatever is a man's own, is absolutely his own; no man hath a right to take it from him without his consent, either expressed by himself or representative; whoever attempts to do it, attempts an injury; whoever does it, commits a robbery; he throws down and destroys the distinction between liberty and slavery. Taxation and representation are coeval with, and essential to, this constitution. There is not a blade of grass growing in the most obscure corner of this kingdom which is not, which was not ever represented since the constitution began; there is not a blade of grass which, when fixed, was not taxed with the consent of the proprietor. Much stress has been laid upon the taxation of Wales, before it was united as it now is, as if the King, standing in the place of the former princes of that country, raised money by his own authority, but the real fact is otherwise; for I find that long before Wales was subdued, the northern part of that principality had representatives, and a parliament, or assembly. As to Ireland, my lords, before that kingdom had a parliament, as it now has, when a tax was to be laid on that country, the Irish sent over here representatives, as your lordships will find if you will examine the old records. For these reasons, my lords,

---

* Lord Camden was only one out of many among British statesmen who maintained, warmly though unsuccessfully, the cause of liberty in our own country, and earned, by their opposition to the ill-judged policy of the Crown, a title to our national gratitude. As there would be little to interest us in the history of most of these defenders, except their attachment to our cause, only those of them who are especially distinguished will hereafter be noticed separately.

I can never give my assent to any bill taxing the American colonies, while they remain unrepresented; for as to the distinction of a virtual representation, it is so absurd as not to deserve an answer; I therefore pass it over with contempt.

The forefathers of the Americans did not leave their native country, and subject themselves to every danger and distress, to be reduced to a state of slavery; they did not give up their rights; they looked for protection, and not for chains, from their mother country; by her they expected to be defended in the possession of their property, and not to be deprived of it; for, should the present power continue, there is nothing which they can call their own; or, to use the words of Mr. Locke: "What property have they in that which another may, by right, take, when he pleases, to himself?"

Ex. VII.—*THE GLORY OF LIBERTY.*

From a Sermon delivered at Boston, May 23, 1766.

JONATHAN MAYHEW.[*]

WE have before this seen times of great adversity. We have known seasons of drought, death, and spreading mortal diseases; the pestilence walking in darkness, and destruction wasting at noon-day. We have seen wide devastations by fire, and amazing tempests; the heaven on flames, the winds and waves roaring. We have known repeated earthquakes, threatening us with destruction. We have been under great apprehensions by reason of formidable fleets of an enemy on our coasts, menacing fire and sword to all our maritime towns. We have known times when the French and savage armies made terrible havoc on our frontiers, carrying all before them; when we have not been without fear, that some capital towns in the colonies would fall into their merciless hands.

Such times as these we have known; at some of which almost every face "gathered paleness," and the knees of all but the good and brave waxed feeble. But never have we

[*] Dr. Mayhew was a clergyman of Boston, highly distinguished for his eloquence, learning and patriotism. He preached a sermon against the Stamp Act from the text, "I would they were even cut off that trouble you!" but disclaimed any sympathy with the rioters who were at the same time engaged in pillaging and destroying houses belonging to officers of the Crown.

known a season of such universal consternation and anxiety, among people of all ranks and ages in these colonies, as was occasioned by that parliamentary procedure which threatened us and our posterity with perpetual bondage and slavery. For what is there in this world more wretched, than for those who were born free, and have a right to continue so, to be made slaves themselves, and to think of leaving a race of slaves behind them; even though it be to masters confessedly the most generous and humane in the world? Or what wonder is it, if, after groaning with a low voice for a while, to no purpose, we have at length groaned so loudly as to be heard more than three thousand miles; and to be pitied throughout Europe, wherever it is not hazardous to mention even the name of liberty, unless it be to reproach it, as only another word for sedition, faction and rebellion?

For myself, having from my childhood up, by the kind providence of my God, and the tender care of a good parent now at rest with him, been educated to the love of liberty, though not of licentiousness, which pure and virtuous passion was still increased in me as I advanced into manhood; I would not, I can not now, though past middle age, relinquish the fair object of my youthful affections, LIBERTY; whose charms, instead of decaying with time in my eyes, have daily captivated me more and more.

Once more hail, then, celestial maid! Welcome to these shores again—welcome to every expanding heart! Long mayst thou reside among us, the delight of the wise, good and brave; the protectress of innocence from wrong and oppression; the patroness of learning, art, eloquence, virtue, rational loyalty, religion! And if any miserable people on the Continent or isles of Europe, after having been weakened by luxury, debauchery, venality, intestine quarrels, or other vices, should, in rude collisions, or now uncertain revolutions of kingdoms, be driven in their extremity to seek a safe retreat from slavery in some distant clime; let them find— oh, let them find one in America, under thy brooding, sacred wings; where *our* oppressed fathers once found it, and we now enjoy it, by the favor of him whose service is the most glorious freedom! Never, oh never, may he permit thee to forsake us, for our unworthiness to enjoy thy enlivening presence. By his high permission, mayst thou attend us through life and death, to the regions of the blessed, thy original abode, there to enjoy forever "the glorious liberty of the sons of God."

Ex. VIII.—*THE WAY TO OBTAIN SUPPLIES FROM AMERICA.*

Speech in Parliament, May 15, 1767.

THOMAS POWNALL.*

ARE you determined, Mr. Speaker, from hence to direct and regulate the quartering of the King's troops in North America? Do it in a way that brings it home to the executive power there to carry your directions and regulations into execution; explain and amend your act; make it practicable; make it effective; and then you may fairly decide whether they deny your sovereignty or not. You will find they do not. And although you represent the assembly of the province of New York alone as having revolted against your power of taxation for the purpose of maintaining the troops—believe me, there is not a province, a colony, or a plantation, that will submit to a tax thus imposed, more than New York will. All have shown their readiness to execute this service as an act of their own; all have, in their zeal to provide for it, by a grant of their own, provided a supply to answer the expense; but not one single assembly has acted or ever will act, under the powers and provisions of this act, as acknowledging, and in consequence thereof apportioning, assessing and levying the supply, as a tax imposed by parliament. They have either acted without taking notice at all of this act of parliament, or have contrived in some way or other to vary it in some particulars, sufficient to make the execution and the tax an act of their own.

Try the conduct of every province and colony through by this rule, and you will find nothing particular in the case of New York. Don't fancy that you can divide the people on this point, and that you need only divide to govern; you will by this conduct only unite them the more inseparably; you will make the cause of New York a common cause, and will call up every other province and colony to stand forth in their justification, while New York, learning from the complexion of your measure how to avoid or evade the purport of your enforcing Bill, will suspend the force of it, in-

---

* Governor Pownall had held by royal appointment the office of Chief Magistrate of Massachusetts Bay, and had done much by his wise and conciliatory measures to suppress the rising spirit of discontent among the colonists. He was not only a statesman and an orator, but an author, a treatise "On the Administration of the Colonies," and a "Description of part of North America," being among his published works.

stead of suspending the Assembly of that province against which it is brought forward.

It is a fact which the House ought to be apprised of, in all its extent, that the people of America, universally, unitedly, and unalterably, are resolved not to submit to any internal tax imposed upon them by any legislature, in which they have not a share by representatives of their own election.

This claim must not be understood as though it were only the pretence of party leaders and demagogues; as though it were only the visions of speculative enthusiasts; as though it were the mere ebullition of a faction that must subside; as though it were only temporary or partial; it is the cool, deliberate, principled maxim, of every man of business in the country.

They say that supplies are of good will, and not of duty: are the free and voluntary act of the giver, having a right to give, not obligations and services to be complied with, which the subject can not in right refuse; they therefore maintain, claim and insist upon it, that whatever is given out of the lands or property of the people of the colonies, should be given and granted by themselves.

Ex. IX.—*EXHORTATION TO SELF-DEFENCE.*

Boston, 1768.

JOSIAH QUINCY.*

IF there ever was a time, this is the hour for Americans to rouse themselves, and exert every ability. Their all is at hazard, and the die of fate spins doubtful. British taxations, suspensions of legislatures, and standing armies, are but some of the clouds which overshadow the northern world. Now is the time for this people to summon every aid, human and

---

* The name of Quincy has long been celebrated in the annals of Boston. The author of this spirit-stirring address was the third of the name who had filled honorable positions in the councils of this country. He died in April, 1775, on his return from a voyage to Europe undertaken partly with the object of advancing the interests of the colonies, and left a son, bearing the same name, who has but now, (July, 1864,) departed from among us, after a dignified and useful life, at the age of ninety-two years.

divine; to exhibit every moral virtue, and call forth every Christian grace. The wisdom of the serpent, the innocence of the dove, and the intrepidity of the lion, with the blessing of God, will yet save us from the jaws of destruction. By the sweat of our brow we earn the little we possess; from nature we derive the common rights of man; and by charter we claim the liberties of Britons! Shall we, dare we, pusillanimously surrender our birthright?

Be not deceived, my countrymen! Believe not those venal hirelings who would cajole you by their subtleties into submission, or frighten you by their vaporings into compliance. When they strive to flatter you by the terms "moderation and prudence," tell them that calmness and deliberation are to guide the judgment, courage and intrepidity command the action. When they endeavor to make us "perceive our inability to oppose our mother country," let us boldly answer: "In defence of our civil and religious rights, we dare oppose the world! With the God of armies on our side, even the God who fought our fathers' battles, we fear not the hour of trial, though the hosts of our enemies should cover the field like locusts. If this be enthusiasm, we will live and die enthusiasts."

O my countrymen! what will our children say, when they read the history of these times, should they find that we tamely gave away, without one noble struggle, the most inestimable of earthly blessings! As they drag the galling chain, will they not execrate us? If we have any respect for things sacred, any regard to the dearest treasure on earth,—if we have one tender sentiment for posterity, if we would not be despised by the whole world,—let us, in the most open, solemn manner, and with determined fortitude, swear,—" We will die, if we can not live, freemen!"

Ex. X.—*A SONG TO THE TUNE OF "HEARTS OF OAK."*

Written July 4th, 1768.*

JOHN DICKINSON.

Come, join hand in hand, brave Americans all,
And rouse your bold hearts at fair LIBERTY's call;

* It is scarcely necessary to remind our young readers that the circumstance of this date's agreeing with that of our national holiday is only a curious coincidence.

No tyrannous acts shall suppress your just claim,
Or stain with dishonor AMERICA's name.

Chorus.—In freedom we're born, and in freedom we'll live;
    Our purses are ready—
    Steady, friends, steady,
  Not as SLAVES, but as FREEMEN, our money we'll give.

Our worthy forefathers—(let's give 'em a cheer,)
To climates unknown did courageously steer;
Through oceans to deserts for freedom they came,
And dying bequeathed us their freedom and fame.

Chorus.—In freedom we're born, &c.

Their generous bosoms all dangers despised,
So highly, so wisely, their birth-rights they prized;
We'll keep what they gave—we will piously keep—
Nor frustrate their toils on the land or the deep.

Chorus.—In freedom we're born, &c.

The tree their own hands had to liberty reared,
They lived to behold growing strong and revered;
With transport they cried, "Now our wishes we gain,
"For our children shall gather the fruits of our pain."

Chorus.—In freedom we're born, &c.

How sweet are the labors that freemen endure,
That they shall enjoy all the profits secure.
No more such sweet labors Americans know,
If Britons shall reap what Americans sow.

Chorus.—In freedom we're born, &c.

Swarms of placemen and pensioners soon will appear,
Like locusts deforming the charms of the year;
Suns vainly will rise, showers vainly descend,
If we are to drudge for what others shall spend.

Chorus.—In freedom we're born, &c.

Then join hand in hand, brave Americans all,
By uniting we stand, by dividing we fall;

In so righteous a cause let us hope to succeed,
For heaven approves of each virtuous deed.

Chorus.—In freedom we're born, &c.

All ages shall speak with amaze and applause,
Of the courage we'll show in support of our laws;
To die we can bear, but to serve we disdain,
For shame is to freemen more dreadful than pain.

Chorus.—In freedom we're born, &c.

This bumper I crown for our sovereign's health,
And this for Britannia's glory and wealth;
That wealth and that glory immortal may be,
If she is but just and if we are but free.

Chorus.—In freedom we're born, &c.

Ex. XI.—*TIMELY WARNINGS.*

Speech in Parliament, April, 1769.

THOMAS POWNALL.

Sir: There is a general dissatisfaction and uneasiness, as well here as in America, at our falling back into that controversy and contest between the government and the colonies, which we were once so happily delivered from. All now are convinced that there are no means of deciding the controversy, that there are no hopes of putting an end to the contest. Every event that arises, raises fresh difficulty; nothing but power can operate, and that can operate only to mischief. Power, thus used, will inflame and unite the colonies, as in one common cause, and every further exertion of that power will only press the people closer together, and render more intense and ardent that heat with which they are already inflamed.

The legislatures of the colonies have been hitherto permitted to hold that check and control upon the government, under which the people whom they represent live, that they have granted, appropriated, and held the disposal of the provision for its support. And although they complain of their being aggrieved in having this power taken away from them, yet they have submitted to your authority, have manifested their obedience to your laws, and have paid your taxes. They have indeed petitioned against the exercise of this power of raising a revenue for this purpose, yet they obeyed before they complained.

They are at the lowest point of submission. If you endeavor to press them down one hair's-breadth lower, like a spring they will fly all to pieces, and they will never be brought to the same point again.

They have humbled themselves in the hope, in the confidence, that as you are strong you will be merciful; but if you continue to exert your strength, you will find them as sturdy as they have been humble. They will not oppose power to your power—they will not go into any acts of sedition—they will not commit any treason—but they will be impracticable.

There have been strange violences and outrages in America—the winds have beaten hard, the storm has been high. The state, like a ship, hath been driven into extreme dangers amidst shoals and breakers, but now all is peace; there is a lull at this moment; now then is the time to refit your rigging, to work out the vessel from amidst these breakers, and to get her under way, in her old safe course, and you may bring her to the harbor that you wish.

Matters are now brought to a crisis at which they never will be again; if this occasion is now lost, it is lost forever. You may exert power over, but you never can govern an unwilling people; they will be able to obstruct and pervert every effort of your policy; they will render ineffectual every exertion of your government, and will shut up every source, one after another, by which you should derive any benefit or advantage from them.

Take, for example, the duty on painters' colors. Can any one imagine that the people of America are under any necessity of importing this article into that country? Can any one imagine that there is no red or yellow ochre on that great continent? Can any one suppose that a country which abounds with mines of lead, iron, and copper, hath not every color that the art of painting hath produced and used? But if they had but one, and that the poorest pigment that was ever used, if a fancy was taken up at once to call this poor color the color of Liberty, every house, carriage, and ship would be painted with it.

In conclusion, as your authority and power has its full effect at this time; as the people have submitted, are paying the taxes, and are at peace; as you have rejected their applications, and renounced their principles; as you are, at this hour, at perfect liberty, and masters of your own motives—this then is the proper time, the suitable occasion, that you should take to recur only to yourselves, to your own motives, to the principles of commerce, policy and justice.

Ex. XII.—*REBUKE OF THE BRITISH MINISTERS.*
Speech in Parliament, Jan. 9, 1770.

COLONEL BARRÉ.

WITH regard to our colonies, the conduct of administration has been weak, irresolute, ineffectual, and disgraceful. Acts have been made by one set of ministers to inflame them, which by those who succeeded, have been repeated to appease them. By a third administration, those unconstitutional acts, that had given birth to the most dangerous contention that ever was set on foot, concerning a subject that never should have been brought into debate, were revived, in order to inflame the colonies and drive them to extremity. When they resisted those unwarrantable acts, troops have been sent and quartered in their towns, in direct violation of the law, to dragoon them into a compliance. And now we hear from his Majesty that " the spirit of faction has broken out afresh in some of the colonies of North America, in one of them proceeding to acts of violence, and of resistance to the execution of the law. The capital town of which colony appears, by late advices, to be in a state of disobedience to all law and government; and has proceeded to measures subversive of the constitution, and attended with circumstances that manifest a disposition to throw off their dependence on Great Britain."

And now, sir, I appeal to the whole House—I appeal to the things upon that bench—that wretched row of no-ministers,—if such a representation was a just one, of the honest, faithful, loyal, and till that moment, as subjects, irreproachable people of the province of Massachusetts Bay ? And if not a just representation, how unfit to be proclaimed by the mouth of Majesty throughout all Europe ! I will venture to say, sir, that all Europe knows it to be false. With what astonishment, then, must they be struck at the daring iniquity of those by whose advice it was made! To crown all, a governor is sent to cure these disorders, and to reconcile this contradictory system of court policy, who, with vinegar in one hand, and oil in the other, was to mix up a mess, which, if it did not remove the cause, was at least to meliorate the symptoms. These were the astonishing measures by which the prejudices of the people in America were to be removed; but his Lordship was instructed to state the proceedings of parliament as his Majesty's measures, and to explain them according to his own notions of prudence. His Lordship's notions of prudence will, indeed, appear to be very extraordinary, for, in consequence of these instructions, he assured the assembly of Virginia, that his Majesty would sooner lose his crown than preserve it by deceit; intimating, that his Majesty would support the measures of his present wise set of ministers at the hazard of his crown.

But, according to the notions which other men have formed of prudence, this declaration was imprudent in itself, and still more imprudent with respect to the situation in which it was made. It was certainly imprudent to involve the measures of his Majesty with those of his ministry; it was still more imprudent, as it was diametrically opposite to the sentiments of the people to whom it was addressed; and it was more than imprudence, it was madness or folly to make any assurance which might lead the people of America to believe that the interposition of any set of ministers could influence the British parliament to impose, or to repeal, any acts of taxation by which the people of America were to be affected.

Is it, therefore, to be wondered at, that from such a governor and such instructions, the affairs of America should still remain in a state of distraction? That the colonies, from such politicians and such politics, should conceive the most sanguine hopes of gaining their point, and shaking off their dependence upon the British senate? To impose duties, one season, with the professed purpose of raising a revenue, and to take them off the next, as being contrary to the true principles of commerce, is an instance of weakness and inconsistency, not to be paralleled, but by other measures of the same ministry, with respect to the government of the same people.

By this pitiful no-management of these no-ministers, the contest remains undecided; and what they have not been able to accomplish by wisdom and good policy, is to be effected by military force; soldiers are sent over *in terrorem*, and because capacity is wanting to give lawful authority its full vigor, unlawful violence is to supply the deficiency.

Ex. XIII.—*FIRST ANNIVERSARY OF THE " BOSTON MASSACRE."* *

Address delivered in Boston, March 5th, 1771.

JAMES LOVELL.

Who are a free people? not those who do not suffer actual oppression; but those who have a constitutional check upon the power to oppress.

Chatham, Camden and others, Gods among men, have owned that England has a right to exercise every power over us but that of taking money out of our pockets without our consent. Those I have named are mighty characters, but they wanted one advantage which Providence has given us. The beam is carried off from our eyes by the flowing blood of our 'fellow-citizens, and now we may attempt to remove the mote from the eyes of our exalted patrons. That mote, we think, is nothing but our obligation to England first, and afterwards Great Britain, for constant kind protection of our lives and birth-rights against foreign danger. We all acknowledge that protection.

Let us once more look into the early history of this prov-

---

* The 5th of March, 1770, the day on which American blood shed by British hands first flowed in the streets of Boston, was long commemorated in the New England States as a crisis in the struggle for our liberties, and the anniversary did not cease to be regularly celebrated, even after the Fourth of July, 1776, formed a new point of attraction around which all the impulses and memories of patriotism might cluster. The battle of Lexington was but a rekindling, after five years of smothered burning, of the fires which raged so fiercely in 1770.

In justice to the British soldiers, it should be remembered that the so-called " massacre" consisted of one volley of musketry, fired by a picket guard of eight men who had been provoked beyond endurance by insults and personal attacks from a disorderly mob, and that the number killed was but five in all. It is to the credit of American candor and moderation, that when these men were tried for murder, all were acquitted but two, who were found guilty of manslaughter in a minor degree, John Adams and Josiah Quincy (honored names!) voluntarily conducting their defence.

ince. We find that our English ancestors, disgusted in their native country at a legislation which they saw was sacrificing all their rights, left its jurisdiction, and sought, like wandering birds of passage, some happier climate. Here at length they settled down. The king of England was said to be the royal landlord of this territory; with him they entered into mutual, sacred compact, by which the price of tenure, and the rules of management, were fairly stated. It is in this compact that we find our only legitimate authority.

It is said that disunited from Britain we shall bleed at every vein. I can not see this consequence. The states of Holland do not suffer thus. But grant it true, Seneca would prefer the lancets of France, Spain, or any other power, to the bowstring, even though applied by the fair hand of Britannia.

A brave nation is always generous. Let us appeal, therefore, at the same time, to the generosity of the people of Great Britain, before the tribunal of Europe, not to envy us the full enjoyment of the rights of brethren.

And now, my friends and fellow-townsmen, having declared myself an American son of liberty and true charter principles; having shown the critical and dangerous situation of our birth-rights, and the true course of speedy redress, I shall take the freedom to recommend, with boldness, one previous step. Let us show that we understand the true value of what we are claiming.

We know ourselves subjects of common law; to that and the worthy executors of it, let us pay a conscientious regard. Past errors in this point have been written with gall, by the pen of malice. May our future conduct be such as to make even that vile imp lay her pen aside.

The right which imposes duties upon us, is in dispute; but whether they are managed by a surveyor-general, a board of commissioners, Turkish janizaries, or Russian Cossacks, let these enjoy, during our time of fair trial, the common personal protection of the laws of our constitution. Let us shut our eyes for the present, to their being executors of claims subversive of our rights.

Watchful, hawk-eyed jealousy ever guards the portal of the temple of the goddess of Liberty. This is known to those who frequent her altars. Our whole conduct, therefore, I am sure, will meet with the utmost candor of her votaries; but I wish we may be able to convert even her basest apostates.

We are slaves until we obtain such redress, through the

justice of our king, as our happy constitution leads us to expect. In that condition, let us behave with the propriety and dignity of freemen; and thus exhibit to the world a new character of a people which no history describes.

May the all-wise and beneficent Ruler of the Universe preserve our lives and health, and prosper all our lawful endeavors in the glorious cause of FREEDOM.

Ex. XIV.—*THE CONTRAST.*

Speech in Parliament, May 1, 1771.

EARL OF CHATHAM.

MY LORDS:—It is not many years since this nation was the envy and the terror of its neighbors. Alone and unassisted, it seemed to balance the half of Europe. Nor was the aspect of its affairs abroad more flattering than at home. Concord and unanimity prevailed throughout the whole extent of the British empire. Whatever heats and animosities might have subsisted between the grandees, the body of the people was satisfied. No complaints, no murmurs were audible. Nothing was heard on every side but one general burst of acclamation and joy. But how is the prospect darkened! How are the mighty fallen! On public days the royal ears are saluted with hisses and hoots, and he sees libels against his person and government written with impunity, juries solemnly acquitting the publishers. What greater mortification can befall a monarch! Yet this sacrifice he makes to his ministers. To their false steps, not to his own, he owes his disgrace.

My lords, were the sacrifice of our honor and interest abroad compensated by the wisdom of our domestic government, it would be some comfort. But the fact is, that Great Britain, Ireland and America, are equally dissatisfied, and have reason to be dissatisfied, with the ministry. The impolitic taxes laid upon America, and the system of violence there adopted, have unfortunately soured the minds of the people, and rendered them disaffected to the present parliament, if not to the king. The imprudence and indeed the absolute madness of these measures demonstrates, not the result of that assembly's calm, unbiassed deliberations, but the dictates of weak, uninformed ministers, influenced by those who mislead the sovereign.

The Americans had almost forgotten, in their excess of gratitude for the repeal of the Stamp Act, any interest but that of the mother country; there seemed an emulation among the different provinces who should be most dutiful and forward in their expressions of loyalty to their real benefactor. This, my lords, was the temper of the Americans; and would have continued so, had it not been interrupted by your fruitless endeavors to tax them without their consent. But the moment they perceived that your intention was renewed to tax them, their resentment got the ascendant of their moderation, and hurried them into actions contrary to law, which in their cooler moments they would have thought upon with horror.

But, my lords, from the complexion of the whole of the proceedings, I think the administration has purposely irritated them into those violent acts for which they now so severely smart, purposely to be revenged on them for the victory they gained by the repeal of the Stamp Act, for this seems to be the only motive they could have had to break in upon that peace and harmony which then so happily subsisted between them and the mother country.

Ex. XV.—*ANNIVERSARY ORATION.*

Delivered March 5th, 1772.

DR. JOSEPH WARREN.

THE infatuation which hath seemed, for a number of years, to prevail in the British councils with regard to us, is truly astonishing! What can be proposed by the repeated attacks made upon our freedom, I really can not surmise—even leaving justice and humanity out of the question. I do not know one single advantage which can arise to the British nation from our being enslaved. I know not of any gains which can be wrung from us by oppression, that they may not obtain equally from us, by our own consent, in the smooth channel of commerce; we wish the health and prosperity of Britain—we contribute largely to both. Does what we contribute lose all its value because it is done voluntarily?

The amazing increase of riches to Britain, the great rise of the value of her lands, the flourishing state of her navy, are striking proofs of the advantages she derives from the commerce of the colonies, and it is our earnest desire that she may continue to enjoy the same emoluments until her streets are paved with American gold, only let us have the pleasure of calling it our own while it is still in our own hands. But this, it seems, is too great a favor; we are to be governed by the absolute command of others; our property is to be taken away without our own consent. If we complain, our complaints are to be treated with contempt, if we assert our rights, that assertion is deemed insolence; if we offer to submit the matter to the impartial decision of reason, the sword is judged the most proper argument to silence our murmurs! Surely this can not long be the case—the British nation will not suffer the reputation of their justice and their honor to be thus sported away by a capricious ministry. No! they will in a short time open their eyes to their true interest; they nourish in their own breasts a noble love of liberty; they hold her dear, and they know that all who have once possessed her charms, would rather die than suffer her to be torn from their embraces. None but they who set a just value upon liberty are worthy to enjoy her; your illustrious fathers were her zealous votaries; when the blasting frown of tyranny drove her from public view, they clasped her in their arms—they cherished her in their generous bosoms—they brought her safe over the rough ocean, and fixed her seat in this then dreary wilderness. They nursed her infant age with the most tender care; for her sake, they patiently endured the severest hardships, for her support they underwent the most rugged toils, in her defence they boldly encountered the most alarming dangers. Neither the ravenous beasts that ranged the woods for prey, nor the more furious savages of the wilderness, could damp their ardor. While with one hand they broke the stubborn glebe, with the other they grasped their weapons, ever ready to protect her from danger. No sacrifice, not even their own blood, was deemed to rich a libation for *her* altar! God prospered their valor; he preserved her brilliancy unsullied; they enjoyed her while they lived, and dying, bequeathed the precious inheritance to your care. And as they left you this glorious legacy, they have undoubtedly transmitted to you some portion of their heroic spirit, to inspire you with virtue to merit, and courage to preserve her; and you surely can not, with such examples before your eyes, suffer your liberties to be ravished from you by lawless force, or cajoled away by flatteries and fraud.

May the Almighty Being who protected our venerable forefathers—who enabled them to turn a barren wilderness into a fruitful field, and so often stretched forth his arm for their salvation,—graciously preside in all our councils. May he direct us to such measures as he himself shall approve, and be pleased to bless. May we ever be a people favored of God. May our land be a land of liberty, the home of virtue, the asylum of the oppressed, a name and a praise in the whole earth, until the last shock of time shall bury the empires of the world in one common undistinguished ruin!

Ex. XVI.—*RULES FOR REDUCING A GREAT EMPIRE TO A SMALL ONE.*

London, Sept. 1773.

GENTLEMAN'S MAGAZINE.

An ancient sage boasted that though he could not fiddle, he knew how to make a great city of a little one. The science that I, a modern simpleton, am about to communicate, is the very reverse.

I address myself to all ministers who have the management of extensive dominions, which, from their very greatness, are become troublesome to govern, because the multiplicity of affairs leaves no time for fiddling.

In the first place, you are to consider that a great empire, like a great cake, is most easily diminished at the edges. Turn your attention, therefore, to your most remote provinces; that as you get rid of them, the rest may follow in order. Take special care that the colonies are never incorporated with the mother country, that they do not enjoy the same common rights, the same privileges in commerce, and that they are governed by severe laws, all of your enacting, and without allowing them any share in the choice of the legislators.

However peaceably your colonies have submitted to your government, shown their affection to your interests, and patiently borne their grievances, you are to suppose them always inclined to revolt, and treat them accordingly.

Quarter troops among them, who by their insolence may provoke the rising of mobs, and by their bullets and bayonets suppress them. If, when you are engaged in war, your colonies should vie in liberal aid of men and money against the common enemy upon your simple requisition, and go far beyond their abilities, reflect that a penny taken from them by your power is more honorable than a pound presented by your benevolence. Despise therefore their voluntary grants, and resolve to harass them by novel taxes. They will probably complain to your parliament that they are taxed by a body in which they have no representation, and that this is contrary to common right. They will petition for redress. Let the Parliament flout their claims, reject their petitions, refuse even to suffer the reading of them, and treat the petitioners with the utmost contempt. Nothing can have a better effect in producing the alteration proposed—for though many can forgive injuries, none ever forgave contempt.

To make your taxes more odious, and more likely to procure resistance, send from the capital a board of officers to superintend the collection, composed of the most indiscreet, ill-bred and insolent men you can find. Let these men, by your order, be exempt from all the common taxes and burdens of the province, though they and their property are protected by its laws. If any revenue officers are suspected of the least tenderness for the people, discard them. If others are justly complained of, protect and reward them.

If the assemblies of your provinces shall dare to claim rights, and to complain of your administration, order them to be harassed by repeated dissolutions. If the same men are continually returned by new elections, adjourn their meetings to some country village where they cannot be accommodated, and keep them there during your pleasure;—for this, you know, is your PREROGATIVE. And an excellent one it is, as you may manage it to promote discontents among the people, diminish their respect, and increase their disaffection.

If you are told of discontents in your colonies, never believe that they are general, or that you have given occasion for them; therefore do not think of applying any remedy, or of changing any offensive measure. Redress no grievance, lest they should be encouraged to demand the redress of some other grievance. Grant no request that is just and reasonable, lest they should make another that is unreasonable. Take all the informations of the state of the colonies from your governors, and officers in enmity with them. Encourage and reward these leasing-makers; secrete their lying accusations, lest they should be confuted; but act upon them as the clearest evidence, and believe nothing you hear from the friends of the people. Suppose all their complaints to be invented and promoted by a few factious demagogues, whom if you could catch and hang all would be quiet. Catch and hang them accordingly, and the blood of the martyrs shall work miracles in favor of your purpose.

Send armies into their country under pretence of protecting the inhabitants; but instead of garrisoning the forts on the frontiers with those troops, order them into the heart of the country, that the savages may be encouraged to attack the frontiers, and that the troops may be protected by the inhabitants; this will seem to proceed from your ill-will or your ignorance, and contribute farther to produce and strengthen an opinion among them that you are no longer fit to govern them.

Ex. XVII.—*PROTEST AGAINST BRITISH AGGRESSION.*

Address to the Public, Dec. 15, 1773.

SONS OF LIBERTY.*

It is essential to the freedom and security of a people that no taxes be imposed upon them but by their own consent, or that of their representatives. For what property have they in that which another may, by right, take when he pleases to himself? And yet, to the astonishment of all the world, and the grief of America, the Commons of Great Britain, after the repeal of the memorable and detestable Stamp Act, reassumed the power of imposing taxes on the American colonies. And thus they who, from time immemorial, have

---

* Associations bearing this title sprang up rapidly over all the northern colonies on the passage of the Stamp Act, with the avowed object of forcible resistance to that measure. The body grew very formidable to the Stamp officers, who were generally obliged to resign, while the Stamps were either destroyed or allowed to remain unopened in the original packages, until after the repeal of the Act. The "Sons of Liberty" did not cease their operations with this repeal, but continued their meetings to keep up the spirit of resistance to other acts of oppression. The address quoted above was published the day before the destruction of the tea in Boston Harbor.

exercised the right of giving to, or withholding from the crown, their aids and subsidies, according to their own free-will and pleasure, do by the act in question deny us, their brethren in America, the enjoyment of the same right. As this denial, and the execution of that act, involves our slavery, and would sap the foundation of our freedom, the merchants and inhabitants of this city, in conjunction with the merchants and inhabitants of the ancient American colonies, have entered into an agreement to decline a part of their commerce with Great Britain, until the above-mentioned act shall be totally repealed. If, after this, the British succeed in procuring the sale of their tea, we shall have no property we can call our own, and then we may bid adieu to American liberty. Therefore, to prevent a calamity which of all others is the most to be dreaded—slavery, and its dreadful concomitants—we, being influenced by a regard to liberty, and disposed to use all lawful endeavors in our power to transmit to our posterity those blessings of freedom which our ancestors have handed down to us, do for this important purpose, agree to associate together under the name and style of "The Sons of Liberty" in New York, and engage our honor to and with each other faithfully to observe and perform the resolutions demanded for our safety in this exigency.

And we hereby declare, that whosoever shall aid or abet, or in any manner assist in the introduction of tea from any place whatever into this colony, while it is subject to the payment of a duty for the purpose of raising a revenue in America, shall be deemed an enemy to the liberties of this country.

And whether the duties on tea, imposed by this act, be paid in Great Britain or in America, our liberties are equally affected. And we declare, furthermore, that whoever shall transgress any of these resolutions, we will not deal with, nor employ, nor have any connection with him.

Ex. XVIII.—*KING GEORGE'S TEA-PARTY.*
1773.

Oh, King George is a very great man!
   A great and a mighty man is he;
He has soldiers and ships at his command,
   But he couldn't make us swallow his Tea!

He sent it here in the year of grace,
   Seventeen Hundred and Seventy-three;
But the nation made a very wry face,
   And said, "I don't like the taste of your Tea."

"I'll give you a taste of gunpowder, then,
   To improve the flavor a bit," said he;
"You're a little cranky and stiff, my men—
   I'll show you the way to drink your Tea!"

But then a thought came into our heads;—
   "King Neptune is always thirsty," said we;
"We'll give *him* a dose of the precious weed—
   It'll suit his Majesty just to a T."

I went to my mother—(God bless her old head!
   Many's the cup she's made for me,)
And I put on a simple face, and I said,
   "Do tell me how you make your Tea."

"Laws bless us all! The boy 's bereaved!
   What on earth do you want to know for?" said she;
"A pint of hot water, a spoonful of leaves;
   That 's the way to make good Tea."

So down we went on board the ships;
   "Here 's a good many gallons of water," said we;
"And not to give old Nep the slip,
   It'll need a good many chests of Tea."

So we hauled them up from the hold in a trice,
   And emptied them all in the deep blue sea;
And we hoped the old gentleman found it nice,
   And liked our way of making his Tea.

King George looked up, and King George looked down;
   A wrathfully angry man was he,
And he said, "As sure as I wear a crown,
   "I'll make those people swallow their Tea!"

But when you do, my merry King,
   Call all your neighbors in to see,
For muskets shall rattle, and swords shall ring,
   Before we swallow a cup of your Tea.

Take off your tax, most gracious King;
  Let free goods come to a people free;
Then call your poets in to sing
  How the Yankees have taken to drinking Tea.

Ex. XIX.—*AN OLD MAN'S ADVICE.*

Speech delivered in Parliament, May 27, 1774.

EARL OF CHATHAM.

My Lords: I am an old man, and would advise the noble lords in office to adopt a more gentle mode of governing America; for the day is not far distant, when America may vie with these kingdoms, not only in arms, but in arts also. It is an established fact, that the principal towns in America are learned and polite, and understand the constitution of the empire as well as the noble lords who are now in office; and consequently, they will have a watchful eye over their liberties, to prevent the least encroachment on their hereditary rights.

This observation is so recently exemplified in an excellent pamphlet, which comes from the pen of an American gentleman, that I shall take the liberty of reading to your lordships his thoughts on the competency of the British parliament to tax America, which, in my opinion, puts this interesting matter in the clearest view: "The high court of Parliament," says he, "is the supreme legislative power over the whole empire; in all free states the constitution is fixed; and as the supreme legislature derives its power and authority from the constitution, it cannot overleap the bounds of it without destroying its own foundation. The constitution ascertains and limits both sovereignty and allegiance; and, therefore, his Majesty's American subjects, who acknowledge themselves bound by the ties of allegiance, have an equitable claim to the full enjoyment of the fundamental rules of the British constitution; and it is an essential unalterable right in nature, engrafted into the English constitution as a fundamental law, and ever held sacred and irrevocable by the subjects within this realm, that what a man has honestly acquired, is absolutely his own; which he may freely give, but which can not be taken from him without his consent."

This, my lords, though no new doctrine, has always been my received and unalterable opinion, and I will carry it to my grave, that this country had no right under heaven to tax America. It is contrary to all the principles of justice and civil policy, which neither the exigencies of the state, nor even an acquiescence in the taxes, could justify upon any occasion whatever. Instead of adding to their miseries, which this bill undoubtedly does, adopt some lenient measures, which may lure them to their duty; proceed like a kind and affectionate parent over a child whom he tenderly loves, and instead of those harsh and severe proceedings, pass an amnesty on all their youthful errors; clasp them once more in your kind and affectionate arms; and I will venture to affirm, you will find them children worthy of their sire.

But should their turbulence exist after your proffered terms of forgiveness, which I hope and expect this House will immediately adopt, I will be among the foremost of your lordships to move for such measures as will effectually prevent a future relapse, and make them feel what it is to provoke a fond and forgiving parent—a parent, my lords, whose welfare has ever been my greatest and most pleasing consolation. This declaration may seem unnecessary; but I will venture to declare, the period is not far distant when she will want the assistance of her most distant friends; but should the all-disposing hand of Providence prevent me from affording her my poor assistance, my prayers shall be ever for her welfare—length of days be ever in her right hand, and in her left hand riches and honor; may her ways be ways of pleasantness, and all her paths be peace!

Ex. XX.—*ABANDONMENT OF TAXATION.*

Speech in Parliament, 1774.

BISHOP OF ST. ASAPH'S.

It has always been a most arduous task to govern distant provinces, with even a tolerable appearance of justice. The viceroys and governors of other nations are usually temporary tyrants, who think themselves obliged to make the most of their time; who not only plunder the people, but carry away their spoils, and dry up all the sources of commerce and industry. Taxation, in their hands, is an unlimited power of oppression; but in whatever hands the power of taxation is lodged, it implies and includes all other powers. Arbitrary taxation is plunder authorized by law; it is the support and the essence of tyranny, and has done more mischief to mankind than those other three scourges from heaven, famine, pestilence, and the sword.

Let us reflect, that before these innovations were thought of, by following the line of good conduct which had been marked out by our ancestors, we governed our colonies in North America with mutual benefit to them and ourselves. It was a happy idea, that made us first consider them rather as instruments of commerce than as objects of government. It was wise and generous to give them the form and spirit of our own constitution; an assembly, in which a greater equality of representation has been preserved than at home, and councils and governors such as were adapted to their situation, though they must be acknowledged to be very inferior copies of the dignity of this house, and the majesty of the crown.

But what is far more valuable than all the rest, we gave them liberty. We allowed them to use their own judgment in the management of their own interests. The idea of taxing them never entered our heads. We made requisitions to them on great occasions, in the same manner as our princes formerly asked benevolences of their subjects; and as nothing was asked but what was visibly for the public good, it was always granted; and they sometimes did more than we expected. And let us not forget that the people of New England were themselves during the last war, the most forward of all in the national cause; that in the preceding war, they alone enabled us to make the treaty of Aix-la-Chapelle, by furnishing us with the only equivalent for the towns that were taken from our allies in Flanders; and that, in times of peace, they alone have taken from us six times as much of our woollen manufactures as the whole kingdom of Ireland.

In order to observe the strictest impartiality, it is but just for us to inquire what we have gained by these taxes as well as what we have lost. I am assured that out of all the sums raised in America the last year but one, if the expenses are deducted which the natives would else have discharged themselves, the net revenue paid into the treasury to go in aid of the sinking fund, or to be employed in whatever public services parliament shall think fit, is eighty-five pounds. Eighty-five pounds, my lords, is the whole equivalent we have received for all the hatred and mischief, and all the infinite losses this kingdom has suffered during that year in her disputes with North America! Money that is earned so dearly as this, ought to be expended with great wisdom and economy. My lords, were you to take up but one thousand pounds more from North America upon the same terms, the nation itself would be a bankrupt. But the most amazing and most alarming circumstances are still behind. It is that our case is so incurable, that all this experience has made no impression upon us.

And yet, my lords, if you could keep these facts, which I have ventured to lay before you, for a few moments in your minds, supposing your right of taxation to be never so clear, yet I think you must necessarily perceive that it can not be exercised in any manner that can be advantageous to ourselves or them. We have not always the wisdom to tax ourselves with propriety, and I am confident we could never tax a people at that distance, without infinite blunders and more oppression. And to own the truth, my lords, we are not honest enough to trust ourselves with the power of shifting our own burdens upon them. Allow me, therefore, to conclude, I think unanswerably, that the inconvenience and distress we have felt in this change of our conduct, no less than the ease and tranquillity we formerly found in the pursuit of it, will force us, if we have any sense left, to return to the good old path we trod in so long and found it the way of pleasantness.

Ex. XXI.—*TRUE AND FALSE DIGNITY.*
Speech in Parliament, April 19th, 1774.

EDMUND BURKE.[*]

THEY tell you, sir, that your dignity is tied to it. I know not how it happens, but this dignity of yours is a terrible in-

---

[*] No name in English Parliamentary history shines with a purer lustre than that of Edmund Burke. His splendid intellect, great acquirements, and brilliant powers of oratory, were all enlisted on the side of the American colonists; while his exemplary private life, his disinterestedness, uprightness and

cumbrance to you; for it has of late been ever at war with your interest, your equity, and every idea of your policy. Show the thing you contend for to be reason; show it to be common sense; show it to be the means of attaining some useful end; and then I am content to allow it what dignity you please. But what dignity is derived from the perseverance in absurdity, is more than ever I could discern. The honorable gentleman has said well—indeed in most of his *general* observations I agree with him—he says that this subject does not stand as it did formerly. Oh, certainly not! every hour you continue on this ill-chosen ground, your difficulties thicken on you; and therefore my conclusion is, remove from a bad position as quickly as you can. The disgrace and the necessity of yielding, both of them, grow upon you every hour of your delay.

Let us, sir, embrace some system or other before we end the session. Do you mean to tax America, and to draw a productive revenue from thence? If you do, speak out; name, fix, ascertain this revenue; settle its quantity; define its objects; provide for its collection; and then fight when you have something to fight for. If you murder, rob; if you kill, take possession; and do not appear in the character of madmen, as well as assassins, violent, vindictive, bloody, without an object. But may better counsels guide you!

Again I say it, revert to your old principles—seek peace and ensue it—leave America, if she has taxable matter in her, to tax herself. Be content to bind her by laws of trade; you have always done it; let this be your reason for binding their trade. Do not burden them with taxes; you were not used to do so from the beginning; let this be your reason for not taxing. These are the arguments of states and kingdoms. Sir, let the gentlemen on the other side call forth all their ability; let the best of them get up and tell me what one character of liberty the Americans have, what one brand of slavery they are free from, if they are bound in their property and industry, by all the restraints you can imagine on commerce, and at the same time are made packhorses of ev-

---

nobleness of character make him a champion which any cause may be proud to own. His speeches are masterpieces of English composition which can not be too carefully studied by any one aspiring to excellence in oratory. But no oratory, though resting on a solid foundation of truth and justice, could restrain the madness of the British Government; and one year from the day when Burke uttered the thrilling speech of which this extract forms a part, the first blood of the Revolution was spilled on the field of Lexington!

ery tax you choose to impose upon them, without the least share in granting them. When they bear the burdens of unlimited monopoly, will you bring them to bear the burdens of unlimited revenue too? The Englishman in America will feel that this is slavery—that it is *legal* slavery, will be no compensation either to his feelings or to his understanding.

If this be the case, ask yourselves this question; "Will they be content in such a state of slavery?" If not, look to the consequences. Reflect how you ought to govern a people, who think they ought to be free, and think they are not. Your scheme yields no revenue; it yields nothing but discontent, disorder, disobedience; and such is the state of America, that after wading up to your eyes in blood, you could only end just where you began, that is, to tax where no revenue is to be found, to—my voice fails me; my inclination indeed carries me no further—I will say no more.

Ex. XXII.—*GREAT BRITAIN'S RIGHT TO TAX AMERICA.*

Speech in Parliament, April 19th, 1774.

EDMUND BURKE.

BUT, Mr. Speaker, we have a *right* to tax America! Oh, inestimable right! Oh! wonderful, transcendent right, the assertion of which has cost this country thirteen provinces, six islands, one hundred thousand lives, and seventy millions of money! Oh, invaluable right! for the sake of which we have sacrificed our rank among nations, our importance abroad, and our happiness at home! Oh, right! more dear to us than our existence, which has already cost us so much, and which seems likely to cost us our all! Infatuated minister! miserable and undone country! not to know that the claim of right, without the power of enforcing it, is nugatory and idle. We have a right to tax America, the noble lord tells us; therefore we ought to tax America. This is the profound logic which comprises the whole chain of his reasoning.

Not inferior to this was the wisdom of him who resolved to shear the wolf. What! shear a wolf! Have you considered the resistance, the difficulty, the danger of the attempt?

No, says the madman, I have considered nothing but the right. Man has a right of dominion over the beasts of the forest; and therefore I will shear the wolf. How wonderful that a nation could be thus deluded! But the noble lord deals in cheats and delusions. They are the daily traffic of his invention; and he will continue to play off his cheats on this House, so long as he thinks them necessary to his purpose, and so long as he has money enough at command to bribe gentlemen to pretend that they believe him. But a black and bitter day of reckoning will surely come; and whenever that day does come, I trust I shall be able, by a parliamentary impeachment, to bring upon the heads of the authors of our calamities, the punishment they deserve.

Ex. XXIII.—*ADDRESS TO THE PEOPLE OF GREAT BRITAIN, SEPT.* 1774.

BY DELEGATES FROM THE AMERICAN CONGRESS.

FRIENDS and Fellow Subjects: When a nation, led to greatness by the hand of liberty, and possessed of all the glory that heroism, munificence and humanity can bestow, descends to the ungrateful task of forging chains for her children, and instead of giving support to freedom, turns advocate for slavery and oppression, there is reason to suspect she has either ceased to be virtuous, or been extremely negligent in the appointment of her rulers.

In almost every age, in repeated conflicts, in long and bloody wars, as well civil as foreign, against many and powerful nations, against the open assaults of enemies, and the more dangerous treachery of friends, have the inhabitants of your island, your great and glorious ancestors, maintained their independence, and transmitted the rights of men and the blessings of liberty, to you their posterity.

Be not surprised, therefore, that we, who are descended from the same common ancestors; that we, whose forefathers participated in all the rights, the liberties, and the constitution you so justly boast of, and who have carefully conveyed the same fair inheritance to us, guaranteed by the plighted faith of government and the most solemn compacts with British sovereigns, should refuse to surrender them to men who found their claims on no principles of reason, and who prosecute them with a design that, by having our lives and properties in their power, they may with the greatest facility, enslave you. The cause of America is now the object of universal attention; it has at length become very serious. This unhappy country has not only been oppressed, but abused and misrepresented; and the duty we owe to ourselves and posterity, to your interest, and the general welfare of the British empire, leads us to address you on this very important subject.

Know then, that we consider ourselves, and do insist that we are and ought to be, as free as our fellow-subjects in Britain, and that no power on earth has a right to take our property from us, without our consent.

That we claim all the benefits secured to the subject by the English constitution, and particularly that inestimable one of trial by jury.

That we hold it essential to English liberty, that no man be condemned unheard, or punished for supposed offences, without having an opportunity of making his defence.

That we think the legislature of Great Britain is not authorized by the constitution to establish a religion fraught with sanguinary and impious tenets, or to erect an arbitrary form of government, in any quarter of the globe. These rights, we, as well as you, deem sacred; and yet, sacred as they are, they have, with many others, been repeatedly and flagrantly violated.

Are not the proprietors of the soil of Great Britain, lords of their own property? can it be taken from them without their consent? will they yield it to the arbitrary disposal of any man, or number of men whatever? You know they will not.

Why then are the proprietors of the soil of America less lords of their property than you are of yours? or why should they submit it to the disposal of your parliament, or any other parliament or council in the world, not of their election? Can the intervention of the sea that divides us, cause disparity in rights, or can any reason be given why English subjects who live three thousand miles from the royal palace, should enjoy less liberty than those who are three hundred miles distant from it?

Reason looks with indignation on such distinctions, and freemen can never perceive their propriety. And yet, however chimerical and unjust such discriminations are, the parliament assert that they have a right to bind us in all cases, without exception, whether we consent or not; that they may take and use our property when and in what manner they please; that we are pensioners on their bounty for all that we possess, and can hold it no longer than they vouchsafe to permit. Such declarations we consider as heresies in English politics, and which can no more operate to deprive us of our property, than the interdicts of the pope can divest kings of sceptres which the laws of the land and the voice of the people have placed in their hands. At the conclusion of the late war—a war rendered glorious by the abilities and integrity of a minister to whose efforts the British empire owes its safety and its fame : at the conclusion of this war, which was succeeded by an inglorious peace, formed under the auspices of a minister of principles and of a family unfriendly to the protestant cause, and inimical to liberty: we say, at this period, and under the influence of that man, a plan for enslaving your fellow-subjects in America was concocted, which has ever since been pertinaciously carrying into execution.

Ex. XXIV.—*GEN. GAGE AND THE MINISTRY.*

Speech in Parliament, Dec. 19, 1774.

EDMUND BURKE.

I can not sit down, Sir, without first saying a word or two on the solicitude which the honorable member has just expressed for General Gage, and the troops under his command. It is, I confess, most humiliating and mortifying, and it is difficult to say whether those who have put them into this position deserve most our compassion or our ridicule. It is, indeed, an absurdity without parallel; a warlike parliament, and a patient, forbearing general. I would not be understood to reflect on the gentleman, who, I understand, is a very worthy, intelligent, deserving man; no, Sir, it is those who have sent him on such an errand that are to blame. The order of things is reversed in this new system. The rule of government now is to determine hastily, violently, and without consideration, and to execute indecisively, or rather not execute at all. And have not the consequences exactly corresponded with such a mode of proceeding?

They have been measures not practicable in themselves in any event, nor has one step been taken to put them in execution. The account we have is that the General is besieging and besieged; that he had cannon sent to him, but they were stolen; that he himself has made reprisals of a similar nature on the enemy; and that his straw has been burnt, and his brick and mortar destroyed. It is painful to dwell on such monstrous and absurd circumstances, which could be only a subject of ridicule, if it did not lead to circumstances of a very alarming nature. In fact, Sir, your army is turned out to be merely an army of observation, and is of no other use but as an asylum for magistrates of your own creation. I have heard of such places for thieves, rogues, and female orphans; but it is the first time I ever heard of an asylum for magistrates. As to the protection of trade, on which the honorable gentleman has laid such stress, to protect trade, in a place where all sorts of trade or commerce are prohibited, is a glorious task, but not a difficult one. The gentleman has also spoken of blocking up the port of Boston. I cannot pretend to deny that the harbor may be blocked up—it is undoubtedly true; but to me this mode of blockade seems rather novel. Such an expression, it is certain, might come with great propriety from me; but I must confess, I never heard such a bull as that in my own country. At the entrance of Dublin harbor there is a north bull and a south bull; but even there or elsewhere, such a bull as this I never heard.

Ex. XXV.—*INEXPEDIENCY OF MAINTAINING TROOPS IN BOSTON.*

Speech in Parliament, Jan. 20, 1775.

EARL OF CHATHAM.

My Lords:—After more than six weeks' possession of the papers now before you, on a subject so momentous, at a time when the fate of this nation hangs on every hour, the ministry have at length condescended to submit to the consideration of the house intelligence from America with which your lordships and the public have long been acquainted.

The measures of last year, my lords, which have produced the present alarming state of America, were founded upon misrepresentation—they were violent, precipitant and vindictive. The nation was told that it was only a faction in Boston, which opposed all lawful government; that an unwarrantable injury had been done to private property, for which the justice of parliament was called upon to order reparation; that the least appearance of firmness would awe the Americans into submission, and upon only passing the Rubicon, we should find ourselves victorious.

But, my lords, we find that instead of suppressing the opposition of the faction at Boston, these measures have spread it over the whole continent. They have united that whole people by the most indissoluble of bands—intolerable wrong. The just retribution is an indiscriminate, unmerciful proscription of the innocent with the guilty, unheard and untried. The bloodless victor is an impotent general, with his dishonored army, trusting solely to the pickaxe and the spade, for security against the just indignation of an injured and insulted people.

My lords, I am happy that a relaxation of my infirmities permits me to seize this earliest opportunity of offering my poor advice to save this unhappy country, at this moment tottering to its ruin. I wish not to lose a day in this urging present crisis; an hour now lost in allaying the ferment in America, may produce years of calamity; but for my own part, I will not desert for a moment the conduct of this mighty business, unless nailed to my bed by the extremity of sickness; I will give it unremitting attention; I will knock at the door of the sleeping or confounded ministry, and will rouse them to a sense of their impending danger.

When I state the importance of the colonies to this country, I desire not to be understood to argue for a reciprocity of indulgence between England and America; I contend not for indulgence, but justice, to America; and I shall ever contend that the Americans owe obedience to us in a limited degree; they owe obedience to our ordinances of trade and navigation; but let the line be skilfully drawn between the objects of those ordinances, and their private, internal property. Let the sacredness of their property remain inviolate; let it be taxable only by their own consent, given in their provincial assemblies, else it will cease to be property. The law that attempts to alter this disposal of it, annihilates it.

When I urge this measure for recalling the troops from Boston, I urge it on this pressing principle, that it is necessarily preparatory to the restoration of your prosperity. It will then appear that you are disposed to treat amicably and equitably, and to consider, revise and repeal, if it should be found necessary, as I affirm it will, those violent acts and declarations which have disseminated confusion throughout your empire. Resistance to your acts was as necessary as it was just; and your vain declarations of the omnipotence of parliament, and your imperious doctrines of the necessity of submission, will be found equally impotent to convince or enslave your fellow-subjects in America, who feel that tyranny, whether ambitioned by an individual part of the legislature, or by the bodies which compose it, is equally intolerable to British principles.

Ex. XXVI.—*TRIBUTE TO THE CONTINENTAL CONGRESS.*

Speech in Parliament, Jan. 20, 1775.

EARL OF CHATHAM.

WHEN your lordships look at the papers transmitted to us from America; when you consider their decency, firmness and wisdom, you can not but respect their cause, and wish to make it your own. For myself, I must declare and avow, that in all my reading and observation, (and it has been my favorite study; I have read Thucydides, and have studied and admired the master states of the world,) I say I must declare, that, for solidity of reasoning, force of sagacity, and wisdom of conclusion, under such a complication of difficult circumstances, no nation or body of men can stand in preference to the General Congress at Philadelphia. I trust it is obvious to your lordships, that all attempts to impose servitude upon such men, to establish despotism over such a mighty continental nation, must be vain, must be fatal.

We shall be forced, ultimately, to retract; let us retract while we *can*, not when we *must*. I say we must necessarily undo these violent oppressive acts. They MUST be repealed. You WILL repeal them. I pledge myself for it, that you will in the end repeal them. I stake my reputation on it. I will consent to be taken for an idiot, if they are not finally repealed.

Avoid, then, this humiliating, disgraceful necessity. With a dignity becoming your exalted situation, make the first advances to concord, to peace and happiness; for it is your true dignity, to act with prudence and justice. That *you* should first concede, is obvious from sound and rational policy. Concession comes with better grace and more salutary effects from superior power; it reconciles superiority of power with the feelings of men, and establishes solid confidence on the foundations of affection and gratitude.

Every motive, therefore, of justice and of policy, of dignity and of prudence, urges you to allay the ferment in America, by a removal of your troops from Boston; by a repeal of your acts of parliament; and by demonstration of amicable dispositions towards your colonies. On the other hand, every danger and every hazard impend, to deter you from perseverance in your present ruinous measures. Foreign war hanging over your heads by a slight and brittle thread; France and Spain watching your conduct, and waiting for the maturity of your errors, with a vigilant eye to America and the temper of your colonies, more than to their own concerns, be they what they may.

To conclude, my lords; if the ministers thus persevere in misadvising and misleading the king, I will not say that they can alienate the affections of his subjects from his crown; but I will affirm that they will make the crown not worth his wearing; I will not say that the king is betrayed, but I will pronounce that the kingdom is undone.

Ex. XXVII.—*ATTITUDE OF AMERICA TOWARDS GREAT BRITAIN.*

Speech in the Continental Congress, Jan. 1775.

JAMES WILSON.[*]

AND what, Sir, has been our course hitherto? When our rights were invaded by her regulation of our internal

[*] Mr. Wilson was a native of Scotland, and emigrated to this country about the time of the first Stamp Act disturbances. He enlisted warmly on the side of the patriots, was appointed a delegate to the Continental Congress, and afterward to the Convention for framing the Constitution. After the Government was established, he resumed the practice of law, which he had pursued on first coming to this country, and became Judge of the Supreme Court of the United States.

policy, we submitted to England; we were unwilling to oppose her. The spirit of Liberty was slow to act. When those invasions were renewed; when the efficacy and malignancy of them were attempted to be redoubled by the Stamp Act; when chains were formed for us, and preparations were made for riveting them on our limbs—what measures did we pursue? The spirit of Liberty found it necessary now to act; but she acted with the calmness and dignity suited to her character. Were we rash or seditious? Did we discover want of loyalty to our sovereign? Did we betray want of affection towards our brethren in Britain? Let our dutiful and reverential petitions to the throne—let our respectful, though firm, remonstrances to the parliament—let our warm and affectionate addresses to our brethren, and (we will still call them) our friends in Great Britain—let all those, transmitted from every part of the continent, testify the truth. By their testimony let our conduct be tried.

As our proceedings during the existence and operation of the Stamp Act prove fully and incontestably the painful sensations that tortured our breasts from the prospect of disunion with Britain; the peals of joy which burst forth universally upon the repeal of that odious statute, loudly proclaim the heartfelt delight produced in us by a reconciliation with her. Unsuspicious, because undesigning, we buried our complaints, and the causes of them, in oblivion, and returned with eagerness to our former unreserved confidence.

But alas, the root of bitterness still remained. The duty on tea was reserved to furnish occasion to the ministry for a new effort to enslave and to ruin us; and the East India Company were chosen, and consented, to be the detested instruments of ministerial despotism and cruelty. A cargo of tea arrived at Boston. By a low artifice of the governor, and by the wicked activity of the tools of government, it was rendered impossible to store it up, or to send it back, as was done at other places. A number of persons unknown destroyed it.

We behold, sir—with the deepest anguish we behold—that our opposition has not been as effectual as it has been constitutional. The hearts of our oppressors have not relented; our complaints have not been heard; our grievances have not been redressed; our rights are still invaded; and have we no cause to dread that the invasions of them will be enforced in a manner against which all reason and argument, and all opposition of every peaceful kind, will be vain? Our opposition has hitherto increased with our oppression; shall it, in the most desperate of all contingencies, observe the same proportion?

Let us pause, sir, before we give an answer to this question; the fate of us, the fate of millions now alive, the fate of millions yet unborn, depends upon the answer. Let it be the result of calmness and of intrepidity; let it be dictated by the principles of loyalty, and the principles of liberty. Let it be such as never, in the worst events, to give us reason to reproach ourselves, or others reason to reproach us for having done too much or too little.

Ex. XXVIII.—*THE CALL TO ARMS.*

Hark! hear ye the sounds that the winds on their pinions
    Exultingly roll from the shore to the sea,
With a voice that resounds through her boundless dominions?
    'Tis Columbia who calls on her sons to be free!

Behold on yon summits where Heaven has throned her,
    How she starts from her proud inaccessible seat,
With nature's impregnable ramparts around her,
    And the cataract's thunder and foam at her feet!

In the breeze of her mountains her loose locks are shaken,
    While the soul-stirring notes of her warrior song
From the rock to the valley reëcho, "Awaken,
    "Awaken, ye hearts that have slumbered too long!"

Yes, despots! too long did your tyranny hold us,
    In a vassalage vile, ere its weakness was known;
Till we learned that the links of the chain that controlled us,
    Were forged by the fears of its captives alone.

That spell is destroyed, and no longer availing,
    Despised as detested—pause well, ere ye dare
To cope with a people whose spirit and feeling
    Are roused by remembrance and steeled by despair.

Go, tame the wild torrent, or stem with a straw
    The proud surges that sweep o'er the strand that confines
        them;

But presume not again to give freemen a law,
  Nor think with the chains they have broken to bind them.

To hearts that the spirit of liberty flushes,
  Resistance is idle, and numbers a dream;
They burst from control, as the mountain stream rushes
  From its fetters of ice, in the summer's warm beam.

Ex. XXIX.—*DIFFERENCE BETWEEN REBELLION AND REVOLUTION.*

Speech in Parliament, Feb. 6th, 1775.

JOHN WILKES.

My Lords: Whether the present state of the American colonies is that of rebellion, or of a fit and just resistance to unlawful acts of power, to our attempts to rob them of their property and liberties, as they imagine, I shall not declare. But I well know what will follow—nor, however strange and harsh it may appear to some, shall I hesitate to announce it, that I may not be accused hereafter of having failed in duty to my country on so grave an occasion, and at the approach of such direful calamities.

Know, then, that a successful resistance is a revolution, not a rebellion. Rebellion, indeed, appears on the back of a flying enemy, but revolution flames on the breast-plate of the victorious warrior. Who can tell whether, in consequence of this day's violent and mad address to his majesty, the scabbard may not be thrown away by them as well as by us; and whether, in a few years, the independent American may not celebrate the glorious era of the revolution of 1775, as we do that of 1688? The generous efforts of our forefathers for freedom, Heaven crowned with success, or their noble blood had dyed our scaffolds, like that of Scottish traitors and rebels; and the period of our history which does us the most honor would have been deemed a rebellion against the lawful authority of the prince, not a resistance authorized by all the laws of God and man; not the expulsion of a detested tyrant.

But suppose the Americans to combat against us with more unhappy auspices than those under which we combated against James, would not victory itself prove pernicious and deplorable? Would it not be fatal to British as well as American liberty? Those armies which should subjugate the colonies, would subjugate also their parent state. Marius, Sylla, Cæsar, Augustus, Tiberius—did they not oppress Roman liberty with the same troops that were levied to maintain Roman supremacy over subject provinces? But the impulse once given, its effects extended much further than its authors expected; for the same soldiery that destroyed the Roman republic, subverted and utterly demolished the imperial power itself. In less than fifty years after the death of Augustus, the armies destined to hold the provinces in subjection, proclaimed three emperors at once; disposed of the empire according to their caprice, and raised to the throne of the Cesars the object of their momentary favor.

I can no more comprehend the policy, than acknowledge the justice of your deliberations. Where is your force, what are your armies—how are they to be recruited, and how supported? The single province of Massachusetts has, at this moment, thirty thousand men, well trained and disciplined, and can bring, in case of emergency, ninety thousand men into the field; and, doubt not, they will do it, when all that is dear is at stake, when forced to defend their liberty and property against their cruel oppressors. Boston, perhaps, you may lay in ashes, or it may be made a strong garrison— but the province will be lost to you. You will hold Boston as you hold Gibraltar, in the midst of a country which will not be yours; the whole American colonies will remain in the power of your enemies. In the great scale of empires you will decline, I fear, from the decision of this day; and the Americans will rise to independence, to power, to all the greatness of the most renowned states; for they build on the solid basis of general public liberty.

I dread the effects of the present resolution; I shudder at our injustice and cruelty; I tremble for the consequences of our imprudence. You will drive the Americans to desperation. They will certainly defend their property and liberties with the spirit of freemen; with the spirit our ancestors did, and which I hope we should exert on a like occasion. They will sooner declare themselves independent, and risk every consequence of such a contest, than submit to the galling yoke which the administration is preparing for them.

You would declare the Americans rebels; and to your injustice and oppression you add the most opprobrious language and the most insulting scoffs. If you persist in your resolution, all hope of a reconciliation is extinct. The Americans will triumph,—the whole continent of North America will be dismembered from Great Britain, and the wide arch of the raised empire fall. But I hope the just vengeance of the people will overtake the authors of these pernicious counsels, and the loss of the first province of the empire be speedily followed by the loss of the heads of those ministers who first invented them.

Ex. XXX.—*OPINIONS OF AN ENGLISH TRAVELLER IN AMERICA.*

Speech in Parliament Feb. 27, 1775.

TEMPLE LUTTRELL.

I AM not, Sir, altogether unacquainted with the people of whom I am now speaking. Curiosity once led me to travel many hundreds of miles along their flourishing and hospitable provinces. I found in most of them the Spartan temperance, in many the urbanity of Athens; and notwithstanding the base and groundless imputations on their spirit which the cankered tongue of prejudice and slander has poured forth against them, they will, I am confident, if set to the proof, evince the Roman magnanimity, ere Rome fell under sceptred usurpation. But, Sir, if a foreign enemy should appear at your gates, will there be found among them many a Coriolanus? He stands single as the prodigy of forgiveness, in the annals of a people whose attachment to their native land was carried to the utmost height of enthusiasm.

How soon that foreign enemy may appear at your gates, I know not. According to the horological predictions of a most enlightened state soothsayer, we have about seven years more of profound tranquillity with the House of Bourbon to trust to; but from the symptoms of our domestic distraction, and the improved state of the government and finances of our neighbors, I should judge it prudent to be somewhat better provided than we are at present for an early rupture; not entirely to dismantle our ports and our coasts of soldiers and seamen, sent to immolate the martyrs to liberty of their own flesh and blood, on the distant continent of America.

It is well known, through melancholy observation, drawn from the fate of the Assyrian, Persian, and Roman empires, that national societies, as well as the individual mortals of whom those societies are composed, have their nonage, their adult vigor, and their decline. Whatever share of indulgence and independency Great Britain shall, in this her florid and athletic stage, generously bestow on her rising colonies, they will no doubt amply repay to her in some future generation when she is verging towards that awful goal which must close her race of glory.

The military coercion of America will be impracticable. What has been the fate of your famous Bills passed in the last session of the deceased parliament? I mean, Sir, the Boston Port Bill, and the one for altering the charter of Massachusetts Bay. America, as an earnest of her triumph over the future labors for which envy and malice may reserve her, has, like another Hercules in the cradle, already grappled with those two serpents sent for her destruction. Neither shall we be long able to sustain the unhallowed war at so remote a distance; unexplored deserts, woodland ambuscades, latitudes to which few of our soldiery have been seasoned; the southern provinces scarcely to be endured in the summer months, the northern provinces not approachable in the winter season; shipwrecks, pestilence, famine,—the unrelenting inveteracy and carnage of York and Lancaster will here be joined to all the elementary hardships and maladies of a bigot crusade.

Now, Sir, who can look forward to a probable epoch in the red volume of Time, when the sword drawn in this quarrel will be sheathed in peace? Without a gift of preternatural foresight, I may remark that these are features in the aspect of infant America which denote at maturer years a most colossal force. And, to adopt their own words, what they contend for is that reasonable portion of liberty with which they were chartered as their birthright, not by any earthly potentate, but by the King of kings, "to make their lives happy in the possession of which liberty they do now hourly invoke that King of kings, or to make their death glorious in its just defence."

Beware how you aggravate a spirit like this! It will grow, it will strengthen, it will gather to itself every stream of patriotic feeling and love of freedom, until, like a roaring torrent, it will overwhelm you and bury you in the abyss of its waters!

Ex. XXXI.—*ANNIVERSARY ORATION.*

Delivered at Boston, March 5, 1775.

DR. JOSEPH WARREN.

My ever honored fellow-citizens: You will not now expect the elegance, the learning, the fire, the enrapturing strains of eloquence, which charmed you when a Lovell or a Hancock spoke; but you will permit me to say, that with a sincerity equal to theirs, I mourn over my bleeding country. With them I weep at her distress, and with them deeply resent the injuries she has received from the hands of cruel and unreasonable men.

Yet, though our country is in danger, it is not to be despaired of. Our enemies are numerous and powerful, but we have many friends, determined to be free—and Heaven and earth will aid the resolution. On *you* depend the fortunes of America. You are to decide the important question on which rest the happiness and liberty of millions yet unborn. Act worthy of yourselves. The faltering tongue of hoary age calls on you to support your country. The lisping infant raises its suppliant hands, imploring defence against the monster slavery. Your fathers look from their celestial seats with smiling approbation on their sons, who boldly stand forth in the cause of virtue; but sternly frown upon the inhuman miscreant who, to secure the loaves and fishes to himself, would breed a serpent to destroy his children!

But pardon me, my fellow citizens, I know you want not zeal or fortitude. You will maintain your rights, or perish in the generous struggle. However difficult the combat, you never will decline it when Freedom is the prize. An independence of Great Britain is not our aim. No! our wish is that Great Britain and the colonies may, like the oak and ivy, grow and increase in strength together. But if pacific measures are ineffectual—if it should appear that the only way to safety is through fields of blood, I know you will never turn your faces from the foe, but will undauntedly press forward until tyranny is trodden under foot, and you have fixed your adored goddess Liberty fast by a Brunswick's side on an American throne.

You then, who nobly have espoused your country's cause —who generously have sacrificed wealth and ease—who have despised the pomp and show of tinselled greatness—refused the summons to the festive board, and been deaf to the alluring calls of luxury and mirth; who have forsaken your downy pillow to keep your vigils by the midnight lamp, for the salvation of your invaded country; you will reap that harvest of renown which you so justly have deserved. Even the children of your most inveterate enemies, ashamed to tell from whence they sprung, shall join the general cry of gratitude to those who broke the fetters that their fathers forged.

Having redeemed your country, and secured the blessing to future generations, who, fired by your example, shall emulate your virtues, and learn from you the heavenly art of making millions happy—with heart-felt joy, with transports all your own, you will cry, "The glorious work is done!" Then drop the mantle to some young Elisha, and take your seats with kindred spirits in your native skies.

Ex. XXXII.—*USELESS TOIL.*

Speech in Parliament, March 16, 1775.

LORD CAMDEN.

MY LORDS:—To conquer a great continent of 1,800 miles in length, containing three millions of people, all indissolubly united on the great Whig foundation of liberty, seems an undertaking not to be rashly engaged in. Where are you to get men and money adequate to the service and expense that the reduction of such a continent must require? What are the ten thousand men you have just voted out to Boston? Merely to save General Gage from the disgrace and destruction of being sacked in his entrenchments. It is obvious, my lords, that you cannot furnish armies, or treasure competent to the mighty purpose of subduing America. It is obvious that your only effort can be by your naval power; and admitting full success to this, what can you effect? Merely the blocking up of their ports, and the suppression of their trade.

But will this procure the conquest of America? No, my lords, they are prepared to meet these severities, and to surmount them. They are applying themselves most diligently to agriculture, that great source of strength and independence. Foreseeing the important crisis, they have provided against its wants; and have imported into their country stores of industry, implements of husbandry and manufactures. They have united in the rejection of luxury and superfluous enjoyment. They have suppressed their public diversions, formerly common enough in their great and wealthy towns; and every man attaches himself wholly to the great business of his country. Such is the state of America. She has curtailed her expenses; she has reduced her table; she has clothed herself in mean and coarse stuffs; she has adopted the wise system of frugal industry. Her wants can be only ideal, imaginary, non-existent.

But, my lords, what will be the state of this civilized, enlightened, dissipated and debauched country? How shall the want of American commerce be supplied, of that commerce which contributes the means of your luxury, of your enjoyments, of the imaginary happiness of this country? We may feel the loss of American connection, a loss which nothing can compensate; but America will have little reason to regret her disconnection from England; and, my lords, it is evident that England must one day lose the dominion of America.

It is impossible that this petty island can retain in dependence that mighty continent increasing daily in numbers and strength. To protract the time of separation to a distant day, is all that can be hoped; and this hope might be obtained by wise and temperate counsels; not by precipitation and violence uniting England against you; for so it is, my lords; there is not a man in America who can endure the idea of being taxed, perhaps to the amount of his whole property, by a legislation three thousand miles distant; or who can separate the idea of taxation from representation.

And when you consider what has been your conduct towards America; when the severest and most comprehensive punishments are inflicted, without examining the offence; when their constitutional liberties are destroyed; when their charters and their rights are sacrificed to the vindictive spirit of the moment; when you thus tear up all their privileges by the roots; is there a country under heaven, breathing the last gasp of freedom, that will not resist such oppressions, and vindicate, on the oppressors' heads, such violations of justice?

And what, my lords, is the state into which the present measures have brought both countries? At home, discontent and division prevail; but in America it was reserved for the wisdom of these times to produce such a union as renders her invincible. The Americans are now united and cemented by the strongest ties. They are allied in the common defence of every thing most dear to them. They are struggling in support of their liberties and properties, and the most sacred rights of mankind. Thus associated by the strongest mutual engagements, and aided by their mutual strength, aided by the justice of their cause, I must assert and repeat, my lords, that your efforts against them must be without success, and your war impracticable.

Ex. XXXIII.—*THE REVENUE QUESTION.*

Speech in Parliament, March 22, 1775.

EDMUND BURKE.

I, FOR one, protest against compounding our demands; I declare against compounding, for a poor limited sum, the immense, ever-growing, eternal debt, which is due to generous government from protected freedom. And so may I speed in the great object I propose to you, as I think it would not only be an act of injustice, but would be the worst economy in the world, to compel the colonies to a sum certain, either in the way of ransom, or in the way of compulsory compact.

But to clear up my ideas on this subject; a revenue from America transmitted hither—do not delude yourselves, you can never receive it—no, not a shilling. We have experience, that from remote countries it is not to be expected. If, when you attempted to extract revenue from Bengal, you were obliged to return in loan what you had taken in imposition; what can you expect from North America? For certainly, if there ever was a country qualified to produce wealth, it is India; or an institution fit for the transmission, it is the East India company. America has none of these aptitudes. If America gives you taxable objects, on which you lay your duties here, and gives you, at the same time, a surplus, by a foreign sale of her commodities to pay the duties on these objects which you tax at home, she has performed her part in the British revenue. But with regard to her own internal establishment; she may, I doubt not she will, contribute in moderation. I say, in moderation; for she ought not to be permitted to exhaust herself. She ought to be reserved to a war, the weight of which, with the enemies we are likely to have, must be considerable in her quarter of the globe. Then she may serve you, and serve you essentially.

For that service, for all service, whether of revenue, trade, or empire, my trust is in her interest in the British constitution. My hold of the colonies is in the close affection which grows from common names, from kindred blood, from similar privileges and equal protection. These are ties which, though light as air, are strong as links of iron. Let the colonies always keep the idea of their civil rights associated with your government,—they will cling and grapple to you, and no force under heaven will be of power to tear them from their allegiance. As long as you have the wisdom to keep the sovereign authority of this country as the sanctuary of liberty, the sacred temple consecrated to our common faith, wherever the chosen race and sons of England worship freedom, they will turn their faces toward you. The more they multiply, the more friends you will have; the more ardently they love liberty, the more perfect will be their obedience.

Slavery they can have anywhere. It is a weed that grows in every soil. They may have it from Spain, they may have it from Prussia. But until you become lost to all feeling of your true interest and your natural dignity, freedom they can have from none but you. This is the commodity of price, of which you have the monopoly. This is the true act of navigation, which binds to you the commerce of the colonies, and through them secures to you the wealth of the world. Deny them this participation of freedom, and you break that sole bond which originally made, and must still preserve, the unity of the empire. It is the spirit of the English constitution, which, infused through the mighty mass, pervades, feeds, unites, invigorates, vivifies, every part of the empire, even down to the minutest member.

Is it not the same virtue that does everything for us here in England? Do you imagine, then, that it is the land-tax act which raises your revenue? that it is the annual vote in the committee of supply which gives you your army? or that it is the mutiny bill which inspires it with bravery and discipline? No! surely no! It is the love of the people; it is their attachment to their government, from the sense of the deep stake they have in such a glorious institution, which gives you your army and your navy, without which your army would be a base rabble and your navy nothing but rotten timber.

Magnanimity in politics is not seldom the truest wisdom; and a great empire and little minds go ill together. If we are conscious of our situation, and glow with zeal to fill our places as becomes our station and ourselves, we ought to auspicate all our public proceedings on America, with the old warning of the church, *Sursum corda!* We ought to elevate our minds to the greatness of that trust to which the order of Providence has called us. By adverting to the dignity of this high calling, our ancestors have turned a savage wilderness into a glorious empire; and have made the most extensive, and the only honorable conquests, not by destroying, but by promoting the wealth, the number, the happiness of the human race. Let us get an American revenue as we have got an American empire. English privileges have made it all that it is; English privileges alone will make it all that it can be.

Ex. XXXIV.—*SPIRIT OF ENTERPRISE IN NEW ENGLAND.*

Speech in Parliament, March 22, 1775.

EDMUND BURKE.

As to the wealth, Mr. Speaker, which the colonies have drawn from the sea by their fisheries, you had all that matter fully opened at your bar. You surely thought those acquisitions of value, for they seemed even to excite your envy; and yet the spirit by which that enterprising employment has been exercised, ought rather, in my opinion, to have raised your esteem and admiration. And pray, Sir, what in the world is equal to it? Pass by the other parts, and look at the manner in which the people of New England have of late carried on the whale fishery.

Whilst we follow them among the tumbling mountains of ice, and behold them penetrating into the deepest frozen recesses of Hudson's Bay, and Davis's Straits, whilst we are looking for them beneath the Arctic Circle, we hear that they have pierced into the opposite region of polar cold, that they are at the antipodes, and engaged under the frozen serpent of the South Falkland Island, which seemed too remote and romantic an object for the grasp of national ambition, but is only a stage and resting place in the progress of their victorious industry.

Nor is the equinoctial heat more discouraging to them than the accumulated winter of both the poles. We know that whilst some of them draw the line and strike the harpoon on the coast of Africa, others run the longitude, and pursue their gigantic game along the coast of Brazil. No sea but what is vexed by their fisheries. No climate that is not witness to their toils. Neither the perseverance of Holland, nor the activity of France, nor the dexterous and firm sagacity of English enterprise, ever carried this most perillous mode of hardy industry to the extent to which it has been pushed by this recent people; a people who are still, as it were, but in the gristle, and not yet hardened into the bone of manhood.

When I contemplate these things; when I know that the colonies in general owe little or nothing to any care of ours, and that they are not squeezed into this happy form by the constraints of a watchful and suspicious government, but that through a wise and salutary neglect, a generous nature has been suffered to take her own way to perfection; when I reflect upon these effects, when I see how profitable they have been to us, I feel all the pride of power sink, and all presumption in the wisdom of human contrivances melt, and die away within me. My rigor relents. I pardon something to the spirit of liberty.

In the character of the Americans, a love of freedom is the predominating feature which marks and distinguishes the whole; and as an ardent is always a jealous affection, your colonies become suspicious, restive, and intractable whenever they see the least attempt to wrest from them by force, or shuffle from them by chicane, what they think the only advantage worth living for.

The people of the colonies are descendants of Englishmen. England, Sir, is a nation, which still, I hope, respects, and formerly adored, her freedom. The colonists emigrated from you, when this part of your character was most predominant; and they took this bias and direction the moment they parted from your hands. They are, therefore, not only devoted to liberty, but to liberty according to English ideas, and on English principles. It happened, you know, Sir, that the great contests for freedom in this country were from the earliest times chiefly upon the question of taxing.

Most of the contests in the ancient commonwealths turned primarily on the right of the election of magistrates; or on the balance among the several orders of the state. But in England it was otherwise. On this point of taxes the ablest pens and the most eloquent tongues have been exercised; the greatest spirits have acted and suffered.

They have taken infinite pains to inculcate, as a fundamental principle, that, in all monarchies, the people must in themselves, mediately or immediately, possess the power of granting their own money, or no shadow of liberty could exist. The colonies draw from you, as with their life-blood, their ideas and principles. Their love of liberty, as with you, is fixed and attached on this specific point of taxing. Liberty might be safe, or might be endangered in twenty other particulars, without their being much pleased or alarmed. Here they felt its pulse; and as they found that beat, they thought themselves sick or sound. I do not say whether they were right or wrong in applying your general arguments to their own case. The fact is, they did thus apply those arguments, and your mode of governing them, whether through lenity or indolence, through wisdom or mistake, confirmed them in the imagination that they, as well as you, had an interest in these common principles.

Ex. XXXV.—*LEXINGTON.**

April 19, 1775.

OLIVER WENDELL HOLMES.

SLOWLY the mist o'er the meadow was creeping,
   Bright on the dewy buds glistened the sun,
When from his couch, while his children were sleeping,
   Rose the bold rebel and shouldered his gun.
      Waving her golden veil
      Over the silent dale
Blithe looked the morning on cottage and spire;

* It having been found impossible to obtain sufficient Revolutionary poetry (of a suitable kind) to give variety to the selections, such as refers to well-known events in our history, although written in more modern times, will be introduced in its appropriate chronological order.

Hushed was his parting sigh,
While from his noble eye
Flashed the last sparkle of liberty's fire.

On the smooth green where the fresh leaf is springing,
    Calmly the first-born of glory have met;
Hark! the death volley around them is ringing!
    Look! with their life-blood the young grass is wet!
        Faint is the feeble breath
        Murmuring low in death,
"Tell to our sons how their fathers have died;"
        Nerveless the iron hand,
        Raised for its native land,
Lies by the weapon that gleams at its side.

Over the hill-sides the wild knell is tolling,
    From their far hamlets the yeomanry come;
As through the storm-clouds the thunder-burst rolling,
    Circles the beat of the mustering drum.
        Fast on the soldier's path
        Darken the waves of wrath;
Long have they gathered and loud shall they fall;
        Red glares the musket's flash,
        Sharp rings the rifle's crash,
Blazing and clanging from thicket and wall.

Gaily the plume of the horseman was dancing,
    Never to shadow his cold brow again;
Proudly at morning the war-steed was prancing,
    Reeking and panting he droops on the rein.
        Pale is the lip of scorn,
        Voiceless the trumpet horn,
Torn is the silken-fringed red cross on high;
        Many a belted breast
        Low on the turf shall rest,
Ere the dark hunters the herd have passed by.

Snow-girdled crags where the hoarse wind is raving,
    Rocks where the weary floods murmur and wail,
Wilds where the fern by the furrow is waving,
    Reeled with the echoes that rode on the gale.
        Far as the tempest thrills
        Over the darkened hills,
Far as the sunshine streams over the plain,

3*

>   Roused by the tyrant band,
>   Woke all the mighty land,
> Girded for battle, from mountain to main.
>
> Green be the graves where her martyrs are lying!
>   Shroudless and tombless they sank to their rest,—
> While o'er their ashes the starry fold flying
>   Wraps the proud eagle they roused from his nest.
>   Borne on her northern pine
>   Long o'er the foaming brine,
> Spread her broad banner to storm and to sun;
>   Heaven keep her ever free,
>   Wide as o'er land and sea
> Floats the fair emblem her heroes have won.

Ex. XXXV.—*ADDRESS OF THE CONGRESS OF MASSACHUSETTS BAY TO THE INHABITANTS OF GREAT BRITAIN.*

April 26, 1775.

FRIENDS AND FELLOW SUBJECTS: Hostilities are at length commenced in this colony by the troops under the command of General Gage, and it being of the greatest importance that an early, true and authentic account of this inhuman proceeding should be known to you, the Congress of this colony think it proper to address you on the alarming occasion.

By the clearest depositions relative to this transaction, it will appear that on the night preceding the 19th of April, instant, a body of the king's troops, under command of Colonel Smith, were secretly landed at Cambridge, with an apparent design to take or destroy the military and other stores, provided for the defence of this colony, and deposited at Concord—that some inhabitants of the colony, on the night aforesaid, whilst travelling peaceably on the road between Boston and Concord were seized and greatly abused by armed men, who appeared to be officers of General Gage's army—that the town of Lexington, by these means, was alarmed, and a company of the inhabitants mustered on the occasion—that the regular troops on their way to Concord, marched into the said town of Lexington, and the said company, on their approach, began to disperse—that, notwithstanding this, the regulars rushed on with great violence and first began hostilities, by firing on said Lexington company, whereby they killed eight, and wounded several others—that the regulars continued their fire, until those of said company who were neither killed nor wounded, had made their escape—that Colonel Smith, with the detachment, then marched to Concord, where a number of provincials were again fired on by the troops, two of them killed and several wounded, before the provincials fired on them—and that these hostile measures of the troops produced an engagement that lasted through the day, in which many of the provincials, and more of the regular troops, were killed and wounded.

To give a particular account of the ravages of the troops, as they retreated from Concord to Charlestown, would be very difficult, if not impracticable; let it suffice to say, that a great number of the houses on the road were plundered and rendered unfit for use; several were burnt; women in child-bed were driven by the soldiery naked into the streets; old men remaining peaceably in their houses were shot dead, and such scenes exhibited as would disgrace the annals of the most uncivilized nation.

These, brethren, are marks of ministerial vengeance against this colony for refusing, with her sister colonies, a submission to slavery; but they have not yet detached us from our royal sovereign. We profess to be his loyal and dutiful subjects, and so hardly dealt with as we have been, are still ready, with our lives and fortunes, to defend his person, family, crown and dignity. Nevertheless, to the persecution and tyranny of his cruel ministry, we will not tamely submit; appealing to Heaven for the justice of our cause, we determine to die or be free.

We can not think that the honor, wisdom and valor of Britons will suffer them to be longer inactive spectators of measures in which they themselves are so deeply interested —measures pursued in opposition to the solemn protests of many noble lords, and expressed sense of conspicuous commoners, whose knowledge and virtue have long characterized them as some of the greatest men in the nation—measures executed contrary to the interests, petitions, and resolves of many large, respectable and opulent counties, cities, and boroughs in Great Britain—measures highly incompatible with justice, but still pursued with a specious pretence of easing the nation of its burthens—measures which, if successful, must end in the ruin and slavery of Britain, as well as the persecuted American colonies.

We sincerely hope that the Great Sovereign of the Universe, who hath so often appeared for the English nation, will support you in every rational and manly exertion with these colonies, for saving it from ruin, and that, in a constitutional connection with the mother country, we shall soon be altogether a free and happy people.

Ex. XXXVI.—*WAR INEVITABLE.*

Speech in the Continental Congress, 1775.

PATRICK HENRY.*

Mr. President: It is natural for man to indulge in the illusions of hope. We are apt to shut our eyes against a painful truth; and listen to the song of that syren till she turns us into beasts. Is this the part of wise men, engaged in a great and arduous struggle for liberty? Are we disposed to be of the number of those who, having eyes, see not, and having ears, hear not, the things which so nearly concern our temporal salvation? For my part, whatever anguish of spirit it may cost, I am willing to know the whole truth; to know the worst, and to provide for it.

I have but one lamp by which my feet are guided; and that is the lamp of experience. I know of no way of judging of the future but by the past. And judging by the past, I wish to know what there has been in the conduct of the British ministry for the last ten years to justify those hopes with which gentlemen have been pleased to solace themselves and the house? Is it that insidious smile with which our petition has been lately received? Trust it not, Sir: it will prove a snare to your feet. Suffer not yourselves to be be-

---

* Patrick Henry was a born orator. With very little preparatory study, and after a youth spent in agricultural and mercantile pursuits, he began to practise law, and distinguished himself so much in his profession that he was soon called into public life, where he filled one office after another until the new government was fairly in operation, after which he resumed his attendance at the bar. His powers of oratory are said by those who heard him to have been indescribable, and this is given as a reason why so few of his speeches have come down to us, except traditionally. He was a native of Virginia, and died in the same year with Washington.

trayed with a kiss. Ask yourselves how this gracious reception of our petition comports with those warlike preparations which cover our waters and darken our land. Are fleets and armies necessary to a work of love and reconciliation? Have we shown ourselves so unwilling to be reconciled that force must be called in to win back our love? Let us not deceive ourselves, Sir. These are the implements of war and subjugation—the last arguments to which kings resort.

I ask gentlemen, Sir, what means this martial array, if its purpose be not to force us to submission? Can gentlemen assign any other possible motive for it? Has Great Britain any enemy in this quarter of the world, to call for all this accumulation of navies and armies? No, Sir, she has none. They are meant for us; they can be meant for no other. They are sent over to bind and rivet upon us those chains which the British ministry have been so long forging. And what have we to oppose to them? Shall we try argument? Sir, we have been trying that for the last ten years. Have we anything new to offer upon the subject? Nothing. We have held the subject up in every light of which it is capable; but it has been all in vain.

Shall we resort to entreaty and humble supplication? What terms shall we find which have not been already exhausted? Let us not, I beseech you, Sir, deceive ourselves longer. Sir, we have done everything that could be done to avert the storm which is now coming on. We have petitioned—we have remonstrated—we have supplicated—we have prostrated ourselves before the throne, and have implored its interposition to arrest the tyrannical hands of the ministry and parliament. Our petitions have been slighted; our remonstrances have produced additional violence and insult: our supplications have been disregarded; and we have been spurned, with contempt, from the foot of the throne.

In vain, after these things, may we indulge the fond hope of peace and reconciliation. *There is no longer any room for hope.* If we wish to be free—if we mean to preserve inviolate those inestimable privileges for which we have been so long contending—if we mean not basely to abandon the noble struggle in which we have been so long engaged, and which we have pledged ourselves never to abandon, until the glorious object of our contest shall be obtained—we must fight! I repeat it, Sir, we must fight!! An appeal to arms, and to the God of Hosts, is all that is left us.

They tell us, Sir, that we are **weak**—unable to cope with

so formidable an adversary. But when shall we be stronger? Will it be the next week, or the next year? Will it be when we are totally disarmed, and when a British guard shall be stationed in every house? Shall we gather strength by irresolution and inaction? Shall we acquire the means of effectual resistance by lying supinely on our backs, and hugging the delusive phantom of hope, until our enemies shall have bound us hand and foot? Sir, we are not weak if we make a proper use of those means which the God of Nature hath placed in our power.

Three millions of people, armed in the holy cause of liberty, and in such a country as that which we possess, are invincible by any force which our enemy can send against us. Besides, Sir, we shall not fight our battles alone. There is a just God, who presides over the destinies of nations, and who will raise up friends to fight our battles for us. The battle, Sir, is not to the strong alone; it is to the vigilant, the active, the brave. Besides, Sir, we have no election. If we were base enough 'to desire it, it is now too late to retire from the contest. There is no retreat but in submission and slavery! Our chains are forged. Their clanking may be heard on the plains of Boston! The war is inevitable, and let it come!! I repeat it, Sir, let it come!!!

It is in vain, Sir, to extenuate the matter. Gentlemen may cry peace, peace—but there is no peace. The war is actually begun! The next gale that sweeps from the north will bring to our ears the clash of resounding arms! Our brethren are already in the field! Why stand we here idle? What is it that gentlemen wish? What would they have? Is life so dear, or peace so sweet, as to be purchased at the price of chains and slavery? Forbid it, Almighty God! I know not what course others may take; but as for me, give me liberty, or give me death!

Ex. XXXVII.—*CONFLICT OF DUTY AND INCLINATION.*

Speech in Parliament, May 18, 1775.

EARL OF EFFINGHAM.*

I confess, my lords, that whatever has been done by the Americans I must deem the mere consequence of our un-

* The Earl of Effingham was bred to arms, and from an eager desire to become a practical soldier, served as a volunteer in the Russian army, during

just demands. They have come to you with fair arguments, you have refused to hear them; they make the most respectful remonstrances, you answer them with pains and penalties; they know they ought to be free, you tell them they shall be slaves. Is it then a wonder if they say in despair, "For the short remainder of our lives we will be free!" Is there one among your lordships who, in a situation similar to that which I have described, would not resolve the same? If there could be such a one, I am sure he ought not to be here.

To bring the history down to the present scene. Here are two armies in presence of each other; armies of brothers and countrymen; each dreading the event, yet each feeling that it is in the power of the most trifling accident to cause the sword to be drawn, and to plunge the whole country into all the horrors of blood, flames and parricide. In this dreadful moment, a set of men more moderate than the rest exert themselves to bring us all to reason. They state their claims and their grievances; nay, if any thing can be proved by law and history, they prove it. They propose oblivion; they make the first concessions; we treat them with contempt; we prefer poverty, blood, and servitude, to wealth, happiness, and liberty.

My lords, I should think myself guilty of offering an insult to your lordships, if I could presume that there is any one among you who could think of what was expedient, when once it appeared what was just. What weight these few observations may have, I do not know; but the candor your lordships have indulged me with, requires a confession on my part which may still lessen that weight. I must own I am not personally disinterested. Ever since I was of an age to have any ambition at all, my highest has been to serve my country in a military capacity. If there was on earth an event I dreaded, it was to see this country so situated as to make that profession incompatible with my duty as a citizen.

That period is, in my opinion, arrived; and I have thought myself bound to relinquish the hopes I had formed by a resignation which appeared to me the only method of avoiding the guilt of enslaving my country, and imbruing

---

the war with the Porte. The regiment of foot in which he held a captain's commission being ordered to America, he resolved, though not possessed of an ample patrimony, to resign a darling profession rather than bear arms in a cause he did not approve. The cities of London and Dublin voted him their thanks for this conduct.

my hands in the blood of her sons. When the duties of a soldier and a citizen become inconsistent, I shall always think myself obliged to sink the character of the soldier in that of the citizen, till such duties shall again, by the malice of our real enemies, become united. It is no small sacrifice which a man makes who gives up his profession; but it is a much greater, when a predilection, strengthened by habit, has given him so strong an attachment to his profession as I feel. I have, however, this one consolation, that by making that sacrifice, I, at least, give to my country an unequivocal proof of the sincerity of my principles.

Ex. XXXIX.—*WARREN'S ADDRESS BEFORE THE BATTLE OF BUNKER HILL.*

J. PIERPONT.

STAND! The ground 's your own, my braves!
Will ye give it up to slaves?
Will ye look for greener graves?
   Hope ye mercy still?
What's the mercy despots feel?
Hear it in that battle peal!
Read it on yon bristling steel!
   Ask it,—ye who will.

Fear ye foes who kill for hire?
Will ye to your *homes* retire?
Look behind you!—they're a-fire!
   And, before you, see
Who have done it! From the vale
On they come!—and will you quail?
Leaden rain and iron hail
   Let their welcome be!

In the God of battles trust!
Die we may,—and die we must:
But, oh! where can dust to dust
   Be consigned so well,
As where heaven its dews shall shed
On the martyred patriot's bed,
And the rocks shall raise their head
   Of his deeds to tell.

Ex. XL.—*EULOGIUM ON GEN. JOSEPH WARREN,* WHO FELL AT THE BATTLE OF BUNKER HILL, JUNE 17th, 1775.*

WHAT spectacle more noble than this, of a hero who has given his life for the safety of his country! Approach, cruel ministers, and contemplate the fruits of your sanguinary edicts. What reparation can you offer to his children for the loss of such a father, to the king for that of so good a subject, to the country for that of so devoted a citizen? Send hither your satellites; come, feast your vindictive rage; the most implacable enemy to tyrants is no more. We conjure you, respect these his honored remains. Have compassion on the fate of a mother overwhelmed with despair and with age. Of him, nothing is left that you can still fear. His eloquence is mute: his arms are fallen from his hand: then lay down yours; what more have you to perpetrate, barbarians that you are? But, while the name of American liberty shall live, that of Warren will fire our breasts, and animate our arms, against the pest of standing armies.

Approach, Senators of America! Come, and deliberate here upon the interests of the United Colonies. Listen to the voice of this illustrious citizen; he entreats, he exhorts, he implores you not to disturb his present felicity with the doubt that he, perhaps, has sacrificed his life for a people of slaves.

Come hither, ye soldiers, ye champions of American liberty, and contemplate a spectacle which should inflame your generous hearts with even a new motive to glory. Remember his shade still hovers, unexpiated, among us. Ten thousand ministerial soldiers would not suffice to compensate his death. Let ancient ties be no restraint: foes of liberty

* The name of this early martyr to liberty is invested with a romantic interest. He was one of those many-sided men whose loss seems to create a separate vacancy in each department adorned by them, and whose death is regretted in proportion to the versatility of their talents. A successful and skilful physician, an eloquent public speaker, a graceful and elegant conversationist, of high literary culture and a brave and patriotic spirit, he had but just enlisted in the military service of his country when the battle of Bunker Hill cut him off in the prime of manhood, at the age of thirty-four. His death was deeply felt by the struggling colony, and a year afterward his remains were removed from the lowly grave dug on the spot where he fell, and interred with much ceremony in Boston. His having been twice selected to deliver the "Fifth of March" oration, extracts from which have already been given in this volume, shows in what estimation his literary endowments were held by his fellow-citizens.

are no longer the brethren of freemen. Give edge to your arms, and lay them not down till tyranny be expelled from the British empire, or America, at least, become the real seat of liberty and happiness.

Approach ye also, American fathers and American mothers; come hither, and contemplate the first fruits of tyranny; behold your friend, the defender of your liberty, the honor, the hope of your country. See this illustrious hero, pierced with wounds, and bathed in his own blood. But let not your grief, let not your tears be sterile. Go, hasten to your homes, and there teach your children to detest the deeds of tyranny; lay before them the horrid scene you have beheld; let their hair stand on end; let their eyes sparkle with fire; let resentment kindle every feature; let their lips vent threats and indignation; then—then put arms into their hands, send them to battle, and let your last injunction be, to return victorious, or to die, like Warren, in the arms of liberty and glory!

Ex. XLI.—*BUNKER HILL.*

ALFRED B. STREET.

THE eve of a deathless day
  Had gather'd o'er the land,
And the clear moon cast her silvery ray
  On banner, plume, and brand;
Ranks of the bold and free
  Were rallying thickly round,
With the stern watchword "Liberty!"
  To drum and trumpet sound.
The hunter left his deer-trod hill,
The hamlet's busy voice was still,
The bark lay idly by the shore,
The city's hum arose no more;
And wild birds in the thicket sung
Where late the woodman's hatchet rung.
All came to swell the patriot's ranks—
  Men who to man ne'er bow'd the knee:
  Like mountain torrents, wild and free,
Fierce bursting from their banks.

Morn breaks. On yon embattled height,
  What form stands towering in the air,
Holding an ægis broad and bright
  O'er the small band collected there?
And whose that banner o'er her streaming,
In striped and starry blazon gleaming?
And whose that eagle at her side,
With arching neck, and glance of pride?
American! 'tis Freedom's form!
Does not thy life-blood kindle warm?
And thine that standard waving high,
And thine that eagle pluming by.
With blast of trump and roll of drum,
Near and more near the foemen come!
Think, sire! thy helpless children throw
Their arms for succor round thee now!
Think, son! thy age-worn parents feel
Their fireside hopes are on thy steel!
And, most of all, oh, think that ye
Defend a nation's liberty!

Smoke veils the view—but flash on flash,
And roar on roar, and crash on crash,
And groan and shriek, and shout and yell,
The progress of the combat tell.
Fitfully through the lurid haze
Shoots fierce and red the cannon's blaze,
And glance, like sparkles on a stream,
Glitter of sword, and bayonet's gleam.
It lifts—wild scene of rushing files,
And dropping forms, and thickening piles.
But, on yon earthen mounds, behold!
That starry flag is still unrolled;
There side by side the patriots stand,
The bulwark of their native land.
In struggling masses—up the hill,
  On the steep glacis, scorch'd and plough'd,
Beneath the tottering ramparts, still
  The eager hosts of England crowd.
Twice had they hurled, with warrior might,
On Freedom's ranks the deadly fight,
And twice, upon their corpse-strewn track,
By Freedom's sons been beaten back.
But see! they rally now; the air

Gleams with the bayonets bristling there.
They come! they come! Brave hearts! who stay'd
That serried torrent undismayed,
   When fiercer in its flow;
By all the dearest ties of earth—
By all the holiest rights of birth,
   Sink not beneath it now.

Once more! once more! ye tried and true,
Bear up, for Freedom strives with you!
Your banner waves before your eye,
Your guardian Eagle hovers nigh.
By every blow a right is freed,
On every effort's glory's meed!
Ha! Warren falls! but waver not—
Pour in your last, your deadliest shot!
Now like a lion, death-beset,
And drenched with blood, unconquer'd yet—
With bristling mane, and rolling eye,
Too weak to rush—too proud to fly,
Scowling more grim, as hasten foes,
Growling more fierce, as thicken blows,
Till, with a roar of deep despair,
He staggers feebly to his lair—
Grasp, grasp again, ye little band,
Each weapon with determined hand!
Though every limb is faint with toil,
And every vein has stained the soil,
With your clench'd muskets, strike once more!
One crushing blow!—'tis o'er—'tis o'er!—
And shouting as they slowly flee,
They leave the humbled king his useless victory.

Ex. XLII.—*DECLARATION OF RIGHTS BY THE CONTINENTAL CONGRESS.*

July 6th, 1775.

WERE it possible for men who exercise their reason, to believe that the Divine Author of our existence intended a part of the human race to hold an absolute property in, and unbounded power over others,—marked out by his infinite goodness and wisdom as the objects of a legal domination never rightfully resistible, however severe and oppressive,—the inhabitants of these colonies might, at least, require from the Parliament of Great Britain some evidence that this dreadful authority over them has been granted to that body. But a reverence for our great Creator, principles of humanity, and the dictates of common sense, must convince all those who reflect upon the subject, that government was instituted to promote the welfare of mankind, and ought to be administered for the attainment of that end.

The Legislature of Great Britain, however, stimulated by an inordinate passion for power, and despairing of success in any mode of contest where regard should be had to truth, law, or right, have at length deserted them all. They have attempted to effect their cruel and impolitic purpose of enslaving these colonies by violence, and have therefore rendered it necessary for us to close with their last appeal from reason to arms. Yet, however blinded that Assembly may be by their intemperate rage for unlimited domination, so to slight justice and the opinion of mankind, we esteem ourselves, by obligations of respect to the rest of the world, to make known the justice of our cause.

We are reduced to the alternative of choosing an unconditional submission to tyranny, or resistance by force. The latter is our choice. We have counted the cost of this contest, and find nothing so dreadful as voluntary slavery. Honor, justice, and humanity forbid us tamely to surrender that freedom which we received from our gallant ancestors, and which our innocent posterity has a right to receive from us.

Our cause is just; our union is perfect; our internal resources are great; and, if necessary, foreign assistance is undoubtedly attainable.

With hearts fortified with these animating reflections, we most solemnly, before God and the world, declare, that exerting the utmost energy of those powers which our beneficent Creator has graciously bestowed upon us, the arms we have been compelled by our enemies to assume, we will, in defiance of every hazard, employ for the preservation of our liberties, being of one mind resolved to die freemen, rather than live slaves.

We fight not for glory, or for conquest, we exhibit to mankind the remarkable spectacle of a people attacked by unprovoked enemies. They boast of their privileges and civilization, and yet proffer no milder conditions than servitude or death.

In our own native land—in defence of the freedom that is our birthright,—for the protection of our property against violence actually offered—we have taken up arms; we shall lay them down when hostilities shall cease on the part of the aggressors, and all danger of their being resumed shall be removed—and not before.

Ex. XLIII.—*PARLIAMENTARY LEVITY REPROVED.*

Speech in Parliament, October 26, 1775.

EARL OF SHELBURNE.

It is with equal astonishment and concern, my lords, that I perceive not the least mention made in the speech which has been this day delivered to us, of a paper, the most important of any that could possibly come under the consideration of this house. I mean the last petition from the general congress in America. How comes it that the colonies are charged with planning independence in the face of their explicit declaration to the contrary, contained in that petition? Is it the intention, by thus perpetually sounding independence in the ears of the Americans, to lead them to it, or by treating them, upon suspicion, with every possible violence, to compel them into that which must be our ruin? For let visionary writers say what they will, it is a plain and incontestable fact that the commerce of America is the vital stream of this great empire.

My lords, you have heard two of his majesty's ministers acknowledge that they were deceived in their information and have erred in their measures respecting America. There wants only a similar acknowledgment from a certain law lord, who was forward to pledge himself last year for the success of their plans. A little blood, indeed, he owned they might cost, but with that their efficacy was inevitable. The noble lord's political sagacity has for once forsaken him. A great deal of blood has been unhappily shed, to no purpose but to sever us more, if not to put us asunder forever.

But is it possible that your lordships should not have marked, and marked with indignation, the levity, and even ridicule, with which the noble lord at the head of the admiralty has treated this most solemn subject? No man who did not feel himself secure in the promise of impunity from some quarter, would proclaim his mistakes in triumph, and sport with the calamities of his country. The noble lord laughs at all proposals of reconciliation—repeats his imputation of cowardice against the Americans—says the idea of rights is to be driven out of their heads by blows, and ridicules the objections against employing foreigners and papists. I appeal to you, my lords, is it decent thus to stigmatize so great a part of the empire with so base a calumny? Is this a language becoming so great an officer of state?

The inevitable consequence of persevering in these measures must be such a depreciation of our estates, that opulence will be reduced to competence, and that to indigence. In contemplation of this adversity, I feel it a happiness that I have been bred a soldier; accustomed to the moderation of that life, my fall from opulence will be easy; so may it be with the rest of your lordships! But as you would avoid this, and still greater calamities, let me beseech you to temper and restrain with your wisdom the violence of this fatal address.

Ex. XLIV.—*EFFECTS OF THE POLICY OF ENGLAND.*

Speech in Parliament, October 26, 1775.

JOHN WILKES.

I speak, Sir, as a firm friend of England and America, but still more to universal liberty and the rights of all mankind. I trust no part of the subjects of this vast empire will ever submit to be slaves. I am sure the Americans are too high-spirited to brook the idea. Your whole power, and that of your allies, if you add any, even of all the German troops, of all the ruffians from the north whom you can hire, can not effect so wicked a purpose. The conduct of the present administration has already wrested the sceptre of America out of the hands of our sovereign, and he has now scarcely even a postmaster left in that whole northern continent. More than half the empire is already lost, and the rest is confusion and anarchy. The ministry have brought our sovereign into a more disgraceful situation than any crowned head now living. He alone has already lost, by their fatal counsels, more territory than the three great united powers of Russia, Austria and Prussia have together by a wicked conspiracy robbed Poland of, and by equal acts of violence and injustice from administration.

England was never engaged in a contest of such importance to our most valuable concerns and possessions. We are fighting for the subjection, the unconditional submission, of a country infinitely more extended than our own, of which every day increases the wealth, the natural strength, the population. Should we not succeed, it will be a loss never enough to be deplored, a bosom friendship soured to hate and resentment. We shall be considered as their most implacable enemies, an eternal separation will follow, and the grandeur of the British empire pass away.

Success, final success, seems to me not equivocal, not uncertain, but impossible. However we may differ among ourselves, they are perfectly united. On this side the Atlantic, party-rage unhappily divides us; but one soul animates the vast northern continent of America, the general congress, and each provincial assembly. An appeal has been made to the sword; and at the close of the last campaign, what have we conquered? Bunker's Hill only, and with the loss of twelve hundred men. Are we to pay as dearly for the rest of America? The idea of the conquest of that immense continent is as romantic as unjust.

We are told, moreover, that "the Americans have been treated with lenity." Will facts justify this assertion? Was your Boston Port Bill a measure of lenity? Was your Fishery Bill a measure of lenity? Was your bill for taking away the charter of the Massachusetts Bay, a measure of lenity, or even justice? I omit your many other gross provocations and insults, by which the brave Americans have been driven into their present state. The honorable gentleman asserts that they avow a disposition to be independent. On the contrary, Sir, all the declarations, both of the late and the present congress, uniformly tend to this one object of being put on the same footing the Americans were on in 1763. This has been their only demand, from which they have never varied. Their daily prayers and petitions are for peace, liberty and safety. They justly expect to be put on an equal footing with the other subjects of the empire, and are willing to come into any fair agreement with you in commercial concerns. If you confine all our trade to yourselves, say they; if you make a monopoly of our commerce; if you shut all the other ports of the world against us, do not tax us likewise. If you tax us, then give us a free trade, such as you enjoy yourselves. Let us have equal advantages of commerce, all other ports open to us; then we can, and will, cheerfully, voluntarily pay taxes.

My wish and hope, therefore, is, that an address may be presented to the King, praying his Majesty that he would sheathe the sword, prevent the further effusion of the blood of our fellow-subjects, adopt some mode of negotiation with the general congress, in compliance with their repeated petition, and thereby restore peace and harmony to this distracted empire.

Ex. XLV.—*SONG*, 1776.

SMILE, Massachusetts, smile!
　Thy virtue still outbraves
The frowns of Britain's isle,
　And rage of home-born slaves.
Thy free-born sons disdain their ease
When purchased by their liberties.

In Hancock's generous mind
　Awakes the noble strife,
Which so conspicuous shined
　In gallant Sydney's life.
While in its cause the hero bled,
Immortal honors crowned his head.

Brave Washington arrives
　Arrayed in warlike fame,
While in his soul revives
　Great Marlb'ro's martial flame,
To lead your conquering armies on
To lasting glory and renown.

To aid the glorious cause
　Experienced Lee has come,
Renowned in foreign wars,
　A patriot at home.

While valiant Putnam's warlike deeds
Among the foe a terror spreads.

Stand firm in your defence;
　Like sons of Freedom fight;
Your haughty foes convince
　That you'll maintain your right.
Defiance bid to tyrant's frown,
And glory will your valor crown.

Ex. XLVI.—*THE DUTIES OF PATRIOTS.*

Speech in the General Assembly of South Carolina, delivered April 11, 1776.

JOHN RUTLEDGE.*

Mr. Speaker and Gentlemen of the General Assembly: A solemn oath has been taken on my part for the faithful discharge of my duty; on yours, a solemn assurance has been given of your determination to support me therein. Thus, a public compact between us stands recorded. You may rest assured that I shall keep this oath ever in mind; the constitution shall be the invariable rule of my conduct; my ears shall be ever open to the complaint of the injured; justice, in mercy, shall be neither denied nor delayed; our laws and religion, and the liberties of America, shall be maintained and defended to the utmost of my power. I repose the most perfect confidence in your engagement.

And now, gentlemen, let me entreat that you will, in your several parishes and districts, use your influence and authority to keep peace and good order, and procure strict observance of, and ready obedience to the law. If any persons therein are still strangers to the nature and merits of the dispute between Great Britain and the colonies, you will ex-

---

* Governor Rutledge, one of the most distinguished patriots of South Carolina, was a native of Ireland, but came to this country at an early age, and identified himself with the interests, not only of his adopted state, but of the united colonies. At the time of the delivery of this speech, he was president of the colony of South Carolina. He must not be confounded with Edward Rutledge, a signer of the Declaration of Independence, who was born in Charleston, S. C., and also occupies a prominent position in the political history of the last century.

plain it to them fully, and teach them, if they are so unfortunate as not to know, their inherent rights. Prove to them that being tried by a jury of the vicinage, acquainted with the parties and witnesses; of being taxed only with their own consent, and of having their internal polity regulated only by laws framed by competent judges of what is best adapted to their situation and circumstances, are inestimable privileges, and derived from that constitution which is the birthright of the poorest man, and the best inheritance of the most wealthy.

Relate to them the various unjust and cruel statutes which the British Parliament, claiming a right to make laws for binding the colonies in all cases whatsoever, have enacted; and it must appear, even to the most illiterate, that no power on earth can rightfully deprive them of the hard-earned fruits of their own industry and toil. Show your constituents the indispensable necessity which there was for establishing some mode of government in these colonies; the benefits of that which a full and free representation has established; and that the consent of the people is the origin, and their happiness the end of government. Remove the apprehensions with which honest and well-meaning, but weak and credulous minds may be alarmed; and prevent false impressions by artful and designing enemies.

Truth, being known, will prevail over artifice and misrepresentation. In such case, no man who is worthy of life, liberty, or property, can or will refuse to join with you in defending them to the last extremity, disdaining every sordid view and the paltry considerations of private interest when placed in competition with the liberties of millions. And although superior force may, by the permission of Heaven, lay waste our towns and ravage our country, it can never eradicate from the breasts of freemen those principles which are ingrafted in their very nature. Such men will do their duty, neither knowing nor regarding consequences; but submitting them with humble confidence to the omnipotent arbiter and director of the fate of empires, and trusting that the almighty arm, which has been so signally stretched out for our defence, will deliver them in a righteous cause.

Ex. XLVII.—*FUNERAL ORATION.*

Delivered April, 1776, at the re-interment of the remains of Dr. Joseph Warren, who was slain in the battle of Bunker Hill.

DR. MORTON.

ILLUSTRIOUS RELICS! What tidings from the grave? Why have ye left the peaceful mansions of the tomb to visit again this troubled earth? Though thy body has long lain undistinguished among the vulgar dead; though not a friendly sigh was uttered o'er thy grave, and though the execration of an impious foe was all thy funeral knell, yet, matchless patriot! thy memory has been embalmed in the affections of thy faithful countrymen, who in their hearts have raised eternal monuments to thy bravery!

We searched in the once bloody field for the murdered son of a widow; and we found him, by the turf and the twig, buried on the brow of a hill, though not in a decent grave. And though we must again commit his body to the tomb, yet our breasts shall be the burying spot of his virtues, and then

An adamantine monument we'll rear,
With this inscription—Warren lieth here.

In public life the sole object of his ambition was to acquire the consciousness of virtuous enterprises; *amor patriæ* was the spring of his actions, and *mens conscia recti* was his guide. When the liberties of America were attacked, he appeared an early champion in the combat; and although his knowledge and abilities would have insured riches and preferment, yet he nobly withstood the fascinating charm, tossed Fortune back her plume, and pursued the inflexible purpose of his soul, in guiltless competence.

When he found that the tools of oppression were obstinately bent on violence; when he saw that the British court must be glutted with blood; then he determined that what he could not effect by his eloquence or his pen, he would bring to purpose by his sword. And on the memorable 19th of April he appeared on the field under the united characters of the general, the soldier, and the physician. Here he was seen animating his countrymen to battle, and fighting by their side; and there he was found administering healing comforts to the wounded. And when he had repelled the unprovoked assaults of the enemy, and had driven them back into their strongholds, like the virtuous chief of Rome he returned to the Senate, and presided again at the councils of the fathers.

When the vanquished foe had rallied their disordered army, and by the acquisition of fresh strength again presumed to fight against freemen, our patriot, ever anxious to be where he might do the most good, again put off the senator, and, in contempt of danger, flew to the field of battle, where after a stern and almost victorious resistance, alas, too soon for his country, he sealed his principles with his blood. Then "Freedom wept that merit could not save;" but the immortal name of Warren shall make forever glorious the field on which he fell, and the heights of Charleston bear perpetual record of the blood shed in the cause of virtue and mankind.

And can *we*, my countrymen, behold with indifference so much valor laid prostrate by the hand of British tyranny, and can we ever grasp that hand in affection again? Are we not yet convinced that he who hunts the woods for prey, the naked and untutored Indian, is less a savage than the king of Britain? Have we not proofs, written in blood, that the corrupted nation from whence we sprang is stubbornly fixed on our destruction, and shall we still court dependence on such a state? still contend for a connection with those who have forfeited not only every kindred claim, but even their title to humanity? Forbid it, spirit of the brave Montgomery! Forbid it, spirit of the immortal Warren! Rather ought we to disclaim forever the forfeited affinity; and by a timely amputation of one limb of the empire, save the mortification of the whole! Let us listen to the voice of our slaughtered brethren, who are now proclaiming aloud to their country:

> "Go tell the king, and tell him from our spirits,
> That you and Britons can be friends no more;
> Tell him, to you all tyrants are the same;
> Or if in bonds the never conquered soul
> Can feel a pang more keen than slavery's self,
> 'Tis when the chains that crush you into dust,
> Are forged by hands from which you hoped for freedom."

Yes, we will assert the blood of our murdered hero against thy hostile oppression, O shameless Britain! and when thy "cloud-capped towers, thy gorgeous palaces" shall, by the teeth of pride and folly be levelled with the ground, and when thy glory shall have faded like the western sunbeam, the name and the virtues of WARREN shall remain immortal!

Ex. XLVIII.—*INSTRUCTIONS TO MR. EZRA SARGENT, A DELEGATE TO THE CONTINENTAL CONGRESS, BY THE INHABITANTS OF THE TOWN OF MALDEN, MASS.*

May 27, 1776.

The time was, Sir, when we loved the king and the people of Great Britain with an affection truly filial; we felt ourselves interested in their glory, we shared in their joys and sorrows; we cheerfully poured the fruit of all our labors into the lap of our mother country, and without reluctance expended our blood and our treasure in her cause.

These were our sentiments toward Great Britain while she continued to act the part of a parent state; we felt ourselves happy in our connection with her, nor wished it to be dissolved; but our sentiments are altered—it is now the ardent wish of our souls that America may become a free and independent state.

A sense of unprovoked injuries will arouse the resentment of the most peaceful. Such injuries these colonies have received from Great Britain. The frantic policy of administration hath induced them to send fleets and armies to America, that by depriving us of our trade, and cutting the throats of our brethren, they might awe us into submission, and erect a system of despotism in America, which should so far enlarge the influence of the crown as to enable it to rivet their shackles upon the people of Great Britain.

This plan was brought to a crisis upon the ever memorable nineteenth of April. We remember the fatal day! The expiring groans of our countrymen yet vibrate in our ears, and we now behold the flames of their peaceful dwellings ascending to heaven! We hear their blood crying to us from the ground for vengeance! The manner in which the war hath been prosecuted, hath confirmed us in these sentiments; piracy and murder, robbery and breach of faith, have been conspicuous in the conduct of the king's troops; defenceless towns have been attacked and destroyed; the ruins of Charlestown, which are daily in our view, daily remind us of this; the cries of the widow and the orphan demand our attention; they demand that the hand of pity should wipe the tear from their eye, and that the sword of the country should avenge their wrongs. We long entertained hopes that the spirit of the British nation would once more induce them to assert their own and our rights, and bring to condign punishment the elevated villains who have trampled upon the sacred rights of man, and affronted the majesty of the people. We hoped in vain; they have lost their love of freedom; they have lost their spirit of just resentment; we therefore renounce with disdain our connection with a kingdom of slaves, and bid a final adieu to Britain.

We have freely spoken our sentiments upon this important subject, but we mean not to dictate; we have unbounded confidence in the wisdom and uprightness of the Continental Congress; with pleasure we recollect that this affair is under their direction; and we now instruct you, Sir, to give them the strongest assurance that if they should declare America to be a free and independent republic, your constituents will support and defend the measure, to the last drop of their blood, and the last farthing of their treasure.

Ex. XLIX.—*SONG.*

THE day is broke; my boys, push on,
And follow, follow Washington.
 'Tis he that leads the way, my boys,
  'Tis he that leads the way;
When he commands we will obey,
Through rain or sun, by night or day,
 Determined to be free, my boys,
 Determined to be free.

Kind Providence our troops inspires
With more than Greek or Roman fires,
 Until our cause prevails, my boys,
  Until our cause prevails.
Heaven favors, aye, a virtuous few,
The tyrant's legions to subdue,
 For justice never fails, my boys,
 For justice never fails.

With heart and hand, and God our trust,
We'll freely fight—our cause is just.
 Push on, my boys, push on,
  Push on, my boys, push on!

Till freedom reigns, our hearty bands
Will fight like true Americans,
And follow Washington, my boys,
And follow Washington.

Ex. L.—*ASSERTION OF THE RIGHTS OF AMERICA.**

Speech delivered in Congress, June 7, 1776.

RICHARD HENRY LEE.

THE Americans may become faithful friends to the English, but subjects, never. And even though union could be restored without rancor, it could not without danger. There are some who seem to dread the effects of the revolution. But will England, or can she manifest against us greater rigor and rage than she has already displayed? She deems resistance against oppression no less rebellion than independence itself. And where are those formidable troops that are to subdue the Americans? What the English could not do, can it be done by Germans? Are they more brave, or better disciplined? The number of our enemies is increased; but our own is not diminished, and the battles we have sustained have given us the practice of arms and the experience of war.

America has arrived at a degree of power which assigns her a place among independent nations; we are not less entitled to it than the English themselves. If they have wealth, so also have we; if they are brave, so are we; if they are more numerous, our population will soon equal theirs; if they

---

* The occasion of this earnest statement of the nation's position in regard to Great Britain, was the introduction into Congress of the following resolution, moved by R. H. Lee, of Virginia, and debated with much warmth, six states out of thirteen voting against it as premature.

"RESOLVED, That the United Colonies are, and ought to be, free and independent States, and that their political connection with Great Britain is, and ought to be, dissolved."

The farther consideration of the subject was postponed until the 1st of July, and a committee of five appointed to draft a Declaration of Independence. On the 4th of July the question came up for final action, the paper prepared by Jefferson was accepted, the Declaration was signed by the delegates from all the colonies, and on that day our country assumed the title of "The United States of America."

have men of renown as well in peace as in war, we likewise have such; political revolutions produce great, brave, and generous spirits. From what we have already achieved in these painful beginnings, it is easy to presume what we shall hereafter accomplish; for experience is the source of sage counsels, and liberty is the mother of great men.

Have you not seen the enemy driven from Lexington by thirty thousand citizens, armed and assembled in one day? Already their most celebrated generals have yielded, in Boston, to the skill of ours; already their seamen, repulsed from our coasts, wander over the sea, where they are the sport of tempests, and the prey of famine. Let us hail the favorable omen, and fight, not for the sake of knowing on what terms we are to be the slaves of England, but to secure ourselves a free existence—to found a just and independent government. Animated by liberty, the Greeks repulsed the innumerable army of Persians; sustained by the love of independence, the Swiss and Dutch humbled the power of Austria and Spain by memorable defeats, and conquered a rank among nations. The sun of America also shines upon the heads of the brave; the point of our weapons is no less formidable than theirs; here also the same union prevails, the same contempt of dangers and of death, in asserting the cause of our country.

Why then do we longer delay—why still deliberate? Let this most happy day give birth to the American republic. Let her arise, not to devastate and conquer, but to reëstablish the reign of peace and the laws. The eyes of Europe are fixed upon us; she demands of us a living example of freedom, that may contrast, by the felicity of the citizens, with the ever-increasing tyranny which desolates her polluted shores. She invites us to prepare an asylum, where the unhappy may find solace, and the persecuted repose. She entreats us to cultivate a propitious soil, where that generous plant which first sprung up and grew in England, but is now withered by the poisonous blasts of tyranny, may revive and flourish, sheltering, under its salubrious and interminable shade, all the unfortunate of the human race.

This is the end presaged by so many omens; by our first victories, by the present ardor and union, by the flight of Howe and the pestilence which broke out among Dunmore's people, by the very winds which baffled the enemy's fleets and transports, and that terrible tempest which engulfed seven hundred vessels on the coast of Newfoundland. If we are not this day wanting in our duty to our country, the names of the American legislators will be placed, by posterity, at the side of those of Theseus, of Lycurgus, of Romulus, of Numa, of the three Williams of Nassau, and of all those whose memory has been, and will be, forever dear to virtuous men and good citizens.

Ex. LI.—*DECLARATION OF INDEPENDENCE, BY THE UNITED STATES OF AMERICA IN CONGRESS ASSEMBLED.*

July 4, 1776.

THOMAS JEFFERSON.*

WHEN, in the course of human events, it becomes necessary for one people to dissolve the political bands which have connected them with another, and to assume among the powers of the earth the separate and equal station to which the laws of nature and of nature's God entitle them, a decent respect to the opinions of mankind requires that they should declare the causes which impel them to the separation.

We hold these truths to be self-evident—that all men are created equal; that they are endowed by their Creator with certain inalienable rights; that among these are life, liberty and the pursuit of happiness. That, to secure these rights, governments are instituted among men, deriving their just powers from the consent of the governed; that when any form of government becomes destructive of these ends, it is the right of the people to alter or to abolish it, and to institute new government, laying its foundation on such principles, and organizing its powers in such form as to them

---

* Jefferson took great pride, as well he might, in this production of his pen, and in an epitaph written by himself and subsequently placed on his tombstone, his titles are " Author of the Declaration of Independence, and of the Statutes of Virginia for Religious Freedom, and Father of the University of Virginia." Few men have served their country in more various capacities. He was successively member of the provincial legislature of Virginia, delegate to the Continental Congress, Envoy to France, Secretary of State, Vice-President of the United States, and, to close his public life, he filled for eight years the office of President—the highest one in the power of the people to bestow. He died on the fiftieth anniversary of American Independence, July 4th, 1826, within a few hours of John Adams, his predecessor in office and warm personal friend.

shall seem most likely to effect their safety and happiness. Prudence, indeed, will dictate, that governments long established should not be changed for light and transient causes; and, accordingly, all experience hath shown, that mankind are more disposed to suffer, while evils are sufferable, than to right themselves by abolishing the forms to which they are accustomed. But when a long train of abuses and usurpations, pursuing invariably the same object, evinces a design to reduce them under absolute despotism, it is their right, it is their duty to throw off such government, and to provide new guards for their future security. Such has been the patient sufferance of these colonies; and such is now the necessity which constrains them to alter their former system of government. The history of the present King of Great Britain is a history of repeated injuries and usurpations, all having in direct object the establishment of an absolute tyranny over these states. To prove this, let facts be submitted to a candid world.

He has refused his assent to laws the most wholesome and necessary for the public good.

He has forbidden his governors to pass laws of immediate and pressing importance, unless suspended in their operation till his assent should be obtained; and when so suspended, he has utterly neglected to attend to them.

He has refused to pass other laws for the accommodation of large districts of people, unless those people would relinquish the right of representation in the legislature—a right inestimable to them, and formidable to tyrants only.

He has called together legislative bodies, at places unusual, uncomfortable, and distant from the depository of their public records, for the sole purpose of fatiguing them into compliance with his measures.

He has dissolved representative houses repeatedly, for opposing with manly firmness his invasions on the rights of the people.

He has refused for a long time after such dissolutions, to cause others to be elected; whereby the legislative powers, incapable of annihilation, have returned to the people at large for their exercise; the state remaining, in the mean time, exposed to all the danger of invasion from without and convulsions within.

He has endeavored to prevent the population of these states; for that purpose obstructing the laws for naturalization of foreigners; refusing to pass others to encourage their migration hither, and raising the conditions of new appropriations of lands.

He has obstructed the administration of justice, by refusing his assent to laws for establishing judiciary powers.

He has made judges dependent on his will alone for the tenure of their offices, and the amount and payment of their salaries.

He has erected a multitude of offices, and sent here swarms of officers to harass our people and eat out their substance.

He has kept among us, in times of peace, standing armies without the consent of our legislatures.

He has affected to render the military independent of, and superior to the civil power.

He has combined with others to subject us to a jurisdiction foreign to our constitution, and unacknowledged by our laws; giving his assent to their acts of pretended legislation:

For quartering large bodies of armed troops among us:

For protecting them by a mock trial, from punishment for any murder they should commit on the inhabitants of these states:

For cutting off our trade with all parts of the world:

For imposing taxes on us without our consent:

For depriving us, in many cases, of the benefits of trial by jury:

For transporting us beyond seas, to be tried for pretended offences:

For abolishing the free system of English law in a neighboring province, establishing therein an arbitrary government, and enlarging its boundaries so as to render it at once an example and fit instrument for introducing the same absolute rule in these colonies:

For taking away our charters, abolishing our most valuable laws, and altering fundamentally the forms of our governments:

For suspending our own legislatures, and declaring themselves invested with power to legislate for us in all cases whatsoever.

He has abdicated government here, by declaring us out of his protection and waging war against us.

He has plundered our seas, ravaged our coasts, burnt our towns, and destroyed the lives of our people.

He is, at this time, transporting large armies of foreign

mercenaries, to complete the works of death, desolation and tyranny, already begun with circumstances of cruelty and perfidy scarcely paralleled in the most barbarous ages, and totally unworthy the head of a civilized nation.

He has constrained our fellow-citizens, taken captive on the high seas, to bear arms against their country, to become the executioners of their friends and brethren, or to fall themselves by their hands.

He has excited domestic insurrections amongst us, and has endeavored to bring on the inhabitants of our frontiers the merciless Indian savages, whose known rule of warfare is an undistinguished destruction of all ages, sexes, and conditions.

In every stage of these oppressions, we have petitioned for redress in the most humble terms; our petitions have been answered only by repeated injury. A prince whose character is thus marked by every act which may define a tyrant, is unfit to be the ruler of a free people.

Nor have we been wanting in attention to our British brethren. We have warned them, from time to time, of attempts made by their legislature to extend an unwarrantable jurisdiction over us. We have reminded them of the circumstances of our emigration and settlement here. We have appealed to their native justice and magnanimity, and we have conjured them by the ties of our common kindred, to disavow these usurpations, which would inevitably interrupt our connexions and correspondence. They, too, have been deaf to the voice of justice and consanguinity. We must, therefore, acquiesce in the necessity which denounces our separation, and hold them, as we hold the rest of mankind, enemies in war—in peace, friends.

We, therefore, the representatives of the United States of America, in general Congress assembled, appealing to the Supreme Judge of the world for the rectitude of our intentions, do, in the name and by the authority of the good people of these colonies, solemnly publish and declare, that these united colonies are, and of right ought to be, free and independent states; that they are absolved from all allegiance to the British crown, and that all political connexion between them and the State of Great Britain, is and ought to be totally dissolved; and that as free and independent states, they have full power to levy war, conclude peace, contract alliances, establish commerce, and do all other acts and things which independent states may of right do. And for the support of this declaration, with a firm reliance on the protection of Divine Providence, we mutually pledge to each other our lives, our fortunes, and our sacred honor.

Ex. LII.—*SUPPOSED SPEECH OF JOHN ADAMS, IN FAVOR OF THE DECLARATION OF INDEPENDENCE.* *

DANIEL WEBSTER.

SINK or swim, live or die, survive or perish, I give my hand and my heart to this vote. It is true, indeed, that in the beginning we aimed not at independence. But "there's a Divinity which shapes our ends." The injustice of England has driven us to arms; and, blinded to her own interest for our good, she has obstinately persisted, till independence is now within our grasp. We have but to reach forth to it, and it is ours. Why, then, should we defer the declaration? Is any man so weak as now to hope for a reconciliation with England, which shall leave either safety to the country and its liberties, or safety to his own life, and his own honor? Are not you, Sir, who sit in that chair; is not he, our venerable colleague near you, are you not both already the proscribed and predestined objects of punishment and of vengeance? Cut off from all hope of royal clemency, what are you, what can you be, while the power of England remains, but outlaws? If we postpone independence, do we mean to carry on, or to give up the war? Do we mean to submit to the measures of Parliament, Boston Port Bill and all? Do we mean to submit and consent that we, ourselves, shall be ground to powder, and our country and rights trodden down in the dust? I know we do not mean to submit. We never shall submit. Do we intend to violate that most

* This splendid specimen of eloquence, like the "Supposed Speech of James Otis," has become so familiar to young readers and speakers in its present form, that it is mistaken by many of them for the production of the eminent statesman whose name is identified with it. It was in fact, however, uttered by Daniel Webster, in a discourse commemorative of Adams and Jefferson, delivered August 2d, 1826, shortly after the death of these great men. He begins by supposing John Adams to have risen in his seat to speak on the subject of the "Declaration," and judging by his well-known spirit what would have been the tenor of his remarks on such an occasion, frames for him a speech which Adams, had he heard it, would not have been ashamed to own.

solemn obligation ever entered into by men, that plighting, before God, of our sacred honor to Washington, when, putting him forth to incur the dangers of war, as well as the political hazards of the times, we promised to adhere to him, in every extremity, with our fortunes and our lives? I know there is not a man here who would not rather see a general conflagration sweep over the land, or an earthquake sink it, than one jot or tittle of that plighted faith fall to the ground. For myself, having, twelve months ago, in this place, moved you that George Washington be appointed commander of the forces raised, or to be raised, in defence of American liberty, may my right arm forget her cunning, and my tongue cleave to the roof of my mouth, if I hesitate or waver in the support I give him.

The war, then, must go on. We must fight it through. And if the war must go on, why put off longer the Declaration of independence? That measure will strengthen us. It will give us character abroad. The nations will then treat with us, which they can never do while we acknowledge ourselves subjects, in arms against our sovereign. Nay, I maintain that England herself will sooner treat for peace with us on the footing of independence, than consent, by repealing her acts, to acknowledge that her whole conduct towards us has been a course of injustice and oppression. Her pride will be less wounded by submitting to that course of things which now predestinates our independence, than by yielding the points in controversy to her rebellious subjects. The former she would regard as the result of fortune, the latter she would feel as her own deep disgrace. Why then, why then, Sir, do we not as soon as possible change this from a civil to a national war? And since we must fight it through, why not put ourselves in a state to enjoy all the benefits of victory, if we gain the victory?

If we fail, it can be no worse for us. But we shall not fail. The cause will raise up armies, the cause will create navies. The people, the people, if we are true to them, will carry us, and will carry themselves, gloriously through this struggle. I care not how fickle other people have been found. I know the people of these colonies, and I know that resistance to British oppression is deep and settled in their hearts, and can not be eradicated. Every colony, indeed, has expressed its willingness to follow, if we take the lead.

Sir, the Declaration will inspire the people with increased courage. Instead of a long and bloody war, for the restoration of privileges, for redress of grievances, for chartered immunities, held under a British king, set before them the glorious object of entire independence, and it will breathe into them anew the breath of life. Read this Declaration at the head of the army; every sword will be drawn from its scabbard, and the solemn vow uttered, to maintain it, or to perish on the bed of honor. Publish it from the pulpit; religion will approve it, and the love of religious liberty will cling round it, resolved to stand with it, or fall with it. Send it to the public halls, proclaim it there; let them hear it who heard the first roar of the enemy's cannon; let them see it who saw their brothers and their sons fall on the field of Bunker Hill, and in the streets of Lexington and Concord, and the very walls will cry out in its support.

Sir, I know the uncertainty of human affairs, but I see, I see clearly, through this day's business. You and I, indeed, may rue it. We may not live to the time when this Declaration shall be made good. We may die; die colonists; die slaves; die, it may be, ignominiously and on the scaffold. Be it so. Be it so. If it be the pleasure of Heaven that my country shall require the poor offering of my life, the victim shall be ready, at the appointed hour of sacrifice, come when that hour may. But while I do live, let me have a country, or at least the hope of a country, and that a free country.

But whatever may be our fate, be assured, be assured that this Declaration will stand. It may cost treasure, and it may cost blood; but it will stand, and it will nobly compensate for both. Through the thick gloom of the present, I see the brightness of the future, as the sun in Heaven. We shall make this a glorious, an immortal day. When we are in our graves, our children will honor it. They will celebrate it with thanksgiving, with festivity, with bonfires and illuminations. On its annual return they will shed tears, copious, gushing tears, not of subjection and slavery, not of agony and distress, but of exultation, of gratitude, and of joy. Sir, before God, I believe that the hour is come. My judgment approves this measure, and my whole heart is in it. All that I have, and all that I hope, in this life, I am now ready here to stake upon it; and I leave off as I began, that, live or die, survive or perish, I am for the Declaration.

It is my living sentiment, and by the blessing of God it shall be my dying sentiment, Independence *now*, and INDEPENDENCE FOREVER!

Ex. LIII.—*WAR AND WASHINGTON.*

JONATHAN MITCHEL SEWALL.

VAIN Britons, boast no longer with proud indignity,
By land your conquering legions, your matchless strength at sea;
Since we, your braver sons, incensed, our swords have girded on,
Hurra, hurra, hurra, hurra, for war and Washington.

Your dark, unfathomed counsels our weakest heads defeat,
Our children rout your armies, our boats destroy your fleet,
And to complete the dire disgrace, cooped up within a town,
You live, the scorn of all our host, the slaves of Washington.

Great heaven! is this the nation whose thundering arms were hurled
Through Europe, Afric, India? whose navy ruled the world!
The lustre of your former deeds, whole ages of renown,
Lost in a moment, or transferred to us and Washington.

Yet think not thirst of glory unsheathes our vengeful swords
To rend your bands asunder, and cast away your cords;
'Tis heaven-born freedom fires us all, and strengthens each brave son,
From him who humbly guides the plough, to god-like Washington.

For this, oh could our wishes your ancient rage inspire,
Your armies should be doubled, in numbers, force, and fire,
Then might the glorious conflict prove which best deserved the boon,
America or Albion; a George, or Washington!

Fired with the great idea, our fathers' shades would rise;
To view the stern contention the gods desert their skies.

And Wolfe, 'mid hosts of heroes, superior bending down,
Cry out with eager transports, God save great Washington!

Should George, too choice of Britons, to foreign realms apply
And madly arm half Europe, yet still we would defy
Turk, Hessian, Jew, and Infidel, or all these powers in one,
While Adams guides our Senate, our camp great Washington!

Should warlike weapons fail us, disdaining slavish fears,
To swords we'll beat our ploughshares, our pruning-hooks to spears,
And rush all desperate on our foe, nor breathe till battle's won;
Then shout, and shout America! and conquering Washington.

Proud France should view with terror, and haughty Spain revere,
While every warlike nation would court alliance here,
And George, his minions trembling round, dismounting from his throne,
Pay homage to America, and glorious Washington.

Ex. LIV.—*ADDRESS TO THE AMERICAN TROOPS BEFORE THE BATTLE OF LONG ISLAND, AUGUST 27th, 1776.*

GEN. WASHINGTON.

THE time is now near at hand which must probably determine whether Americans are to be freemen or slaves; whether they are to have any property they can call their own; whether their houses and farms are to be pillaged and destroyed, and themselves consigned to a state of wretchedness from which no human efforts will deliver them. The fate of unborn millions will now depend, under God, on the courage and conduct of this army. Our cruel and unrelenting enemy leaves us only the choice of a brave resistance, or the most abject submission. We have, therefore, to resolve to conquer or to die.

Our own, our country's honor, calls upon us for a vigorous and manly exertion; and if we now shamefully fail, we shall become infamous before the whole world. Let us, then, rely on the goodness of our cause, and the aid of the Supreme Being, in whose hands victory is, to animate and encourage us to great and noble actions. The eyes of all our countrymen are now upon us; and we shall have their blessings and praises, if happily we are the instruments of saving them from the tyranny meditated against them. Let us, therefore, animate and encourage each other, and show the whole world that a freeman contending for liberty on his own ground, is superior to any slavish mercenary on earth.

Liberty, property, life, and honor are all at stake. Upon your courage and conduct rest the hopes of our bleeding and insulted country. Our wives, children, and parents, expect safety from us only; and they have every reason to believe that heaven will crown with success so just a cause. The enemy will endeavor to intimidate us by show and appearance; but remember they have been repulsed on various occasions by a few brave Americans. Their cause is bad—their men are conscious of it; and, if opposed with firmness and coolness on their first onset, with our advantage of works and knowledge of the ground, the victory is most assuredly ours. Every good soldier will be silent and attentive, wait for orders and reserve his fire until he is sure of doing execution.

Ex. LV.—*CHARGE TO THE GRAND JURY OF SOUTH CAROLINA.*

October 15th, 1776.

JUDGE DRAYTON.

A DECREE is now gone forth, not to be recalled! And thus has suddenly arisen in the world a new empire, styled the United States of America. An empire, that as soon as started into existence, attracts the attention of the rest of the universe, and bids fair, by the blessing of God, to be the most glorious of any upon record. America hails Europe, Asia, and Africa! She proffers peace and plenty.

When, in modern times, Philip of Spain became the tyrant of the Low Countries in Europe, of seventeen provinces which composed those territories, seven only effectually confederated to preserve their liberties, or to perish in the attempt. They saw Philip the most powerful prince in the Old World, and master of Mexico and Peru in the New—nations incessantly pouring into his territories floods of gold and silver. They saw him possessed of the best troops and the most formidable navy in the universe, and aiming at no less than universal monarchy. But these seven provinces, making but a speck upon the globe, saw themselves without armies, fleets, or funds of money—yet nobly relying upon Providence and the justice of their cause, they resolved to oppose the tyrant's whole force, and at least *deserve* to be free. They fought, they bled, and were often brought to the door of destruction. But they redoubled their efforts in proportion to their danger. And the inhabitants of that speck of earth compelled the master of dominions so extensive that it was boasted the sun was never absent from them, to treat them as a free and independent people!

For a moment, and with the aid of a fearful imagination, let us suppose that the American States are now as defenceless as the Hollanders then were; and that the king of Great Britain is now as powerful as Philip then was. Yet even such a state of things could not be a plea for any degree of submission on our part. Did not the Hollanders oppose their weakness to the strength of Spain? Are not the Americans engaged in as good a cause as the Hollanders fought in? Are the Americans less in love with liberty than the Hollanders were? Shall we not in this, a similar cause, dare those perils that they successfully combated? Shall we not *deserve* freedom? Our past actions presage our future achievements, and animate us in our military efforts for peace, liberty and safety.

America is possessed of resources for the war, which appear as soon as inquired after; are found only by being sought for; and are but scarce imagined even when found. Strong in her union, on each coast and frontier she meets the invaders, whether British or Indian savages, repelling their allied attacks. The Americans can live without luxury. They engage in the war from principle. They follow their leaders to battle with personal affection. Natives of the climate, they bear the vicissitudes and extremities of the weather. Hardy and robust, they need no camp equipage, and they march with celerity. From such a people, everything is to be hoped for, nothing is to be doubted of. Such a people, though young in the practice of war, were ever superior to veteran troops—and if the conduct of America is worthy of herself, I see no cause to fear the enemy. However, in such a conflict, we ought to expect difficulties, dangers and defeats. Let us remember, that it was to the danger in which the Roman state was reared, that she owed her illustrious men and imperial fortune. The Roman dignity was never so majestic, her glory never so resplendent, her fortitude and exertions never so conspicuous and nervous, as when, Hannibal, in the successive battles of Trabia, Thrasymenus and Cannæ, having almost extirpated their whole military force, the very state was on the brink of dissolution. The Romans *deserved*, and they *acquired* victory!

Ex. LVI.—*SONG OF MARION'S MEN.**

WILLIAM CULLEN BRYANT.

Our band is few, but true and tried,
   Our leader frank and bold;
The British soldier trembles
   When Marion's name is told.
Our fortress is the good greenwood,
   Our tent the cypress tree;
We know the forest round us,
   As seamen know the sea.
We know its walls of thorny vines,
   Its glades of reedy grass,
Its safe and silent islands
   Within the dark morass.

Woe to the English soldiery
   That little dread us near!

---

* Francis Marion, a general in the Revolutionary war, was no less distinguished by his personal valor and the extraordinary influence he acquired over the soldiers under his command, than by his skill in conducting military operations. He had, like Washington, served in the French and Indian war, and brought into the war of Independence the experience gained in his previous service. He was what would be called at the present day a "raider," and the attachment between himself and his soldiers was of a closer and more personal nature than that which is formed under the ordinary routine of military discipline. The marshy country between the Pedee and Santee rivers, in South Carolina, was the scene of his principal operations.

On them shall light at midnight
  A strange and sudden fear:
When waking to their tents on fire
  They grasp their arms in vain,
And they who stand to face us
  Are beat to earth again.
And they who fly in terror, deem
  A mighty host behind,
And hear the tramp of thousands
  Upon the hollow wind.

Then sweet the hour that brings release
  From danger and from toil;
We talk the battle over,
  And share the battle's spoil.
The woodland rings with laugh and shout,
  As if a hunt were up,
And woodland flowers are gathered
  To crown the soldier's cup.
With merry songs we mock the wind
  That in the pine-top grieves,
And slumber long and sweetly
  On beds of oaken leaves.

Well knows the fair and friendly moon
  The band that Marion leads—
The glitter of their rifles,
  The scamper of their steeds.
'Tis life to guide the fiery barb
  Across the moonlight plain;
'Tis life to feel the night-wind
  That lifts his tossing mane.
A moment in the British camp—
  A moment—and away!
Back to the pathless forest
  Before the peep of day.

Grave men there are by broad Santee,
  Grave men with hoary hairs,
Their hearts are all with Marion,
  For Marion are their prayers.
And lovely ladies greet our band
  With kindest welcoming,

> With smiles like those of summer,
> And tears like those of spring.
> For them we wear these trusty arms,
> And lay them down no more,
> Till we have driven the Briton
> Forever from our shore.

Ex. LVII.—*EXPOSTULATION WITH PARLIAMENT.*

Speech in Parliament, April 3, 1777.

EDMUND BURKE.

I THINK I know America. If I do not, my ignorance is incurable, for I have spared no pains to understand it; and I feel most solemnly assured that everything that has been done there has arisen from a total misconception of the object: that our means of originally holding America, of reconciling with it after quarrel, of recovering it after separation, of keeping it after victory, did depend, and must depend upon a total renunciation of that unconditional submission which has taken such possession of the minds of violent men. Nothing, indeed, can place us in our former situation. That hope must be laid aside. But there is a difference between bad and the worst of all.

If I had not lived long enough to be little surprised at anything, I should have been in some degree astonished at the continued rage of several gentlemen, who, not satisfied with carrying fire and sword into America, are animated with nearly the same fury against those neighbors of theirs, whose only crime it is that they have charitably and humanely wished them to entertain more reasonable sentiments, and not always to sacrifice their interest to their passion.

All this rage against unresisting dissent convinces me, that at bottom, they are far from satisfied that they are in the right. For what is it they would have? A war? They certainly have at this moment the blessing of something that is very like one; and if the war they enjoy at present be not sufficiently hot and extensive, they may shortly have it as warm and as spreading as their hearts can desire. Is it the force of the kingdom they call for? They have it already; and if they choose to fight their battles in their own person, nobody prevents their setting sail to America in the next transport. Do they think that the service is stinted for want of liberal supplies? Indeed, they complain without reason. The table of the House of Commons will glut them, let their appetite for expense be never so keen. And I assure them further, that those who think with them in the House of Commons are full as easy in the control, as they are liberal in the vote of these expenses. If this be not supply or confidence sufficient, let them open their own private purse strings and give, from what is left to them, as largely and with as little care as they think proper.

I am charged with being an American. If warm affection towards those over whom I claim any share of authority, be a crime, I am guilty of this charge. But I do assure you (and they who know me publicly and privately will bear witness to me), that if ever one man lived, more zealous than another for the supremacy of parliament, it was myself. But in the comprehensive dominion which Divine Providence has put into our hands, it is our duty, in all soberness, to conform our government to the character and circumstances of the several peoples who compose this mighty and strangely diversified mass. If there be one fact in the world perfectly clear, it is this: "That the disposition of the people of America is wholly averse to any other than a free government;" and this is indication enough, to any honest statesman, how he ought to adapt any power he finds in his hands, to their case. If any ask me what a free government is, I answer that, for any practical purpose it is what the people think so; and that they, and not I, are the natural, lawful and competent judges of this matter. If they practically allow me a greater degree of authority over them than is consistent with any correct ideas of perfect freedom, I ought to thank them for so great a trust and not to endeavor to prove from thence, that they have reasoned amiss, and that having gone so far, by analogy, they must hereafter have no enjoyment but by my pleasure.

It is impossible that a nation should remain long in a situation which breeds such notions and dispositions, without some great alteration in the national character. Many things have been long operating towards a gradual change in our principles, but this American war has done more in a very few years than all the other causes could have effected in a century. It is not, therefore, on its own separate account, but because of its attendant circumstances, that I consider its continuance, or its ending in any way but that of an honorable and liberal accommodation, as the greatest evils that can befall us. For that reason I entreat you again and again, neither to be persuaded, shamed, or frighted, out of the principles that have hitherto led so many of you to abhor the war, its cause, and its consequences. Let us not be amongst the first who renounce the maxims of our forefathers.

Ex. LVIII.—*PROCLAMATION*,[*]

By John Burgoyne, esquire, Lieutenant General of His Majesty's armies in North America, Colonel of the Queen's regiment of light dragoons, Governor of Fort William in North Britain, one of the representatives of the Commons of Great Britain, and commanding an army and fleet employed on an expedition from Canada, &c., &c., &c. Given at the Camp at Ticonderoga, July 2, 1777.

The forces intrusted to my command are designed to act in concert, and upon a common principle, with the numerous armies and fleets which already display in every quarter of America the power, the justice, and when properly sought, the mercy of the king.

The cause in which the British arms are thus exerted appeals to the most affecting interests of the human heart; and the military servants of the crown, at first called forth for the sole purpose of restoring the rights of the constitution, now combine with the love of their country and duty to their sovereign, the other extensive incitements which form a due sense of the general privileges of mankind. To the eyes and ears of the temperate part of the public, and the breasts of suffering thousands in the provinces, be the melancholy appeal whether the present unnatural rebellion has not been made a foundation for the completest system of tyranny that ever God, in his displeasure, suffered to be exercised over a froward and stubborn generation.

Arbitrary imprisonment, confiscation of property, persecution and torture, unprecedented in the Inquisition of the

---

[*] The arrogant style of this proclamation is in ludicrous contrast with the fact that in little more than three months from the time it was issued, Burgoyne and his whole army surrendered to the American forces. It is not perhaps generally known that this unlucky general had better success in the field of literature than in that of arms, having ended his life as a popular dramatic author.

Romish church, are among the palpable enormities that verify the affirmation. These are inflicted by assemblies and committees, who dare to profess themselves friends to liberty, upon the most quiet subjects, without distinction of age or sex, for the sole crime, often for the sole suspicion, of having adhered in principle to the government under which they were born, and to which, by every tie, divine and human, they owe allegiance. To consummate these shocking proceedings, the profanation of religion is added to the most profligate prostitution of common reason; the consciences of men are set at nought, and multitudes are compelled not only to bear arms, but also to swear subjection to an usurpation they abhor.

Animated by these considerations—at the head of troops in the full powers of health, discipline and valor—determined to strike where necessary, and anxious to spare where possible—I, by these presents, invite and exhort all persons, in all places where the progress of this army may point—and by the blessing of God I will extend it far—to maintain such a conduct as may justify me in protecting their lands, habitations and families. The intention of this address is to hold forth security, not depredation, to the country. To those whom spirit and principle may induce to partake the glorious task of redeeming their countrymen from dungeons, and reëstablishing the blessings of legal government, I offer encouragement and employment; and upon the first intelligence of their associations, I will find means to assist their undertakings. The domestic, the industrious, the infirm, and even the timid, I am desirous to protect, provided they remain quietly at their houses; that they do not suffer their cattle to be removed, nor their corn or forage to be secreted or destroyed; that they do not break up their bridges or roads; nor by any other act, directly or indirectly, endeavor to obstruct the operations of the king's troops, or supply or assist those of the enemy.

Every species of provision brought to my camp will be paid for at an equitable rate, and in solid coin.

In consciousness of Christianity, my royal master's clemency, and the honor of soldiership, I have dwelt upon this invitation, and wished for more persuasive terms to give it impression. And let not people be led to disregard it, by considering their distance from the immediate situation of my camp. I have but to give stretch to the Indian forces under my direction—and they amount to thousands—to overtake the hardened enemies of Great Britain and America. I consider them the same, wherever they may lurk.

If, notwithstanding these endeavors and sincere inclination to effect them, the phrenzy of hostility should remain, I trust I shall stand acquitted in the eyes of God and men in denouncing and executing the vengeance of the state against these wilful outcasts. The messengers of justice and of wrath await them in the field; and devastation, famine and every concomitant horror, that a reluctant, but indispensable prosecution of military duty must occasion, will bar the way to their return.

Ex. LIX.—*ANSWER TO BURGOYNE'S PROCLAMATION.*

Saratoga, July 10, 1777.

MOST HIGH, MOST MIGHTY, MOST PUISSANT AND SUBLIME GENERAL:

When the forces under your command arrived at Quebec in order to act in concert and upon a common principle with the numerous fleets and armies which already display in every quarter of America the justice and mercy of your king, we, the reptiles of America, were struck with unusual trepidation and astonishment. But what words can express the plenitude of our horror, when the colonel of the queen's regiment of light dragoons advanced towards Ticonderoga? The mountains shook before thee, and the trees of the forest bowed their lofty heads—the vast lakes of the north were chilled at thy presence, and the mighty cataracts stopped their tremendous career, and were suspended in awe at thy approach. Judge, then, O ineffable governor of Fort William in North Britain! what must have been the terror, dismay and despair that overspread this paltry continent of North America, and us, its wretched inhabitants. Dark and dreary indeed was the prospect before us, till, like the sun in the horizon, your most gracious, sublime and irresistible proclamation opened the doors of mercy and snatched us, as it were, from the jaws of annihilation.

We foolishly thought, blind as we were, that your gracious master's fleets and armies were come to destroy us and our liberties, but we are happy in hearing from you (and who can doubt what you assert?) that they were called forth for the sole purpose of restoring the rights of the constitution to a froward and stubborn generation.

And is it for this, O sublime lieutenant-general! that you have given yourself the trouble to cross the wide Atlantic, and with incredible fatigue traverse uncultivated wilds? And we ungratefully refuse the proffered blessing? To restore the rights of the constitution, you have called together an amiable host of savages, and turned them loose to scalp our women and children and lay our country waste—this they have performed with their usual skill and clemency, and yet we remain insensible to the benefit, and unthankful for so much goodness.

Our Congress have declared independence, and our assemblies, as your highness justly observes, have most wickedly imprisoned the avowed friends of that power with which they are at war, and most profanely compelled those whose consciences will not allow them to fight, to pay some small part of the expenses their country is at, in supporting what is called a necessary defensive war. If we go on thus in our obstinacy and ingratitude, what can we expect but that you should, in your anger, give a stretch to the Indian forces under your direction amounting to thousands, to overtake and destroy us? Or, which is ten times worse, that you should withdraw your fleets and armies, and leave us to our own misery, without completing the benevolent task you have begun of restoring to us the rights of the constitution.

We submit, we submit, most puissant colonel of the queen's regiment of light dragoons, and governor of Fort William in North Britain! We offer our heads to the scalping-knife, and our bodies to the bayonet. Who can resist the force of your eloquence? Who can withstand the terror of your arms? The invitation you have made, in the consciousness of Christianity, your royal master's clemency, and the honor of soldiership, we thankfully accept. The blood of the slain, the cries of injured virgins and innocent children, and the never-ceasing sighs and groans of starving wretches, now languishing in the jails and prison-ships of New York, call on us in vain, while your sublime proclamation is sounded in our ears. Forgive us, O our country! Forgive us, dear posterity! Forgive us, all ye foreign powers, who are anxiously watching our conduct in this important struggle, if we yield implicitly to the persuasive tongue of the most elegant colonel of her majesty's regiment of light dragoons.

Forbear then, thou magnanimous lieutenant-general! Forbear to denounce vengeance against us—forbear to give a stretch to those restorers of constitutional rights, the Indian forces under your direction; let not the messengers of justice and wrath await us in the field; and devastation, and every concomitant horror, bar our return to the allegiance of a prince who, by his royal will, would deprive us of every blessing of life, with all possible clemency.

We are domestic, we are industrious, we are infirm and timid, we shall remain quietly at home, and not remove our cattle, our corn, or forage, in hopes that you will come, at the head of troops in the full powers of health, discipline and valor, and take charge of them for yourselves. Behold our wives and daughters, our flocks and herds, our goods and chattels, are they not at the mercy of our lord the king, and of his lieutenant-general, member of the House of Commons, and governor of Fort William in North Britain?

Ex. LX.—*A CAMP BALLAD.*

FRANCIS HOPKINSON.[*]

Make room, oh ye kingdoms! in history renowned,
Whose arms have in battle with glory been crowned;
Make room,—for America, another great nation,
Arises to claim in your council a station.

Her sons fought for freedom, and by their own bravery
Have rescued themselves from the shackles of slavery.
America's free, and though Britain abhorred it,
Yet Fame a new volume prepares to record it.

Fair Freedom in Britain her home had erected,
But her sons growing venal, and she not respected,

---

[*] Judge Hopkinson was a member of the Continental Congress, and signed the Declaration of Independence. He did great service to this country by his pen during the War for Freedom, and left, besides political essays, satires, &c., many songs, very popular in their day, some of them set to music by himself.

The goddess offended forsook the base nation,
And fixed on our mountains a more honored station.

With glory immortal she here sits enthroned,
Nor fears the vain vengeance of Britain disowned;
Whilst Washington guards her with heroes surrounded,
Her foes shall with shameful defeat be confounded.

To arms then! to arms! 'tis fair Freedom invites us;
The trumpet shrill sounding to battle excites us:
The banners of virtue unfurled shall wave o'er us,
Our hero lead on, and the foe fly before us.

On Heaven and Washington placing reliance,
We'll meet the bold Briton and bid him defiance;
Our cause we'll support, for 'tis just and 'tis glorious—
When men fight for freedom, they must be victorious.

Ex. LXI.—*CHARGE TO THE GRAND JURY OF NEW YORK.*
September 9, 1777.

JOHN JAY.*

GENTLEMEN: It affords me very sensible pleasure to congratulate you on the dawn of that free, mild and equal government which now begins to rise and break from amidst those clouds of anarchy, confusion and licentiousness which the arbitrary and violent dominion of the king of Great Britain had spread, in a a greater or less degree, over all of these States. This is one of those signal instances in

---

* An idea of the value of Judge Jay's services to the Republic, especially in a diplomatic capacity, may be acquired by the following passage from Hildreth, in reference to the person to be selected to negotiate the Treaty with Great Britain in 1794, afterwards called Jay's Treaty: "In point of Revolutionary services, only the President himself stood upon higher ground. In lofty disinterestedness, in unyielding integrity, in superiority to the illusions of passion, no one of the great men of the Revolution approached so near to Washington. Profound knowledge of the law, inflexible sense of justice, and solidity of judgment, had especially marked him out for the office which he held. Having played a very active part in a State (New York), the seat of hostilities during the whole struggle of the Revolution, he know what war was, and dreaded it accordingly." Jay was a native of New York, and held several important appointments in that state.

which Divine Providence has made the tyranny of princes instrumental in breaking the chains of their subjects; and rendered the most inhuman designs productive of the best consequences to those against whom they were intended.

The infatuated sovereign of Britain, forgetful that kings were the servants, not the proprietors, and ought to be the fathers, not the incendiaries, of their people, has, by destroying our former constitutions, enabled us to erect more eligible systems of government on their ruins; and, by unwarrantable attempts to bind us in all cases whatsoever, has reduced us to the happy necessity of being free from his control in any.

Whoever compares our present with our former constitution, will find abundant reason to rejoice in the exchange, and readily admit that all the calamities incident to this war will be amply compensated by the many benefits arising from this glorious revolution,—a revolution which, in the whole course of its rise and progress, is distinguished by so many marks of the Divine favor and interposition, that no doubt can remain of its being finally accomplished.

It was begun, and has been supported, in a manner so singular, and I may say miraculous, that when future ages shall read its history, they will be tempted to consider a great part of it as fabulous. What, among other things, can appear more unworthy of credit, than that in an enlightened age, in a civilized and Christian country, in a nation so celebrated for humanity, as well as love of liberty and justice, as the English *once* justly were, a prince should arise, who, by the influence of corruption alone, should be able to seduce them into a combination to reduce three millions of his most loyal and affectionate subjects to absolute slavery, under pretence of a right appertaining to God alone, of binding them in all cases whatever, not even excepting cases of conscience and religion? What can appear more improbable, though true, than that this prince, and this people, should obstinately steel their hearts and shut their ears against the most humble petitions and affectionate remonstrances; and unjustly determine, by violence and force, to execute designs which were reprobated by every principle of humanity and policy; designs which would have been execrable, if intended against savages and enemies, and yet formed against men descended from the same common ancestors with themselves; men who had liberally contributed to their support, and cheerfully fought their battles, even in remote and baleful climates? Will it not appear extraordinary that thirteen colonies, the objects of their wicked designs, divided by variety of governments and manners should immediately become one people; and though without funds, without magazines, without disciplined troops, in the face of their enemies, unanimously determine to be free; and undaunted by the power of Britain, refer their cause to the justice of the Almighty, and resolve to repel force by force. Will it not be matter of doubt and wonder that, notwithstanding these difficulties, they should raise armies, establish funds, carry on commerce, grow rich by the spoils of their enemies, and bid defiance to the armies of Britain, the mercenaries of Germany and the savages of the wilderness? But, however incredible these things may appear, we know them to be true, and we should always remember that the striking proofs of the interposition of Heaven in delivering us from the threatened bondage of Britain, ought to make us ascribe our salvation to its true cause, and instead of swelling our breasts with arrogant ideas of our own prowess and importance, kindle in them a flame of gratitude and piety which may consume all remains of vice and irreligion.

Ex. LXII.—*BARBARITY OF EMPLOYING INDIANS IN WAR.*

Speech in Parliament, Nov. 18, 1777.

EARL OF CHATHAM.

MY LORDS: I am astonished! shocked! to hear such principles confessed—to hear them avowed in this house, or in this country; principles equally unconstitutional, inhuman and unchristian!

My lords, I did not intend to have encroached again upon your attention; but I could not repress my indignation. I feel myself impelled by every duty. My lords, we are called upon as members of this house, as men, as Christian men, to protest against such notions standing near the throne, polluting the ear of Majesty. "That God and nature put into our hands!" I know not what ideas that lord may entertain of God and nature, but I know that such abominable principles are equally abhorrent to religion and humanity. What! to attribute the sacred sanction of God and nature to the massacre of the Indian scalping-knife, to the cannibal savage, torturing, murdering, roasting and eating, literally, my lords, eating the mangled victims of his barbarous battles! Such horrible notions shock every precept of religion, divine or natural, every generous feeling of humanity, and every sentiment of honor.

These abominable principles, and this more abominable avowal of them, demand the most decisive indignation. I call upon that right reverend bench, those holy ministers of the gospel, and pious pastors of our church, I conjure them to join in this holy work, and vindicate the religion of their God. I appeal to the wisdom and law of this learned bench, to defend and support the justice of their country. I call upon the bishops to interpose the unsullied sanctity of their lawn; upon the learned judges to interpose the purity of their ermine, to save us from this pollution. I call upon the honor of your lordships to reverence the dignity of your ancestors, and to maintain your own. I call upon the spirit and humanity of my country to vindicate the national character. I invoke the genius of the constitution. From the tapestry that adorns these walls the immortal ancestors of this noble lord frown with indignation at the disgrace of his country. In vain he led your victorious fleets against the boasted Armada of Spain; in vain he defended and established the honor, the liberties, the religion, the protestant religion of this country, against the arbitrary cruelties of popery and the Inquisition, if these more than popish cruelties and inquisitorial practices are let loose among us. To turn forth into our settlements, among our ancient connexions, friends and relations, the merciless cannibal, thirsting for the blood of man, woman and child! to send forth the infidel savage, against whom? against your protestant brethren, to lay waste their country, to desolate their dwellings, and extirpate their race and name, with these horrible hell-hounds of savage war! —hell-hounds, I say, of savage war. Spain armed herself with blood-hounds to extirpate the wretched natives of America; and we improve on the inhuman example even of Spanish cruelty; we turn loose these savage hell-hounds against our brethren and countrymen in America, of the same language, laws, liberties and religion, endeared to us by every tie that should sanctify humanity.

My lords, this awful subject, so important to our honor, our constitution and our religion, demands the most solemn and effectual inquiry. And I again call upon your lordships, and the united powers of the state, to examine it thoroughly and decisively, and to stamp upon it an indelible stigma of the public abhorrence. And I again implore these holy prelates of our religion to do away these iniquities from among us. Let them perform a lustration, let them purify this house, and this country, from this sin.

My lords, I am old and weak, and unable at present to say more, but my feelings and indignation were too strong to have said less. I could not have slept this night in my bed, nor reposed my head on my pillow, without giving this vent to my eternal abhorrence of such preposterous and enormous principles.

Ex. LXIII.—*PROTEST AGAINST MINISTERIAL MISCONDUCT.*

Speech in Parliament, Nov. 18th, 1777.

EARL OF CHATHAM.

I RISE, my lords, to declare my sentiments on this most solemn and serious subject. It has imposed a load upon my mind which, I fear, nothing can remove; but which impels me to endeavor its alleviation, by a free and unreserved communication of my sentiments.

In the first part of the address, I have the honor of heartily concurring with the noble earl who moved it. No man feels sincerer joy than I do, nor can offer more genuine congratulation on every accession of strength to the succession of the house of Brunswick. I therefore join in every congratulation on the birth of another princess, and the happy recovery of her majesty. But I must stop here. My courtly complaisance will carry me no further. I will not join in congratulation on misfortune and disgrace. I can not concur in a blind and servile address, which approves and endeavors to sanctify the monstrous measures which have heaped disgrace and misfortune upon us. This, my lords, is a perilous and tremendous moment! It is not a time for adulation. The smoothness of flattery can not now avail; cannot *save* us in this rugged and awful crisis. It is now necessary to instruct the throne in the language of truth. We must dispel the delusion and the darkness which envelop it; and display, in its full danger and true colors, the ruin that is brought to our doors.

This, my lords, is our duty. It is the proper function of this noble assembly, sitting, as we are, upon our honors in this house, the hereditary council of the crown. *Who* is the minister—*where* is the minister, that has dared to suggest to the throne the contrary unconstitutional language this day delivered from it? The accustomed language from the throne has been application to parliament for advice, and a reliance on its constitutional advice and assistance. As it is the right of parliament to give, so it is the duty of the crown to ask it. But on this day, and in this extreme momentous exigency, no reliance is placed on our constitutional counsels! no advice is asked from the sober and enlightened care of parliament! but the crown, from itself, and by itself, declares an unalterable determination to pursue measures—and what measures, my lords? The measures that have produced the imminent perils that threaten us; the measures that have brought ruin to our doors.

Can the minister of the day now expect a continuance of support in this ruinous infatuation? Can parliament be so dead to its dignity and its duty, as to be thus deluded into the loss of the one, and the violation of the other? To give an unlimited credit and support for the steady perseverance in measures not proposed for our parliamentary advice, but dictated and forced upon us—in measures, I say, my lords, which have reduced this flourishing empire to ruin and contempt! "But yesterday, and England might have stood against the world; now none so poor as to do her reverence." I use the words of a poet; but though it be poetry, it is no fiction. It is a shameful truth, that not only the power and strength of this country are wasting away and expiring; but her well-earned glories, her true honor, and substantial dignity are sacrificed.

Ex. LXIV.—*FOLLY OF ATTEMPTING TO CONQUER AMERICA.*

Speech in Parliament, Nov. 18, 1777.

EARL OF CHATHAM.

FRANCE, my lords, has insulted you; she has encouraged and sustained America, and whether America be wrong or right, the dignity of this country ought to spurn at the officious insult of French interference. The ministers and ambassadors of those who are called rebels and enemies, are in Paris, in Paris they transact the reciprocal interests of America and France. Can there be a more mortifying insult? Can even our ministers sustain a more humiliating disgrace! Do they dare to resent it? Do they presume even to hint a vindication of their honor and the dignity of the state by requiring the dismission of the plenipotentiaries of America? Such is the degradation to which they have reduced the glories of England.

The people whom they affect to call contemptible rebels, but whose growing power has at last obtained the name of enemies; the people with whom they have engaged this country in war, and against whom they now command our implicit support in every measure of desperate hostility, this people, despised as rebels, or acknowledged as enemies, are abetted against you, supplied with every military store, their interests consulted, and their ambassadors entertained, by your inveterate enemy! and our ministers dare not interpose with dignity or effect. Is this the honor of a great kingdom? Is this the indignant spirit of England, who " but yesterday " gave law to the house of Bourbon? My lords, the dignity of nations demands a decisive conduct in a situation like this.

Even when the greatest prince that perhaps this country ever saw, filled our throne, the requisition of a Spanish general on a similar subject was attended to, and complied with. For, on the spirited remonstrance of the Duke of Alva, Elizabeth found herself obliged to refuse the Flemish exiles all countenance, support, or even entrance into her dominions; and the Count le Marque, with his few desperate followers, was expelled the kingdom. Happening to arrive at the Brille, and finding it weak in defence, they made themselves masters of the place; and this was the foundation of the United Provinces.

My lords, this ruinous and ignominious situation, where we can not act with success, nor suffer with honor, calls upon us in the strongest and loudest language of truth, to rescue the ear of majesty from the delusions which surround it. The desperate state of our army abroad is in part known; no man thinks more highly of it than I do. I love and honor the English troops. I know their virtues and their valor. I know they can achieve anything except impossibilities; and I know that the conquest of English America *is an impossibility.* You can not, I venture to say it, you *can not* conquer America.

Your armies in the last war effected everything that could be effected, and what was it? It cost a numerous army, under the command of a most able general, now a noble lord in this house, a long and laborious campaign, to expel five thousand Frenchmen from French America. My lords, you can not conquer America. What is your present situation there? We do not know the worst; but we know, that in three campaigns we have done nothing and suffered much. Besides the sufferings, perhaps total loss, of the northern force, the best appointed army that ever took the field, commanded by Sir William Howe, has retired from the American lines. He was obliged to relinquish his attempt, and with great delay and danger to adopt a new and distant plan of operations.

We shall soon know, and in any event have reason to lament, what may have happened since. As to conquest, therefore, my lords, I repeat, it is impossible. You may swell every expense, and every effort, still more extravagantly; pile and accumulate every assistance you can buy or borrow; traffic and barter with every little pitiful German prince, that sends and sells his subjects to the shambles of a foreign despot; your efforts are forever vain and impotent; doubly so from this mercenary aid upon which you rely. For it irritates, to an incurable resentment, the minds of your enemies, to overrun them with the mercenary sons of rapine and plunder; devoting them and their possessions to the rapacity of hireling cruelty! If I were an American, as I am an Englishman, while a foreign troop was landed in my country, I would lay down my arms *never*, NEVER, NEVER.

Ex. LXV.—*A HYMN.*

Written 1778.

WILLIAM BILLINGS.

LET tyrants shake their iron rod,
  And slavery clank her galling chains;
We fear them not; we trust in God—
  New England's God forever reigns.

The foe comes on with haughty stride;
  Our troops advance with martial noise;
Their veterans flee before our youth,
  And generals yield to beardless boys.

When God inspired us for the fight,
  Their ranks were broken—fled their host;
Their ships were shattered in our sight,
  Or swiftly driven from our coast.

What grateful offering shall we bring?
  What shall we render to the Lord?
Loud hallelujahs let us sing,
  And praise his name on every chord.

Ex. LXVI.—*ON THE CHOICE OF A WAR WITH AMERICA OR WITH FRANCE.*

Speech in Parliament, February 17, 1778.

CHARLES JAMES FOX.*

You have now two wars before you, of which you must choose one, for both you can not support. The war against America has been hitherto carried on by her alone, unassisted by any ally; yet notwithstanding she stood alone, you have been obliged uniformly to increase your exertions, and to push your efforts to the extent of your power, without being able to bring it to any favorable issue. You have exerted all your strength hitherto without effect, and you can not now divide a force already found inadequate to its object; the war with America is against your own countrymen; every blow you strike there is against yourselves, even though you should be able (which you never will be) to force them to submit.

The war of the Americans is a war of passion; it is of a nature to be supported by the most powerful virtues—love of liberty and of country—and at the same time by those passions in the human heart which give courage, strength and

---

* Fox was one of the most renowned of English Parliamentary orators; and, like Chatham, Burke, and Pitt, his abilities were always enlisted on the side of the Americans. He died in the same year with William Pitt, 1806.

perseverance to man; the spirit of revenge for the injuries you have done them, of retaliation for the hardships inflicted on them, and of opposition to the unjust powers you would have exercised over them; everything combines to animate them to this war, and such a war is without end; for whatever obstinacy enthusiasm ever inspired man with, you now have to contend against in America. No matter what gives birth to that enthusiasm—whether the name of religion or of liberty—the effects are the same; it inspires a spirit that is unconquerable, and solicitous to undergo difficulties and dangers; and as long as there is a man in America, so long will you have him against you in the field. The war with France is of another sort; it is a war of interest. It was interest that first induced her to engage in it, and it is by that same interest she will measure its continuance.

Nobody is more sensible than I am of the necessity of unanimity at this juncture; and I wish I had the opportunity afforded me of supporting the ministry with justice to the country; but that, Sir, can never be the case with the present; I know them too well to do so, and shall feel it my duty to give them every opposition in my power. I know that doing so at this time will be called clogging the wheels of government at a time when they ought to be assisted by every man; but, Sir, they have reduced us to that paradoxical situation that I must choose one of two evils, for they have not left us the power of choosing any good. It is a paradox in fact, and I will choose that part which seems to me, though bad, the best; I must, consequently, use all my exertions to remove the present ministry, by using every means in my power to clog them in this House, to clog them out of this House, and to clog everything they engage in while they continue in office; and I will do so because I consider this course to be less ruinous than to submit any longer to their blundering system of politics.

Ex. LXVII.—*AMERCIA LOST TO GREAT BRITAIN.*

Speech in Parliament, Nov. 26, 1778.

JOHN WILKES.

THE honorable gentleman, Sir, has told us that the Americans were determined to separate their rights from ours, to dissolve all connection between us. The fact is truly stated. They no longer consider themselves embarked with us in the sinking vessel of this state. They avoid us as a tyrannical, unprincipled, rapacious and ruined nation. Their only fear is that the luxury and profligacy of this country should gain their people. It was a long patience and forbearance they practised before the idea of being dissevered from the mother country gained ground among the Americans. They were driven into it by our injustice and violence. Repeated violations of their rights, accumulated injuries, wanton insults, and cruelties shocking to human nature, have brought about this wonderful revolution.

Now it appears to me an impossibility to bring back the Americans to any dependence on this kingdom. Since the declaration of independence, firmness and vigor have governed all the counsels of the Congress. That declaration was made at a moment which proved them strangers to fear, and in their idea superior to all the efforts of which we were capable. From that fatal era, July, 1776, has the Congress, or any one of the thirteen United States, discovered the faintest wish of returning to the obedience of our sovereign? No man will be bold enough to assert it. On the contrary, the Americans have increased in their hatred of us, and aversion to the yoke of bondage which we were preparing for them.

Torrents of noble blood have already flowed in this quarrel; yet the few conquests we made we were obliged to abandon. Towards the close of the last year, we congratulated ourselves on the taking of Philadelphia, the seat of the vacant Congress, in the insulting language of administration. Before the present year is half expired, Sir Henry Clinton evacuated Philadelphia at three o'clock in the morning, and escaped through infinite difficulties to New York, very judiciously avoiding the direct road, where he knew the enemy was in force. The Congress returned in triumph to Philadelphia, and congratulated the inhabitants of North America on the important victory of Monmouth over the British grand army, and the evacuation of Philadelphia, as they had before done on the evacuation of Boston by General Howe. Sir, the Americans have suffered greatly; but their sufferings were borne with temper and courage, for they were in the cause of public virtue. They bore adversity like men of, fixed principle and honor engaged in a righteous cause, and determined never to crouch to oppression.

A series of four years' disgraces and defeats are surely sufficient to convince us of the absolute impossibility of conquering America by force, and I fear the gentler means of persuasion have equally failed. America is, in my opinion, irrecoverably lost. It is indifferent to her whether you think proper to acknowledge her independency, or to call her children your subjects, and her provinces your colonies. The rest of the world will hear those appellations with derision. The very expense of your fleets and armies must exhaust this country. You experienced this for four years, with raw, undisciplined farmers and countrymen. You are now to combat hardy, experienced soldiers. Let pride therefore yield to prudence, withdraw your fleets and armies, give up this unjust, barbarous and destructive war, and inquire who deluded you into this unhappy system of policy.

Ex. LXVIII.—*ADDRESS TO THE STATES, BY THE CONTINENTAL CONGRESS, MAY 26, 1779.*

AMERICA, without arms, ammunition, discipline, revenue, government or ally, almost totally stript of commerce, and in the weakness of youth, as it were with "a staff and a sling" only, dared, in the name of the Lord of Hosts, to engage a gigantic adversary, prepared at all points, boasting of his strength, and of whom even mighty warriors were greatly afraid. * * Infatuated as your enemies have been from the beginning of this contest, do you imagine that they can now flatter themselves with a hope of conquering you, unless you are false to yourselves?

Rouse yourselves, therefore, that this campaign may finish the great work you have so nobly carried on for several years past. What nation ever engaged in such a contest under such a complication of disadvantages, so soon surmounted many of them, and in so short a period of time had a certain prospect of a speedy and happy conclusion? Consider how much you have done, and how little comparatively remains to be done to crown you with success. Persevere; and you insure peace, freedom, safety, glory, sovereignty and felicity, to yourselves, your children, and your children's children.

Encouraged by favors already received from Infinite

Goodness, gratefully acknowledging them, and earnestly imploring their continuance, vigorously employ the means placed by Providence in your hands, for completing your labors.

Fill up your battalions—be prepared in every part to repel the incursions of your enemies—place your several quotas in the continental treasury—lend money for public uses—provide effectually for expediting the conveyance of supplies to your armies and fleets and for your allies—prevent the produce of the country from being monopolized—diligently promote piety, virtue, brotherly love, learning, frugality and moderation—and may you be approved before Almighty God worthy of those blessings we devoutly wish you to enjoy.

Ex. LXIX.—*EULOGIUM ON THOSE WHO HAVE FALLEN IN THE CONTEST WITH GREAT BRITAIN, DELIVERED JULY 5, 1779.*

HUGH HENRY BRACKENRIDGE.*

It is the high reward of those who have risked their lives in a just and necessary war, that their names are sweet in the mouths of men, and every age shall know their actions. I know my abilities rise not on a level with so great a subject, but I love the memory of the men, and it is my hope that the affection I feel will be to me instead of genius, and give me warm words to advance their praises.

For what cause did these brave men sacrifice their lives? For that cause which in all ages has engaged the hopes, the wishes, the endeavors of the hearts of men—the cause of liberty? What was in our power we have done with the bodies of these men; we have paid them military honors—we have placed them in their native earth, and it is with veneration that we yet view their tombs upon the lonely glade, or the distant hill. Their names shall be read with those of Pelopidas, Epaminondas, and the worthies of the world. Posterity shall quote them for parallels and for examples. When they mean to dress the hero with the fairest praises, they

* Judge of the Supreme Court of Pennsylvania.

shall say he was gallant and distinguished in his early fall, like Warren; prudent and intrepid as Montgomery; faithful and generous as Washington; he fell in the bold and resolute advance, like Mercer; he saw the honor which his valor had acquired, and fainted in the arms of victory, like Herkimer; having gallantly repulsed the foe, he fell covered with wounds, in his old age, like Wooster.

Having paid our tribute to the memory of these men, it remains for us to soothe the grief of those who have been deprived of a father, bereaved of a son, or who have lost a husband, brother, or lover in the contest. Fathers, whose heroic sons have offered up their lives on the altar of freedom, it is yours to recollect, that these lives were given them for the service of their country. Sons, whose heroic fathers have early left you, and in the conflict of war have mixed with departed heroes; be congratulated on the fair inheritance of fame which you are entitled to possess. If it is ever lawful for us to array ourselves in borrowed honor, surely it is best drawn from those who have acted a distinguished part in the service of their country. If it is at all consistent with the feeling of philosophy and reason to boast of lineal glory, surely it is most allowable in those who boast it as flowing from such a source.

We despise the uninstructed mind of that man who shall obtrude upon our ears the idea of a vain ancestral honor; but we love the youth, and transfer to him the reputation of his father, who, when the rich and haughty citizen shall frown upon him as ignobly descended, shall say, "I had a father who fell in the service of his country."

And you, my gallant countrymen, your fame shall ascend on the current of the stream of time. It shall play with the breezes of the morning. Men at rest, in the cool age of life, from the fury of a thousand wars finished by their fathers, shall observe the spreading ensign. They shall hail it, as it waves with variegated glories; and feeling all the warm rapture of the heart, shall give it their plaudit from the shores.

Ex. LXX.—*HYMN AT THE CONSECRATION OF PULASKI'S BANNER, 1779.*

H. W. LONGFELLOW.

WHEN the dying flame of day
Through the chancel shot its ray,
Far the glimmering tapers shed
Faint light on the cowlèd head;
And the censer burning swung,
Where, before the altar, hung
The blood-red banner, that with prayer
Had been consecrated there.
And the nuns' sweet hymn was heard the while,
Sung low in the dim, mysterious aisle.

"Take thy banner! may it wave
Proudly o'er the good and brave;
When the battle's distant wail
Breaks the silence of our vale,
When the clarion's music thrills
To the hearts of these lone hills,
When the spear in conflict shakes,
And the strong lance quivering breaks.

"Take thy banner! and beneath
The battle cloud's encircling wreath,
Guard it!—till our homes are free—
Guard it!—God will prosper thee!
In the dark and trying hour,
In the breaking forth of power,
In the rush of steeds and men,
His right hand will shield thee then.

"Take thy banner! but when night
Closes round the ghastly fight,
If the vanquished warrior bow,
Spare him! by our holy vow,

---

* Many noble foreigners, inspired by a kindred love of liberty to that which actuated the Americans, came to this country to volunteer their services in our revolutionary struggle. Count Pulaski was a Pole, highly distinguished in his own country for his bravery and patriotism. He received a mortal wound at the second attack on Savannah, Oct., 1779. The banner here celebrated was embroidered for him by the Moravian nuns at Bethlehem, Penn., and was a very elegant one of crimson silk.

By our prayers and many tears,
By the mercy that endears,
Spare him!—he our love hath shared!
Spare him!—as thou wouldst be spared!

"Take thy banner!—and if e'er
Thou shouldst press the soldier's bier,
And the muffled drum should beat
To the tread of mournful feet,
Then this crimson flag shall be
Martial cloak and shroud for thee."

The warrior took that banner proud:
It was his martial cloak and shroud!

Ex. LXXI.—*ANSWER TO INQUIRIES AS TO THE CONDITION OF AMERICA, PARIS,* 1780.

JOHN ADAMS.[*]

Your first proposition, Sir, is "to prove, by striking facts, that an implacable hatred and aversion reigns throughout America."

In answer to this, I beg leave to say, that the Americans are animated by higher principles, and better and stronger motives than hatred and aversion. They universally aspire after a free trade with all the commercial world, instead of that mean monopoly in which they were shackled by Great Britain, to the disgrace and mortification of America, and to the injury of all the rest of Europe, to whom it seems as if God and nature intended that so great a magazine of productions, so great a source of commerce, and so rich a nursery

[*] Mr. Adams was sent to Europe in 1779, to endeavor to negotiate a peace and a treaty of commerce with Great Britain. While abroad he wrote and published many letters on subjects similar to that of the present one, with the purpose of enlightening public sentiment as to the character of the contest going on in America. Peace was declared in 1783, and two years afterwards Mr. Adams was appointed the first minister to England. He was subsequently elected Vice-President, and then President, of the United States. After leaving the latter office, he passed his time mainly in retirement, his last public service being to attend as delegate a convention for revising the Constitution of Massachusetts, his native state. This was in 1820, when he was in the eighty-sixth year of his age.

of seamen, as America is, should be open. They despise, Sir, they disdain the idea of being again monopolized by any one nation whatsoever; and this contempt is at least as powerful a motive for action as any hatred.

Moreover, Sir, they consider themselves contending for the purest principles of liberty, civil and religious; for those forms of government under the faith of which their country was planted, and for those great improvements of them which have been made by their new constitutions. They consider themselves not only as contending *for* these great blessings, but *against* the greatest evils that any country ever suffered; for they know, if they were to be deceived by England into breaking their union among themselves, and their faith with their allies, they would ever after be in the power of England, who would bring them into the most abject submission to a parliament, the most corrupted in the world, in which they have no voice or influence, at three thousand miles distance from them.

But if hatred must come into consideration, I know not how to justify their hatred better than by showing the provocations they have had to hatred.

If tearing up from the foundation those forms of government under which they were born and educated, and thrived and prospered, to the infinite emolument of England; if imposing taxes upon them, or endeavoring to do it, for twenty years, without their own consent; if commencing hostilities upon them—burning their towns—butchering their people—deliberately starving prisoners—exciting hosts of Indians to torture and scalp them, and purchasing Germans to destroy them, and hiring negro servants to murder their masters;—if all these, and many other things as bad, are not provocations enough to hatred, I would request to be informed what is or can be. And all these horrors the English have practised in America, from Boston to Savannah.

To learn the present state of America, it is necessary to read the public papers. The present state of Great Britain and its dependencies may be learned in the same way. The omnipotence of the British army, and the omnipotence of the British navy, are likely to go the same way.

Ex. LXXII.—*ANNIVERSARY ORATION, DELIVERED MARCH 5, 1781.*

THOMAS DAWES.

May the name of Washington continue steeled, as it ever has been, to the dark slanderous arrow that "flieth in secret." As it ever has been! for none have offered to eclipse his glory but have afterwards sunk away diminished and "shorn of their beams."

Justice to other characters forbids our stopping to gaze at the constellation of heroes who shine brightest in our country's annals, and would fain draw forth a eulogium upon all who have gathered true laurels from the fields of America.

> "Thousands the tribute of our praise
> Demand; but who can count the stars of heaven?
> Who speak their influence on this lower world?"

Whither has our gratitude borne us? Let us behold a contrast;—the army of an absolute prince—a profession distinct from the citizen, and in a different interest—a haughty phalanx, whose object of warfare is pay, and who, the battle over, and if perchance they conquer, return to slaughter the sons of peace. Oh, our bleeding country! was it for this our hoary sires sought thee through all the elements, and having found thee sheltering away from the western wave, disconsolate, cheered thy sad face, and decked thee out like the garden of God? There was a time when we were all ready to cry out that our fathers had done a vain thing—I mean upon that unnatural night which we now commemorate—when the fire of Brutus was in many a heart—when the strain of Gracchus was on many a tongue. "Wretch that I am, where shall I retreat? Whither shall I turn me? To the capitol? The capitol swims in my brother's blood! To my family? There must I see a wretched, a mournful and afflicted mother!"

Misery loves to brood over its own woes; and so peculiar were the horrors of that night, so expressive the pictures of despair, so various the face of death, that not all the grand tragedies that have since been acted, can crowd from our minds that era of the human passions, that preface to the general conflict that now rages. May we never forget to offer a sacrifice to the memories of our friends who bled so early at the foot of liberty. Hitherto we have nobly avenged their fall; but as ages can not expunge the debt, their melancholy ghosts still rise at a stated season, and will forever wander in the night of this noted anniversary. Hark! even now in the hollow wind I hear the voice of the departed. "Oh, ye who listen to wisdom and aspire to immortality, as ye have avenged our blood, thrice blessed! As ye still war against the mighty hunters of the earth, your names are recorded in heaven!"

Let justice then be done to our country, let justice be done to our great leader; and as the only means, under Heaven, of his salvation, let his army be replenished. That grand duty done, we will once more adopt an enthusiasm sublime in itself, but still more so as coming from the lips of a first patriot—the chief magistrate of this commonwealth. "I have," said he, "a most animating confidence that the present noble struggle for liberty will terminate gloriously for America." Aspiring to such a confidence,

> "I see the expressive leaves of Fate thrown wide,
> Of future times I see the mighty tide;
> And borne triumphant on its buoyant wave,
> A godlike number of the great and brave.
> The bright, wide ranks of martyrs—here they rise;
> Heroes and patriots move before my eyes;
> These crowned with olive, those with laurel come,
> Like the first fathers of immortal Rome.
> Fly, Time! oh, lash thy fiery steeds away—
> Roll rapid wheels, and bring the smiling day
> When these blest states, another promised land,
> Chosen and fostered by the Almighty hand,
> Supreme shall rise—their crowded shores shall be
> The fixed abodes of empire and of liberty."

Ex. LXXIII.—*ADDRESS FROM THE LEGISLATURE OF THE STATE OF NEW YORK TO THEIR CONSTITUENTS, MARCH 13, 1781.**

LISTEN, friends, fellow-citizens, and countrymen, to the recommendations of that great and good man, whose virtues

---

* In the stormy and anxious days of the Revolution there were always some discontented spirits who gave more annoyance to the devoted patriots at the head of affairs than even their foreign enemies, because the effect of their murmurs was to clog the wheels of government and prevent those in office

and patriotism, as the soldier and the citizen, have drawn down the admiration, not of America only, but all Europe; whose well-earned fame will roll down the tide of time until it is absorbed in the abyss of eternity. Listen to what he recommended to your army on a recent and an alarming occasion, and seriously apply it to yourselves and to us :

"The general is deeply sensible of the sufferings of the army; he leaves no expedient unused to relieve them; and he is persuaded that Congress and the several States are doing everything in their power for the same purpose. But while we look to the public for the fulfilment of its engagements, we should do it with proper allowance for the embarrassments of public affairs; we began a contest for liberty and independence ill provided with the means of war, relying on our patriotism to supply deficiencies; we expected to encounter many wants and difficulties, and we should neither shrink from them when they happen, nor fly in the face of law and government to procure redress. There is no doubt the public will, in the event, do ample justice to the men fighting and suffering in their defence; but it is our duty to bear present evils with fortitude, looking forward to the period when our country will have it more in its power to reward our services. History is full of examples of armies suffering, with patience, extremities of distress which exceed those we have experienced, and those in the cause of ambition and conquest, not in that of the rights of humanity, of their country, of their families, and of themselves. Shall we, who aspire to the distinction of a patriot army, who are contending for everything precious in society, against everything hateful and degrading in slavery; shall we, who call ourselves citizens, discover less constancy and military virtue than the mercenary instruments of ambition?"

These are the sentiments of a Washington; and although he had us not immediately in view, yet every sentence is replete with wholesome admonition to all orders of men in these States. The force and artifice of the enemy have hitherto proved equally abortive. Britain's proud boasts of conquest are no more, and all Europe detests her cause. You are already within sight of the promised land, and, by the blessing of Heaven, and adequate efforts on your part, you

---

from making the most of the scanty means at their command. We have here an earnest appeal from one of the perturbed and weary councils of the nation, in which the noblest incentives are held up to the malcontents in the hope of allaying their restless spirit of discontent.

may shortly hope, under your own vine and your own fig-tree, to spend the remainder of your days in tranquillity and ease; when the dangers you have passed, and the difficulties you sustain, will only seem to heighten your enjoyments; when you will look forward to the applauses of succeeding ages, and extend your happiness to the most remote period, by anticipating that which your exertions shall transmit to posterity.

But, friends, fellow-citizens, and countrymen, vain is your hope to experience these glorious rewards for all your toils, and quaff the cup of bliss; in vain has our hardy ancestor traversed the trackless ocean to seek in the wilds of the new world a refuge from the oppression of the old; in vain for our sakes has he fled from that tyranny which, by taxing industry, transmits poverty as an inheritance from one generation to another; in vain has he striven with the ruthless barbarian, and with the various difficulties incident on the emigration to countries untrodden by civilized man, if, by internal discord, by a pusillanimous impatience under unavoidable burdens, by an immoderate attachment to perishable property, by an intemperate jealousy of those servants whom each revolving year may displace from your confidence, by forgetting those fundamental principles which induced America to separate from Britain, we play into the hands of a haughty nation, spurred on to perseverance in injury by a despairing and unrelenting tyrant, and his rapacious minions.

Your representatives feel themselves incapable of believing that any but the misguided, the weak and the unwary amongst our fellow citizens, can be guilty of so foully staining the honor of their State, and wantonly becoming parricides of their own peace and happiness, and that of their posterity. Let us then all, for our interest is the same, with one heart and one voice, mutually aid and support each other. Let us steadily, unanimously, and vigorously prosecute the great business of establishing our independence. Thus shall we be free ourselves, and leave the blessings of freedom to millions yet unborn.

Ex. LXXIV.—*AN ENGLISHMAN'S OPINION OF THE AMERICAN WAR.*

Speech in the House of Commons, June 12, 1781.

WILLIAM PITT.*

A NOBLE lord, in the heat of his zeal, has called it a holy war. For my part, though the honorable gentleman who made the motion has been more than once in the course of the debate severely reprehended for calling it a wicked and accursed war, I am persuaded, and will affirm, that it is a most accursed, wicked, barbarous, cruel, unnatural, unjust and diabolical war!- It was conceived in injustice; it was nurtured and brought forth in folly; its footsteps are marked with blood, slaughter, persecution and devastation; in truth, everything which goes to constitute moral depravity and human turpitude, are to be found recorded there. But the mischief of it recoils òn the unhappy people of this country, who are made the instruments by which the wicked purposes of its authors are to be effected. The nation is drained of its best blood, its most vital resources of men and money. The expenses of it are enormous, much beyond any former experience; and what has the British nation received in return? Nothing but a series of ineffective victories, or severe defeats; victories celebrated only by a temporary triumph over our brethren whom we would trample down and destroy; which have filled the land with mourning for the loss of dear and valuable relations, slain in the impious cause of enforcing unconditional submission, or with narratives of the glorious exertions of men struggling in the holy cause of liberty, though struggling under all the difficulties and disadvantages which are in general deemed the necessary concomitants of victory and success. Where is the Englishman who, on reading the narratives of those bloody and well-fought contests, can refrain from lamenting the loss of so much British blood spilt in such a cause; or from

---

* William Pitt, "the illustrious son of an illustrious father," was second son of the great Earl of Chatham, and inherited, with his father's great abilities, his love of constitutional liberty. He was elected to Parliament in 1781, and therefore displayed his sympathy with America only during the latter part of the war; but his voice was always raised on the side of freedom and justice. He was called "The Great Commoner," from the fact that, being a second son, he was not entitled to a seat in the House of Lords, but won all his distinction in the Commons.

weeping, on whatever side victory might be declared? Add to this melancholy consideration, that on whichever side we look, we can perceive nothing but our natural and powerful enemies, or lukewarm and faithless friends, rejoicing in our calamities, or meditating our ultimate downfall.

Ex. LXXV.—*THE ATTACK ON FORT GRISWOLD.**

September 7, 1781.

T. K. POTTER.

"RISE! man the wall! our clarion's blast
   Now sounds the final reveillé;
This dawning morn must be the last
   Our fated band shall ever see.
To life, but not to hope, farewell!
   Yon trumpet-clang, and cannon's peal,
   And storming shout, and clash of steel,
Is ours, but not our country's, knell.
   Welcome the Spartan's death!
   'Tis no despairing strife;
   We fall! we die! but our expiring breath
   Is Freedom's breath of life.

"Here, on this new Thermopylæ,
   Our monument shall tower on high,
And Griswold's Fort hereafter be
   In bloodier fields the battle-cry."
Thus Ledyard from the rampart cried;
   And when his warriors saw the foe
   Like whelming billows move below,
At once each dauntless heart replied,

---

* After the treason of Benedict Arnold, he was rewarded by the British with the rank of Brigadier-General in their army, and in this capacity was sent to ravage and lay waste the coast of his native state, Connecticut. Among other valiant deeds he assaulted and took by storm Fort Griswold, opposite New London, and caused its brave commander, Col. Ledyard, with sixty of his garrison, to be slaughtered in cold blood after the surrender. Informed of this outrage, the militia of the neighborhood assembled to avenge it; but Arnold did not choose to risk an encounter with them, and reëmbarked on board his ships with most undignified haste.

"Welcome the Spartan's death!
'Tis no despairing strife;
We fall! we die! but our expiring breath
Is Freedom's breath of life."

They come! like autumn leaves they fall,
Yet hordes on hordes they onward rush;
With gory tramp they mount the wall,
Till numbers the defenders crush—
Till falls their flag when none remain.
Well may the ruffians quake to tell
How Ledyard and his hundred fell
Amid a thousand foemen slain.
They died the Spartan's death,
But not in hopeless strife;
Like brothers died; and their expiring breath
Was Freedom's breath of life.

Ex. LXXVI.—*IN MEMORIAM.**

PHILIP FRENEAU.

At Eutaw Springs the valiant died:
Their limbs with dust are covered o'er;
Your waves may tell, oh, tearful tide,
How many heroes are no more!

If in this wreck of hope, the brave
Can yet be thought to claim a tear,
Oh, smite thy gentle breast, and say,
The friends of freedom slumber here!

Thou, who shalt trace this bloody plain,
If goodness rules thy generous breast,
Sigh for the rural wasted reign;
Sigh for the shepherds, sunk to rest!

Stranger! their humble graves adorn;
You too may fall, and ask a tear:

---

* This poem is inscribed by the author, "To the memory of the brave Americans under General Greene, in South Carolina, who fell in the action of September 8, 1781."

'Tis not the beauty of the morn
  That proves the evening shall be clear.

They saw their injured country's woe,
  The flaming town, the wasted field;
Then rush'd to meet the insulting foe,
  They took the spear—but left the shield.

But, like the Parthian, famed of old,
  Who, flying, still their arrows threw,
These routed Britons fierce as bold,
  Retreated, but retreating slew.

Now rest in peace our patriot band;
  Though far from nature's limits thrown,
We trust, they find a happier land,
  A brighter sunshine of their own.

Ex. LXXVII.—*CIRCULAR LETTER FROM CONGRESS TO THE STATES, DECEMBER 17, 1781.*

SEVEN years have nearly passed since the sword was first unsheathed. The sums expended in so long a period in a just and necessary war must appear moderate; nor can any demand for pecuniary aid be deemed exorbitant by those who compute the extent of the public exigencies and the proportion of the requisition to the ability of the States. Suppose not that funds exist for our relief beyond the limits of these states. As the possessions of the citizens constitute our natural resources, and from a sense of their sufficiency the standard of war was erected against Great Britain, so on them alone we now rely.

But the want of money is not the only source of our difficulties; nor do the enemy gather consolation from the state of our finances alone. We are distressed by the thinness of our battalions. Tardiness in the collection of our troops has constantly encouraged in our enemy a suspicion that American opposition is on the decline. Hence money from time to time is poured into the coffers of our enemy; and the lender is perhaps allured by the prospect of receiving it with a usurious interest from the spoils of confiscation.

To whom then rather than to yourselves, who are called to the guardianship and sovereignty of your country, can these considerations be addressed? Joint laborers, as we are, in the work of independence, duty impels us to admonish you of the crisis. We possess no funds which do not originate with you. We can command no levies which are not raised under your acts. How shall we acquit ourselves to the world, should peace, towards the acquisition of which so illustrious a point hath been gained, now escape our embraces, by the inadequacy of our army, or our treasure? An appeal to this exposition of our affairs will demonstrate our watchfulness of your happiness.

We conjure you to remember what confidence we shall establish in the breast of that great monarch who has become a party in our political welfare, by a bold, energetic display of our ability.

We, therefore, trust in your attention and zeal to avail yourselves, at this important crisis, of the glorious advantages lately obtained, by a full compliance with these requisitions of men and money which we have made to you, and the necessity of which hath been pointed out to us by the maturest consideration on the present circumstances of these United States.

Ex. LXXVIII.—*RETURN OF BRITISH FUGITIVES ADVOCATED.*

Speech in Congress, 1782.

PATRICK HENRY.

I venture to prophesy that there are now those living who will see this favored land amongst the most powerful on earth—able, Sir, to take care of herself, without resorting to that policy, which is always so dangerous, though sometimes unavoidable, of calling in foreign aid. Yes, Sir, they will see her great in arts and arms—her golden harvests waving over fields of immeasurable extent, her commerce penetrating the most distant seas, and her cannon silencing the vain boasts of those who now proudly affect to rule the waves. But, Sir, you must have *men*—you can not get along without them. Those heavy forests of valuable timber, under which your lands are groaning, must be cleared away.

Those vast riches which cover the face of your soil, as well as those that lie hid in its bosom, are to be developed and gathered only by the skill and enterprise of men. Your timber, Sir, must be worked up into ships, to transport the productions of the soil from which it has been cleared. Then, you must have commercial men and commercial capital, to take off your productions, and find the best markets for them abroad. Your great want, Sir, is the want of men; and these you must have, and will have speedily, if you are wise.

Do you ask how you are to get them? Open your doors, Sir, and they will come in! The population of the Old World is full to overflowing. That population is ground, too, by the oppressions of the governments under which they live. Sir, they are already standing on tip-toe on their native shores, and looking to your coasts with a wistful and longing eye. They see here a land blessed with natural and political advantages, which are not equalled by those of any other country upon earth; a land on which a gracious Providence hath emptied the horn of abundance—a land over which Peace hath now stretched forth her white wings, and where Content and Plenty lie down at every door.

Sir, they see something still more attractive than all this. They see a land in which Liberty hath taken up her abode—that Liberty whom they had considered as a fabled goddess, existing only in the fancies of poets. They see her here a real divinity—her altars rising on every hand, throughout these happy States; her glories chanted by three millions of tongues, and the whole region smiling under her blessed influence. Sir, let but this, our celestial goddess, Liberty, stretch forth her fair hand toward the people of the Old World—tell them to come, and bid them welcome—and you will see them pouring in from the North, from the South, from the East, and from the West. Your wildernesses will be cleared and settled, your deserts will smile, your ranks will be filled, and you will soon be in a condition to defy the power of any adversary.

But gentlemen object to any accession from Great Britain, and particularly to the return of the British refugees. Sir, I feel no objection to the return of these deluded people. They have, to be sure, mistaken their own interests most wofully; and most wofully have they suffered the punishment due to their offences. But the relations which we bear to them, and to their native country, are now changed. Their

King hath acknowledged our independence; the quarrel is over, peace hath returned and found us a free people. Let us have the magnanimity, Sir, to lay aside our antipathies and prejudices, and consider the subject in a political light.

Those are an enterprising, moneyed people. They will be serviceable in taking off the surplus produce of our lands, and supplying us with necessaries, during the infant state of our manufactures. Even if they be inimical, in point of feeling and principle, I can see no objection, in a political view, in making them tributary to our advantage. And, as I have no prejudices to prevent my making this use of them, so, Sir, I have no fear of any mischief that they can do us. Afraid of *them!* What, Sir, shall *we*, who have laid the proud British *lion* at our feet, now be afraid of *his whelps?*

Ex. LXXIX.—*ELECTION SERMON.*

Delivered before the Connecticut Legislature, May, 1783.

DR. STILES.*

WHILE we render our supreme honors to the Most High, the God of armies, let us recollect, with affectionate honor, the bold and brave sons of freedom, who willingly offered themselves, and bled in the defence of their country. Our fellow-citizens, the officers and soldiers of the patriot army, who, with other gallant commanders and brave seamen of the American navy, have heroically fought by sea and by land, merit of their once bleeding but now triumphant country, laurels, crowns, rewards, and the highest honors. Never was the profession of arms used with more glory, or in a better cause, since the days of Joshua the son of Nun.

O Washington! how do I love thy name! how often have I adored and blessed thy God, for creating and forming thee, the great ornament of human kind! Upheld and protected by the Omnipotent, by the Lord of Hosts, thou hast been sustained and carried through one of the most arduous and important wars in all history. The world and posterity will, with admiration, contemplate thy deliberate, cool, and stable judgment, thy virtues, thy valor and heroic achievements, as far surpassing those of Cyrus, whom the world

* President of Yale College.

loved and adored. The sound of thy fame shall go out into all the earth, and extend to distant ages. Thou hast convinced the world of the beauty of virtue—for in thee this beauty shines with distinguished lustre. There is a glory in thy disinterested benevolence, which the greatest characters would purchase, if possible, at the expense of worlds, and which may indeed excite their emulation, but can not be felt by the venal great—those who think everything, even virtue and true glory, may be bought and sold, and trace our every action to motives terminating in *self*—

> " Find Virtue local, all relation scorn,
> See all in self, and but for self be born."

But thou, O Washington! forgottest thyself when thou lovedst thy bleeding country. Not all the gold of Ophir, nor a world filled with rubies and diamonds, could affect or purchase the sublime and noble feelings of thy heart in that single self-moved act, when thou didst deliberately cast the die for the dubious, the very dubious alternative of a gibbet or a triumphal arch! But, beloved, enshielded and blessed by the great Melchisedec, the king of righteousness as well as peace, thou hast triumphed gloriously. Such has been thy military wisdom in the struggles of this arduous conflict, such the noble rectitude of thy character; something is there so singularly glorious and venerable thrown by Heaven about thee, that not only does thy country love thee, but our very enemies stop the madness of their fire in full volley, stop the illiberality of their slander, at thy name, as if rebuked from Heaven with "Touch not mine anointed, and do my HERO no harm." Thy fame is of sweeter perfume than Arabian spices in the gardens of Persia. A Baron de Steuben shall waft its fragrance to the monarch of Prussia— a Marquis de La Fayette shall bear it to a much greater monarch, and diffuse thy renown throughout Europe. Listening angels shall catch the odor, waft it to heaven, and perfume the universe.

Ex. LXXX.—*ADDRESS*

To the Officers of the Army on an insidious attempt to seduce them from their allegiance to their country, in 1783.

GEN. WASHINGTON.*

GENTLEMEN: If my conduct heretofore has not evinced to you that I have been a faithful friend to the army, my declaration of it at this time would be equally unavailing and improper. But as I was among the first who embarked in the cause of our common country, as I have never left your side for one moment but when called from you on public duty; as I have been the constant companion and witness of your distresses, and not among the last to feel and acknowledge your merits; as I have ever considered my own military reputation as inseparably connected with that of the army, and my heart has ever expanded with joy when I heard its praises, and my indignation has arisen when the mouth of detraction has been opened against it, it can scarcely be supposed, at this last stage of the war, that I am indifferent to its interests.

With respect to the advice given by the author, to suspect the man who shall recommend longer moderation and forbearance, I *spurn it*, as every man, who regards that liberty, and reveres that justice for which we contend, undoubtedly must; for if a man is to be precluded from offering his sentiments on a matter which may involve the destiny of our country, reason is of no use to us. I cannot, in justice to my own belief, conclude this address without giving it as

---

* Towards the close of the war, great dissatisfaction arose among the officers of the army on the subject of their pay, and these discontents being artfully inflamed by interested persons, a meeting was called to consider their grievances, which might have resulted in open mutiny had not Washington's wise and conciliatory measures prevented. He denounced the anonymous call for a meeting as irregular, but appointed a meeting himself, for an earlier day, at which the matter should be considered. The officers being assembled at this time, he entered the room, with the above address in his hand, prepared to read to them. As he looked around upon his companions in arms, his feelings overcame him, his eyes grew dim, and he could not see to read his notes. Recovering himself, he took his glasses from his pocket, and said quietly, "I have grown gray in your service, and now I am growing blind, but I never doubted the justice of my country, or its gratitude." He then read his address; no reply was made to it, but, after he had left the room, resolutions were passed which entirely counteracted the effect of the mutinous conspiracy, and shortly afterward the news of a glorious peace set the matter permanently at rest.

my decided opinion, that Congress entertains an exalted sentiment of the services of the army, and, from a full conviction of its merits and sufferings, will do it complete justice: that their endeavors to discover and establish funds have been unwearied, and that they will never cease until they have succeeded.

Why should we distrust them? And why, in consequence of that distrust, adopt measures which will cast a shade over that glory which has been so justly acquired, and tarnish the reputation of an army which has been celebrated throughout all Europe for its fortitude and patriotism?

While I pledge myself in the most unequivocal manner, to exert whatever ability I am possessed of in your favor, let me entreat you, gentlemen, on your part, not to take any measures which, viewed in the calm light of reason, will lessen the dignity and sully the glory you have hitherto maintained. Let me request you to rely on the *plighted* faith of your country—to place a full confidence in the purity of the intentions of Congress—and to assure yourselves that they will adopt the most effectual measures in their power to render ample justice to you, for your faithful and meritorious services.

By thus determining and thus acting, you will pursue the plain and direct road to the attainment of your wishes. You will give one more proof of unexampled patriotism and patient virtue, rising superior to the pressure of the most complicated sufferings; and you will, by the dignity of your conduct, afford occasion for posterity to say, when speaking of the glorious example you have exhibited to mankind, "Had this day been wanting, the world would never have seen the last stage of perfection to which human nature is capable of attaining."

Ex. LXXXI.—*ON DISBANDING THE ARMY*—1783.

DAVID HUMPHREYS.*

YE brave Columbian bands! a long farewell!
Well have ye fought for freedom—nobly done

* Col. Humphreys served during the Revolutionary war, principally in the capacity of aid to different generals. At the close of the war he entered the

Your martial task; the meed immortal won;
And Time's last records shall your triumphs tell.

Once friendship made their cup of sufferings sweet—
  The dregs how bitter, now those bands must part!
Ah! never, never more on earth to meet;
  Distilled from gall that inundates the heart,
What tears from heroes' eyes are seen to start!

Ye, too, farewell, who fell in fields of gore,
  And changed tempestuous toil for rest serene;
Soon shall we join you on that peaceful shore,
  (Though gulfs unmeasured darkly roll between,)
Thither by death tides borne, as ye full soon have been.

Ex. LXXXII.—*NATIONAL DEPENDENCE UPON GOD.*

Speech in the Convention for framing the Constitution, 1787.

BENJAMIN FRANKLIN.

Mr. President: The small progress we have made after four or five weeks' close attendance and continual reasonings with each other—our different sentiments on almost every question, several of the last producing as many noes as ayes —is, methinks, a melancholy proof of the imperfection of the human understanding. We indeed seem to feel our own want of political wisdom, and we have been running about in search of it. We have gone back to ancient history for models of government, and examined the different forms of those republics which, having been formed with the seeds of their own dissolution, now no longer exist. And we have viewed modern states all around Europe, but found none of their constitutions suitable to our circumstances.

In this situation of this Assembly, groping in the dark to find political truth, and scarcely able to distinguish it when presented to us, how has it happened; Sir, that we have not hitherto once thought of humbly applying to the Father of Light, to illuminate our understandings? In the begin-

diplomatic service, being appointed successively Secretary of Legation at Paris, Ambassador to Portugal, and Minister Plenipotentiary to Spain. Amidst his various duties he found time for literary composition, and left several poems, of which the present one is a very pleasing specimen.

ning of the contest with Great Britain, when we were sensible of danger, we had daily prayer in this room for the Divine protection. Our prayers, Sir, were heard, and they were graciously answered. All of us who were engaged in the struggle must have observed frequent instances of a superintending Providence in our favor. To that kind Providence we owe this happy opportunity of consulting in peace on the means of establishing our future national felicity. And have we now forgotten that powerful Friend? or do we imagine that we no longer need his assistance? I have lived, Sir, a long time, and the longer I live the more convincing proofs I see of this truth—that God governs in the affairs of men. And if a sparrow cannot fall to the ground without his notice, is it possible that an empire can rise without his aid? We have been assured, Sir, in the sacred writings, that "except the Lord build the house, they labor in vain that build it." I firmly believe this; and I also believe that without His concurring aid, we shall succeed in this political building no better than the builders of Babel. We shall be divided by our little partial local interests; our projects will be confounded, and we ourselves shall become a reproach and a by-word down to future ages. And what is worse, mankind may hereafter, from this unfortunate instance, despair of establishing governments by human wisdom, and leave it to chance, war and conquest.

I therefore beg leave to move—that henceforth prayers imploring the assistance of Heaven, and its blessings upon our deliberations, be held in this assembly every morning before we proceed to business, and that one or more of the clergy of this city be requested to officiate in that service.*

Ex. LXXXIII.—*THE FEDERAL CONSTITUTION.*
Speech in Convention, 1787.

JAMES WILSON.†

NEED I call to your remembrance, my fellow citizens, the contrasted scenes of which we have been witnesses? On the

---

* Strange to say, the motion was not adopted, because, in the words of a writer of the time, "the members of the Convention, with three or four exceptions, thought prayer unnecessary." We cannot suppose WASHINGTON to have sided with the majority!

† It is scarcely possible for us, with whom the Constitution has become a household word, to imagine the long and laborious consideration, the stormy

glorious conclusion of our conflict with Britain, what high expectations were formed concerning us by others! What high expectations did we form concerning ourselves! Have those expectations been realized? No! What has been the cause? Did our citizens lose their perseverance and magnanimity? No. Did they become insensible of resentment and indignation at any high-handed attempt that might have been made to injure and enslave them? No. What then has been the cause? The truth is, we dreaded danger only on one side: this we manfully repelled. But on another side, danger, not less formidable, but more insidious, stole in upon us; and our unsuspicious tempers were not sufficiently attentive, either to its approach or to its operations. Those whom foreign strength could not overpower, have well nigh become the victims of internal anarchy.

When we had baffled all the menaces of foreign power, we neglected to establish among ourselves a government that would ensure domestic vigor and stability. What was the consequence? The commencement of peace was the commencement of every disgrace and distress that could befall a people in a peaceful state. Devoid of national power, we could not prohibit the extravagance of our importations, nor could we derive a revenue from their excess. Devoid of national importance, we could not procure for our exports a tolerable sale at foreign markets. Devoid of national credit, we saw our public securities melt in the hands of the holders, like snow before the sun. Devoid of national dignity, we could not, in some instances, perform our treaties on our parts; and in other instances we could neither obtain nor compel the performance of them on that of others. Devoid of national energy, we could not carry into execution our own resolutions, decisions, nor laws.

But the years of languor are past. We have felt the dishonor with which we have been covered; we have seen the destruction with which we have been threatened. Under these impressions, and with these views, was the late Convention appointed; and under these impressions, and with these views, the late Convention met.

debates, the variety of conflicting opinions, which combined to mould it into its present form. It was a matter of compromises, scarcely any one considering it absolutely perfect, yet each willing to yield his judgment on minor points, for the sake of re-establishing the government, then fast drifting into ruin under the inefficient "Articles of Confederation." But few of the speeches delivered during this period have come down to us, the Convention holding its deliberations under injunctions of the strictest secrecy.

We now see the great end which they proposed to accomplish. It was to frame, for the consideration of their constituents, our federal and national constitution—a constitution that would produce the advantages of good, and prevent the inconveniences of bad government—a constitution whose beneficent energy would pervade the whole Union, and bind and embrace the interests of every part—a constitution that would ensure peace, freedom, and happiness to the States and people of America.

---◆---

Ex. LXXXIV.—*THE FEDERAL CONSTITUTION.*

Speech in Convention, 1787.

BENJAMIN FRANKLIN.*

Sir: I agree to this constitution with all its faults,—if they are such,—because I think a general government necessary for us, and there is no form of government but what may be a blessing to the people, if well administered; and I believe, further, this is likely to be well administered for a course of years, and can only end in despotism, as other forms have done before it, when the people shall become so corrupted as to need despotic government, being incapable of any other. I doubt, too, whether any other Convention we can obtain may be able to make a better constitution. For, when you assemble a number of men, to have the advantage of their joint wisdom, you inevitably assemble with those men all their prejudices, their passions, their errors of opinion, their local interests, and their selfish vices. From such an assembly, can a perfect production be expected? It, therefore, astonishes me, Sir, to find this system approaching so near to perfection as it does, and I think it will astonish our enemies, who are awaiting with confidence to hear that

---

* It must have been an affecting sight to see the philosopher and statesman, at the age of eighty-one years, still taking an active part in the councils of the nation, and always lending his voice and influence to the side of conciliation and liberality. His aim was to harmonize conflicting opinions, and to be satisfied with the best result that could be attained, on the whole, confident that it was impossible ever to bring a large body of men into perfect unanimity. He lived to see the new system of government in successful operation, and died in 1790, the second year of Washington's presidency.

our counsels are confounded, like those of the builders of Babel, and that our States are on the point of separation, only to meet hereafter for the purpose of cutting one another's throats.

Thus I consent, Sir, to this Constitution, because I expect no better, and because I am not sure that this is not the best. The opinion I have had of its errors I sacrifice to the public good. I have never whispered a syllable of them abroad. Within these walls they were born, and here they shall die. If every one of us, in returning to his constituents, were to report the objections he has had to it, and endeavor to gain partisans in support of them, we might prevent its being generally received, and thereby lose all the salutary effects and great advantages resulting naturally in our favor among foreign nations, as well as among ourselves, from our real or apparent unanimity.

Much of the strength and efficacy of any government, in procuring and securing happiness to the people, depends on opinion, on the general opinion of the goodness of that government, as well as of the wisdom and integrity of its governors. I hope, therefore, that for our own sakes, as a part of the people, and for the sake of our posterity, we shall act heartily and unanimously in recommending this constitution, wherever our influence may extend, and turn our future thoughts and endeavors to the means of having it well administered.

Ex. LXXXV.—*THE FEDERAL CONSTITUTION.*

Speech in Convention, June, 1788.

EDMUND RANDOLPH.[*]

Let us consider the definition of a republican government, as laid down by a highly esteemed political philoso-

[*] This debate between Randolph and Patrick Henry did not take place at the time of framing the Constitution, but in the following year, when a Convention was held in Virginia, (as in the other states,) for the purpose of ratifying it. Mr. Randolph had voted against the Constitution in the original Convention, but yielded his opinion in deference to what he believed to be the public good. He was afterwards Governor of Virginia, Attorney-General of the United States, and Secretary of State.

pher. Montesquieu, so celebrated among politicians, says, "that a republican government is that in which the body, or only a part of the people, is possessed of the supreme power; a monarchical, that in which a single person governs by fixed and established laws; a despotic government, that in which a single person, without law and without rule, directs everything by his own will and caprice." This great man has not distinguished a republican government from a monarchy by the extent of its boundaries, but by the nature of its principles.

When laws are made with integrity, and executed with wisdom, the question is, whether a great extent of country will tend to abridge the liberty of the people. If defensive force be necessary in proportion to the extent of country, I conceive that in a judiciously constructed government, be the country ever so extensive, the inhabitants will be proportionably numerous and able to defend it. Extent of country, in my conception, ought to be no bar to the adoption of a good government. No extent on earth seems to me to be too great, provided the laws be wisely made and executed. The principles of representation and responsibility may pervade a large as well as a small territory; and tyranny is as easily introduced into a small as into a large district. If it be answered, that some of the most illustrious and distinguished authors are of a contrary opinion, I reply, that authority has no weight with me until I am convinced; that not the dignity of names, but the force of reasoning, gains my assent.

I have labored for the continuance of the Union—the rock of our salvation. I believe that as surely as there is a God in heaven, our safety, our political happiness and existence depend on the union of the States; and that without that union, the people of this and the other States will undergo all the unspeakable calamities which discord, faction, turbulence, war and bloodshed have produced in other countries. The American spirit ought to be mixed with American pride—pride to see the Union magnificently triumph. Let that glorious pride which once defied the British thunder, re-animate you again! Let it not be recorded of Americans, that after having performed the most gallant exploits —after having overcome the most astonishing difficulties— after having gained the admiration of the world by their incomparable valor and policy, they lost their acquired reputation by their own indiscretion. Let no future historian inform posterity that they wanted wisdom and virtue to concur in any regular efficient government.

Should any writer, doomed to so disagreeable a task, feel the indignation of an honest historian, he would reprehend and recriminate our folly, with equal severity and justice. Catch the present moment, seize it with avidity and eagerness, for it may be lost, never to be regained. If the union be now abandoned, I fear it will remain so forever. I believe gentlemen are sincere in their opposition, and actuated by pure motives; but when I maturely weigh the advantages of the union, and dreadful consequences of its dissolution; when I see safety on my right, and destruction on my left; when I behold respectability and happiness acquired by the one, but annihilation by the other, I can not hesitate to decide in favor of the former.

Ex. LXXXVI.—*THE FEDERAL CONSTITUTION.*

Speech in Convention, June, 1788.

PATRICK HENRY.

THE honorable gentleman, Sir, has said a great deal about the figure we cut in the eyes of foreign nations, and the contemptible aspect in which we must be viewed by France and Holland; all of which, according to the notes I have taken, he attributes to the imbecility of our government. It appears, then, that an opinion has gone forth that we are a contemptible people. The time has been, Sir, when we were thought otherwise. Under this very same despised government, we commanded the respect of all Europe; wherefore are we now reckoned otherwise? Why, because the American spirit has flown from us, and gone to regions where it never was expected.

It has gone to the people of France in search of a splendid government—a strong and energetic government. Shall we imitate the example of those nations who have fallen from a simple to a splendid government? Are those nations so very worthy of our imitation? What can make an adequate satisfaction to them for the evils they have suffered in purchasing such a government at the loss of their liberty? If we admit this consolidated government, it can be for no other reason but because we like a great and gorgeous one. In some way or other, it seems we *must* have a great and mighty empire; we must have an army; we must have a navy; we must have a number of fine things. When the American spirit was in its youth the language of America was different; liberty, Sir, liberty was then the primary object. We then acted as they might be expected to act, who are descended from a people that founded their government on liberty. Our glorious forefathers of Great Britain made liberty the foundation of everything. That country is become a great, a mighty and a splendid nation; not because its government is strong and energetic, but because liberty is its direct end and its foundation. We derived the spirit of liberty from our British ancestors; by that spirit we have triumphed over every difficulty.

But now, Sir, the American spirit, assisted by the ropes and chains of consolidation, is about to convert this country into a powerful and mighty empire. If you make the citizens of this country agree to become the subjects of one great consolidated "EMPIRE OF AMERICA," your government will not have sufficient energy to keep them together. Such a government is incompatible with the genius of republicanism.

Ex. LXXXVII.—*THE FEDERAL CONSTITUTION.*

Speech in Convention, June, 1788.

PATRICK HENRY.

THE gentleman has said a great deal about disunion and of the dangers that are to arise from it—when we are on the subject of union and dangers, let me ask him how will his present doctrine hold with what has happened. Is it consistent with that noble and disinterested conduct which he displayed on a former occasion? Did he not tell us that he withheld his signature? Where, then, were the dangers that now appear to him so formidable? He saw all America eagerly confident that the result of their deliberations would remove their distresses. He saw all America acting under the impulses of hope, expectation and anxiety, arising from their situation, and their partiality for the members of that convention; yet his enlightened mind, knowing that system to be defective, magnanimously and nobly refused its approbation.

He was not led by the *illumined*—the *illustrious few*. He was actuated by the dictates of his own judgment; and a better judgment than I can form. He did not stand out of the way of information. He must have been possessed of every intelligence. What alteration has a few months brought about? The internal difference between right and wrong does not fluctuate: that is immutable. I ask this question as a public man, and out of no particular view. I wish as such, to consult every source of information, in order to form my judgment on so awful a question. I had the highest respect for the honorable gentleman's abilities. I considered his opinion as a great authority. He taught me, Sir, in spite of the approbation of that great federal convention, to doubt the propriety of that system. When I found my honorable friend in the number of those who doubted, I began to doubt also. I coincided with him in opinion. I shall be a stanch and faithful disciple of his. I applaud that magnanimity which led him to withhold his signature. If he thinks now differently, he is as free as I am. Such is my situation that, as a poor individual, I look for information everywhere.

This government is so new, Sir, that it wants a name. I wish its other novelties were as harmless as this. He told us we had an American dictator in 1781. We never had an American president. In making a dictator we follow the example of the most glorious, magnanimous and skilful nations. In great dangers this power has been given. Rome has furnished us with an illustrious example. America wanted a person worthy of that trust—she looked to Virginia for him, and she found him there. We gave a dictatorial power to hands that used it gloriously; and which was rendered still more glorious by surrendering it up.

We have seen the sons of Cincinnatus, without splendid magnificence or parade, going, with the genius of their great progenitor, to the plough. Men who served their country without ruining it—men who had served it to the destruction of their private patrimonies—their country owing them amazing amounts, for the payment of which no adequate provision was then made. We have seen such men throw prostrate their arms at your feet. They did not call for those emoluments which ambition presents to sordid imaginations. The soldiers, who were able to command everything, instead of trampling on those laws which they were instituted to defend, most strictly obeyed them. The hands of justice have not been laid on a single American soldier.

Perhaps I shall be told that I have gone through the regions of fancy—that I deal in noisy declamation, and mighty professions of patriotism. Gentlemen are welcome to their opinions; but I look upon that paper as containing the most fatal plan that ingenuity can devise for enslaving a free people. If such be your rage for novelty, take it—indulge yourselves—but you never shall have my consent. My sentiments may appear extravagant, but I can tell you, that a number of my fellow-citizens have kindred sentiments —and I am anxious, if my country should come into the hands of tyranny, to exculpate myself from being in any degree the cause of it; and to exert my faculties to the utmost to extricate her. Whether I am gratified or not in my beloved form of government, I consider that the more she is plunged into distress, the more it is my duty to combat for her. Whatever be the result, I shall wait with patience; perhaps the day may come, when an opportunity shall offer to exert myself in her cause.

Ex. LXXXVIII.—*THE FEDERAL CONSTITUTION.*

Speech in Convention, June, 1788.

EDMUND RANDOLPH.

MR. CHAIRMAN: I am a child of the Revolution. At an early age, and when I most wanted it, my country took me under its protection; and by a succession of favors and honors, prevented even my most ardent wishes. For those favors, I feel the highest gratitude. My attachment to my country is, as it ought to be, unbounded, and her felicity is the most fervent prayer of my heart. Conscious of having exerted my faculties to the utmost in her behalf, if I have not succeeded in securing the esteem of my countrymen, I shall derive abundant consolation from the rectitude of my intentions.

Honors, when compared to the satisfaction arising from a conscious independence of spirit and rectitude of conduct, are as nothing. The unwearied study of my life shall be to promote the happiness of America. As a citizen, ambition and popularity are, at this time of day, no objects with me. I can truly declare to the whole world, that in the part I take in this very important question, I am actuated by no other motive than a regard for what I conceive to be the best interests of these States. I can also, with equal sincerity, declare, that I would join heart and hand in rejecting this system, were I not convinced that it will promote our happiness; but having a strong conviction on my mind, at this time, that by a disunion we shall throw away all those blessings we have so resolutely fought for, and that a rejection of the constitution will occasion disunion—I am determined to discharge the obligation I owe to my country, by voting for its adoption.

We are told that the report of dangers is false. The cry of peace, Sir, is false; what they call peace is but a deceitful calm. The tempest lowers over you—look around—wherever you cast your eyes you see danger. Recollect the extreme debility of our merely nominal government. We are, Sir, indeed we are, too despicable to be regarded by foreign nations. Without adequate powers vested in Congress, America can not be respectable in the eyes of other nations. Congress, Sir, ought to be fully vested with powers to support the Union—protect the interest of the United States—maintain their commerce—and defend them from external invasions and insults, and internal insurrections; to maintain justice, and promote harmony and public tranquillity among the States.

A government not vested with these powers will ever be found unable to make us happy or respectable; how far the Confederation is different from such a government, is known to all America. Instead of being able to cherish and protect the States, it has been unable to defend itself against the encroachments made upon it by them. What are the powers of Congress? They have full authority to recommend what they please; this recommendatory power reduces them to the condition of poor supplicants. Is this the dignified language of the members of the American Congress:—"May it please your high-mightinesses of Virginia to pay your just proportionate quota of our national debt; we humbly supplicate you that it may please you to comply with your federal duties! We implore, we beg, your obedience!" And is not this, Sir, a very fair representation of the powers of Congress? Their opinions are of no validity, when counteracted by the States. Their authority to recommend is a mere mockery of government.

If anything were wanting to complete this farce, it would be that a resolution of Virginia, and of the other legislatures, should be necessary to confirm and render valid the acts of Congress. This would at once develop the weakness and inefficiency of the general government, to all the world. But, in fact, its imbecility is now nearly the same as if such acts were formally requisite. An act of Virginia, controverting a resolution of Congress, would certainly prevail. I therefore conclude, that the Confederation is too defective to be rendered tolerable even by correction. Let us take our farewell of it, with reverential respect, as an old benefactor. It is gone, whether this House says so, or not. It has perished, Sir, by its own weakness.

Ex. LXXXIX.—*DEFINITION OF GOVERNMENT.*

WM. GILMORE SIMMS.

Government
We hold to be the creature of our need,
Having no power but where necessity
Still, under guidance of the charter, gives it.
Our taxes raised to meet our exigence,
And not for waste or favorites. Our people
Left free to share the commerce of the world,
Without one needless barrier on their prows.
Our industry at liberty for venture,
Neither abridged nor pampered; and no calling
Preferred before another, to the ruin
Or wrong of either. These, Sir, are my doctrines;
They are the only doctrines which shall keep us
From anarchy, and that worst peril yet,
That threatens to dissever, in the tempest,
That married harmony of hope with power
That keeps our starry Union o'er the storm,
And, in the sacred bond that links our fortunes,
Makes us defy its thunders! Thus in one,
The foreign despot threatens us in vain.
His ministers of state may fret to see us,

Grasping the empires which they vainly covet,
And stretching forth our trident o'er the seas
In rivalry with Britain. They may confine,
But cannot chain us. Balances of power,
Framed by corrupt and cunning monarchists,
Weigh none of our possessions; and the seasons
That mark our mighty progress East and West,
Show Europe's struggling millions fondly seeking
The better shores and shelters that are ours.

Ex. XC.—*INAUGURAL ADDRESS TO BOTH HOUSES OF CONGRESS, APRIL* 30, 1789.*

WASHINGTON.

AMONG the vicissitudes incident to life, no event could have filled me with greater anxieties than that of which the notification was transmitted by your order, and received on the 14th day of the present month.

On the one hand, I was summoned by my country, whose voice I can never hear but with veneration and love, from a retreat which I had chosen with the fondest predilection, and, in my flattering hopes, with an immutable decision, as the asylum of my declining years; a retreat which was rendered every day more necessary as well as more dear to me, by the addition of habit to inclination, and of frequent interruptions in my health to the gradual waste committed on it by time. On the other hand, the magnitude and difficulty of the trust to which the voice of my country called me, being sufficient to awaken in the wisest and most experienced of her citizens a distrustful scrutiny into his qualifications, could not but overwhelm with despondence one who, inheriting inferior endowments from Nature, and unpractised in the duties of civil ad-

---

* The regret expressed by Washington on this occasion at being recalled from his chosen retirement, was no idle form of words, but an utterance of sentiments which the whole tenor of his life, when relieved from the pressure of official business, showed to have been sincere. He preferred the fields and groves of Mount Vernon to any presidential mansion, with its attendant cares and labors; but he did not feel at liberty to disregard the call of his people, and no sacrifice was too great for him to endure for their good. He was the only President whose election has been unanimous.

ministration, ought to be peculiarly conscious of his own deficiencies.

In this conflict of emotions, all I dare aver is, that it has been my faithful study to collect my duty from a just appreciation of every circumstance by which it might be affected. All I dare hope is, that if, in executing this task, I have been too much swayed by a grateful remembrance of former instances, or by an affectionate sensibility to this transcendent proof of the confidence of my fellow-citizens, and have thence too little consulted my incapacity as well as disinclination for the weighty and untried cares before me,—my error will be palliated by the motives which misled me, and its consequences be judged by my country with some share of the partiality in which they originated.

Such being the impressions under which I have, in obedience to the public summons, repaired to the present station, it would be peculiarly improper to omit, in this first official act, my fervent supplications to that Almighty Being who rules over the universe, who presides in the councils of nations, whose providential aids can supply every human defect, that his benediction may consecrate to the liberties and happiness of the people of the United States a government instituted by themselves for these essential purposes, and may enable every instrument employed in its administration to execute with success the functions allotted to his charge. In tendering this homage to the great Author of every public and private good, I assure myself that it expresses your sentiments not less than my own; nor those of my fellow-citizens at large less than either. No people can be bound to acknowledge and adore the invisible hand which conducts the affairs of men, more than the people of the United States. Every step by which they have advanced to the character of an independent nation, seems to have been distinguished by some token of providential agency. And, in the important revolution just accomplished in the system of their united government, the tranquil deliberations and voluntary consent of so many distinct communities, from which the event has resulted, can not be compared with the means by which most governments have been established, without some return of pious gratitude along with an humble anticipation of the future blessings which the past seem to presage.

These reflections, arising out of the present crisis, have forced themselves too strongly on my mind to be suppressed. You will join with me, I trust, in thinking that there are none under the influence of which the proceedings of a new and free government can more auspiciously commence.

Having thus imparted to you my sentiments, as they have been awakened by the occasion which brings us together, I shall take my present leave, but not without resorting once more to the benign Parent of the human race, in humble supplication, that as He has been pleased to favor the American people with opportunities for deliberating in perfect tranquillity, and dispositions for deciding with unparalleled unanimity on a form of government for the security of their Union and the advancement of their happiness, so His divine blessing may be equally conspicuous in the enlarged views, the temperate consultations, and the wise measures, on which the success of this Government must depend.

Ex. XCI.—*WASHINGTON AS PRESIDENT.*

Speech in Parliament, 1794.

CHARLES JAMES FOX.

How infinitely superior must appear the spirit and principles of General Washington, in his late address to Congress, compared with the policy of modern European courts! Illustrious man! deriving honor less from the splendor of his situation than from the dignity of his mind! Grateful to France for the assistance received from her in that great contest which secured the independence of America, he yet did not choose to give up the system of neutrality in her favor. Having once laid down the line of conduct most proper to be pursued, not all the insults and provocations of the French minister could at all put him out of his way or change him from his purpose. It must, indeed create astonishment that, placed in circumstances so critical, and filling a station so conspicuous, the character of Washington should not once have been called in question; that he should, in no one instance, have been accused either of improper insolence or of mean submission, in his transactions with foreign nations. It has been reserved for him to run the race of glory without experiencing the smallest interruption to the brilliancy of his career. The breath of censure has not dared to impeach the purity of his conduct, nor the eye of envy to raise its malignant glance to the elevation of his virtues. Such has been the transcendent merit and the unparalleled fate of this illustrious man!

How did he act when insulted by Genet?* Did he consider it necessary to avenge himself for the misconduct or madness of an individual by involving a whole continent in the horrors of war? No; he contented himself with procuring satisfaction for the insult by causing Genet to be recalled; and thus at once consulting his own dignity and the interests of his country. Happy Americans! while the whirlwind flies over one quarter of the globe and spreads everywhere desolation, you remain protected from its baneful effects by your own virtues and the wisdom of your Government. Separated from Europe by an immense ocean, you feel not the effect of those prejudices and passions which convert the boasted seats of civilization into scenes of horror and bloodshed. You profit by the folly and madness of the contending nations, and afford, in your more congenial clime, an asylum to those blessings and virtues which they wantonly contemn, or wickedly exclude from their bosom! Cultivating the arts of peace under the influence of freedom, you advance, by rapid strides, to opulence and distinction; and if, by any accident, you should be compelled to take part in the present unhappy contest,—if you should find it necessary to avenge insult or repel injury,—the world will bear witness to the equity of your sentiments and the moderation of your views; and the success of your arms will, no doubt, be proportioned to the justice of your cause.

---

* Genet was minister from the French Revolutionary Government, and misused the privileges of his diplomatic station to enlist soldiers and fit out privateers in this country to serve against England, in direct contravention of our treaty with that nation, which bound us to the strictest neutrality. He set the United States Government openly at defiance, continuing his practices in spite of repeated remonstrances, and caused a letter to be published from himself to the President, reflecting severely on the conduct of the latter. In this course of conduct he was upheld by a large party of French sympathizers, who wished for a war with England, but the Administration finally triumphed, and he was recalled in 1794.

Ex. XCII.—*THE TOAST.*

FRANCIS HOPKINSON.

'Tis Washington's health,—fill a bumper around,
 For he is our glory and pride;
Our arms shall in battle with conquest be crowned,
 With virtue and him on our side.

'Tis Washington's health—and cannons should roar,
 And trumpets the truth should proclaim;
There can not be found, search all the world o'er,
 His equal in virtue and fame.

'Tis Washington's health—our hero to bless,
 May heaven look graciously down;
Oh long may he live, our glad hearts to possess,
 And freedom still call him her own.

Ex. XCIII.—*ON THE DANGER OF VIOLATING OUR TREATIES.*

Speech in Congress, April, 1796.

FISHER AMES.*

On this theme my emotions are unutterable. If I could find words for them, if my powers bore any proportion to my zeal, I would swell my voice to such a note of remonstrance, it should reach every log-house beyond the mountains. I would say to the inhabitants, wake from your false security; your cruel dangers, your more cruel apprehensions are soon to be renewed; the wounds, yet unhealed, are to be

---

* The treaty with Great Britain concluded by John Jay in 1794, was very unpopular with a part of the people, who considered its terms too favorable to England; and a strong party arose in Congress, in favor of refusing to fulfil its provisions. A long and excited debate ensued. Among the last speakers was Mr. Ames, Member of Congress from Massachusetts, and one of the most eloquent and influential of American statesmen, who urged strongly the duty and expediency of ratification. His speech, though uttered under the pressure of distressing illness, produced a thrilling effect, and silenced, if it did not convince, those who wished to break the national faith. The treaty was ratified, and the threatened war with England put off until the country was better able to sustain it.

torn open again; in the daytime, your path through the woods will be ambushed; the darkness of midnight will glitter with the blaze of your dwellings. You are a father—the blood of your sons shall fatten your corn-field; you are a mother—the war-whoop shall waken the sleep of the cradle.*

On this subject, you need not suspect any deception on your feelings; it is a spectacle of horror which can not be overdrawn. If you have nature in your hearts, they will speak a language compared with which all I have said or can say will be poor and frigid.

Will it be whispered that the treaty has made me a new champion for the protection of the frontiers? It is known that my voice, as well as vote, have been uniformly given in conformity with the ideas I have expressed. Protection is the right of the frontiers; it is our duty to give it.

Who will accuse me of wandering out of the subject? Who will say that I exaggerate the tendencies of our measures? Will any one answer by a sneer, that this is all idle preaching? Will any one deny that we are bound, and I hope, to good purpose, by the most solemn sanctions of duty for the vote we give? Are despots alone to be reproached for unfeeling indifference to the tears and blood of their subjects? Are republicans irresponsible? Have the principles upon which you ground the reproach of cabinets and kings, no practical influence, no binding force? Are they merely themes of idle declamation, introduced to decorate the morality of a newspaper essay, or to furnish pretty topics of harangue from the windows of that state house? I trust it is neither too presumptuous nor too late to ask, Can you put the dearest interest of society at risk, without guilt and without remorse?

It is vain to offer as an excuse, that public men are not to be reproached for the evils that may happen to ensue from their measures. That is very true, where they are unforeseen or inevitable. Those I have depicted are not unforeseen; they are so far from inevitable, we are going to bring them into being by our vote; we choose the consequences, and become as justly answerable for them, as for the measures that we know will produce them.

By rejecting the posts, we light the savage fires—we bind

---

* The frontier posts, in case of a war with the British, would have been exposed to the ravages of the Indians, who were with difficulty restrained from hostilities even when both nations were at peace.

the victims. This day we undertake to render account to the widows and orphans whom our decision will make; to the wretches that will be roasted at the stake; to our country; and I do not deem it too serious to say, to conscience and to God. We are answerable; and if duty be anything more than a word of imposture, if conscience be not a bugbear, we are preparing to make ourselves as wretched as our country.

There is no mistake in this case, there can be none; experience has already been the prophet of events, and the cries of our future victims have already reached us. The western inhabitants are not a silent and uncomplaining sacrifice. The voice of humanity issues from the shade of the wilderness; it exclaims, that while one hand is held up to reject this treaty, the other grasps the tomahawk. It summons our imagination to the scenes that will open. It is no great effort of the imagination to conceive that events so near are already begun. I can fancy that I listen to the yells of savage vengeance and the shrieks of torture; already they seem to sigh in the western wind; already they mingle with every echo from the mountains.

Ex. XCIV.—*SHALL WE BREAK OUR FAITH?*

Speech in Congress, April, 1796.

FISHER AMES.

It would be strange that a subject which has roused in turn all the passions of the country, should be discussed without the interference of any of our own. We are men, and therefore not exempt from those passions; as citizens and representatives, we feel the interest that must excite them. The hazard of great interest can not fail to agitate strong passions; we are not disinterested; it is impossible we should be dispassionate. The warmth of such feelings may becloud the judgment, and, for a time, pervert the understanding. But the public sensibility and our own has sharpened the spirit of inquiry, and given animation to the debate. The public attention has been quickened to mark the progress of the discussion, and its judgment, often hasty and erroneous on first impressions, has become solid and enlightened at last.

Our result will, I hope, on that account be the safer and more mature, as well as more accordant with that of the nation. The only constant agents in political affairs are the passions of men. Shall we complain of our nature? Shall we say that man ought to have been made otherwise? It is right already, because He, from whom we derive our nature, ordained it so; and because, thus made and thus acting, the cause of truth and the public good is the more surely promoted.

The question is: SHALL WE BREAK THE TREATY?

The treaty is bad, fatally bad, is the cry. It sacrifices the interest, the honor, the independence of the United States, and the faith of our engagements to France. If we listen to the clamor of party intemperance, the evils are of a number not to be counted, and of a nature not to be borne, even in idea. The language of passion and exaggeration may silence that of reason in other places; it has not done it here. The question here is, whether the treaty be really so very fatal as to oblige the nation to break its faith. I admit that such a treaty ought not to have been made. I admit that self-preservation is the first law of society, as well as of individuals. It would, perhaps, be deemed an abuse of terms to call that a treaty which violates such a principle. I content myself with pursuing the inquiry whether the nature of the compact be such as to justify our refusal to carry it into effect. A treaty is the promise of a nation. Now, promises do not always bind him who makes them.

The undecided point is, shall we break our faith? And while our country, and enlightened Europe, await the issue with more than curiosity, we are employed to gather, piece-meal, and article by article, from the instrument, a justification for the deed by trivial calculations of commercial profit and loss. No government, not even a despotism, will break its faith without some pretext; and it must be plausible—it must be such as will carry the public opinion along with it. Reasons of policy, if not of morality, dissuade even Turkey and Algiers from breaches of treaty in mere wantonness of perfidy, in open contempt of the reproaches of their subjects. Surely a popular government will not proceed more arbitrarily as it is more free, nor with less shame and scruple in proportion as it has better morals. It will not proceed against the faith of treaties at all unless the strong and decided sense of the nation shall pronounce, not simply that the treaty is not advantageous, but that it ought to be broken and annulled.

And who, I would inquire, is hardy enough to pretend that the public voice demands the violation of the treaty? The evidence of the sense of the great mass of the nation is often equivocal; but when was it ever manifested with more energy and precision than at the present moment? The voice of the people is raised against the measure of refusing the appropriations. If gentlemen should urge, nevertheless, that all the sound of alarm is a counterfeit expression of the sense of the public, I will proceed to other proofs. Is the treaty ruinous to our commerce? What has blinded the eyes of the merchants and traders? Surely they are not enemies to trade, nor ignorant of their own interests. Their sense is not so liable to be mistaken as that of a nation, and they are almost unanimous. The articles stipulating the redress of our injuries by captures on the sea, are said to be delusive. By whom is this said? The very men whose fortunes are staked upon the competency of that redress say no such thing. They wait with anxious fear, lest you should annul that compact on which all their hopes are rested.

Thus we offer proof, little short of absolute demonstration, that the voice of our country is raised, not to sanction, but to depreciate, the non-performance of our engagements. It is not the nation; it is one, and but one, branch of the government that proposes to reject them. With this aspect of things, to reject is an act of desperation.

Ex. XCV.—*HAIL! COLUMBIA.*

JOSEPH HOPKINSON.*

Hail! Columbia, happy land!
Hail! ye heroes, heav'n born band
  Who fought and bled in Freedom's cause;
And when the storm of war was done
Enjoyed the peace your valor won.
  Let Independence be our boast,
    Ever mindful what it cost;
  Ever grateful for the prize,
Let its altar reach the skies.
    Firm united let us be;
    Rallying round our liberty,

* Son of Francis Hopkinson, the Revolutionary Poet.

As a band of brothers joined,
Peace and safety we shall find.

Immortal Patriots ! rise once more !
Defend your rights, defend your shore,
  Let no rude foe with impious hand
Invade the shrine where sacred lies
Of toil and blood the well-earned prize.
  While offering peace sincere and just,
  In heaven we place a manly trust
That truth and justice will prevail,
And every scheme of bondage fail.

Sound, sound the trump of Fame !
Let Washington's great name
  Ring through the world with loud applause ;
Let every clime to Freedom dear
Listen with a joyful ear.
  With equal skill, with god-like power,
  He governs in the fearful hour
Of horrid war, or guides with ease
The happier times of honest peace.

Behold the Chief, who now commands,
Once more to serve his country stands—
  The rock on which the storm will beat.
But armed in virtue, firm and true,
His hopes are fixed on Heaven and you.
  When hope was sinking in dismay,
  When glooms obscured Columbia's day,
His steady mind, from changes free,
Resolved on death or liberty !

Ex. XCVI.—*FAREWELL ADDRESS.**

To the people of the United States, Sept. 17, 1796.

WASHINGTON.

IN looking forward to the moment which is to terminate the career of my political life, my feelings do not permit me

* This masterpiece of political wisdom is throughout so excellent, so replete with sound statesmanship, sterling good sense, lofty patriotism and fatherly affection, that it has been difficult to decide what portions should be left out. We recommend it as a whole, to the study of all young Americans.

to suspend the deep acknowledgment of that debt of gratitude which I owe to my beloved country, for the many honors it has conferred upon me; still more for the steadfast confidence with which it has supported me; and for the opportunities I have thence enjoyed of manifesting my inviolable attachment by services faithful and persevering, though in usefulness unequal to my zeal. If benefits have resulted to our country from these services, let it always be remembered to your praise, and as an instructive example in your annals, that under circumstances in which the passions, agitated in every direction, were liable to mislead amidst appearances sometimes dubious, vicissitudes of fortune often discouraging—in situations in which not unfrequently want of success has countenanced the spirit of criticism—the constancy of your support was the essential prop of the efforts, and a guarantee of the plans by which they were effected.

Profoundly penetrated with this idea, I shall carry it with me to my grave, as a strong incitement to unceasing vows that heaven may continue to you the choicest tokens of its beneficence—that your union and brotherly affection may be perpetual—that the free constitution, which is the work of your hands, may be sacredly maintained—that its administration in every department may be stamped with wisdom and virtue—that, in fine, the happiness of the people of these States, under the auspices of liberty, may be made complete by so careful a preservation, and so prudent a use of this blessing, as will acquire to them the glory of recommending it to the applause, the affection, and adoption of every nation which is yet a stranger to it.

Here, perhaps, I ought to stop. But a solicitude for your welfare, which can not end but with my life, and the apprehension of danger natural to that solicitude, urge me, on an occasion like the present, to offer to your solemn contemplation, and to recommend to your frequent review, some sentiments which are the result of much reflection, of no inconsiderable observation, and which appear to me all important to the permanency of your felicity as a people. These will be offered to you with the more freedom, as you can only see in them the disinterested warnings of a parting friend, who can possibly have no personal motive to bias his counsel. Nor can I forget, as an encouragement to it, your indulgent reception of my sentiments on a former and not dissimilar occasion.

Interwoven as is the love of liberty with every ligament

of your hearts, no recommendation of mine is necessary to fortify or confirm the attachment. The unity of government which constitutes you one people, is also now dear to you. It is justly so; for it is a main pillar in the edifice of your real independence; the support of your tranquillity at home; your peace abroad; of your safety; of your prosperity; of that very liberty which you so highly prize.

But, as it is easy to foresee, that from different causes and from different quarters, much pains will be taken, many artifices employed, to weaken in your minds the conviction of this truth; as this is the point in your political fortress against which the batteries of internal and external enemies will be most constantly and actively (though often covertly and insidiously) directed; it is of infinite moment, that you should properly estimate the immense value of your national union to your collective and individual happiness; that you should cherish a cordial, habitual, and immovable attachment to it; accustoming yourselves to think and speak of it as of the palladium of your political safety and prosperity; watching for its preservation with jealous anxiety; discountenancing whatever may suggest even a suspicion that it can, in any event, be abandoned; and indignantly frowning upon the first dawning of every attempt to alienate any portion of our country from the rest, or to enfeeble the sacred ties that now link together the various parts.

For this you have every inducement of sympathy and interest. Citizens by birth or choice, of a common country, that country has a right to concentrate your affections. The name of American, which belongs to you in your national capacity, must always exalt the just pride of patriotism, more than any appellation derived from local discriminations. With slight shades of difference, you have the same religion, manners, habits, and political principles. You have, in a common cause, fought and triumphed together; the independence and liberty you possess, are the work of joint counsels and joint efforts, of common dangers, sufferings, and successes.

Ex. XCVII.—*FAREWELL ADDRESS—CONTINUED.*

But these considerations, however powerfully they address themselves to your sensibility, are greatly outweighed by those which apply more immediately to your interest. Here, every portion of our country finds the most commanding motives for carefully guarding and preserving the union of the whole.

The *North*, in an unrestrained intercourse with the *South*, protected by the equal laws of a common government, finds in the productions of the latter great additional resources of maritime and commercial enterprise, and precious materials of manufacturing industry. The *South*, in the same intercourse, benefiting by the same agency of the *North*, sees its agriculture grow, and its commerce expand. Turning partly into its own channels the seamen of the *North*, it finds its particular navigation invigorated; and while it contributes, in different ways, to nourish and increase the general mass of the national navigation, it looks forward to the protection of a maritime strength, to which itself is unequally adapted. The *East*, in a like intercourse with the *West*, already finds, and in the progressive improvement of interior communications by land and water, will more and more find, a valuable vent for the commodities which it brings from abroad, or manufactures at home. The *West* derives from the *East* supplies requisite to its growth and comfort—and what is perhaps of still greater consequence, it must of necessity owe the *secure* enjoyment of indispensable *outlets* for its own productions, to the weight, influence, and the future maritime strength of the Atlantic side of the union, directed by an indissoluble community of interest as *one nation*. Any other tenure by which the *West* can hold this essential advantage, whether derived from its own separate strength or from an apostate and unnatural connexion with any foreign power, must be intrinsically precarious.

While then every part of our country thus feels an immediate and particular interest in union, all the parts combined can not fail to find in the united mass of means and efforts, greater strength, greater resource, proportionably greater security from external danger, a less frequent interruption of their peace by foreign nations, and, what is of inestimable value, they must derive from union an exemption from those broils and wars between themselves, which so frequently afflict neighboring countries not tied together by the same government, which their own rivalships alone would be sufficient to produce, but which opposite foreign alliances, attachments and intrigues, would stimulate and imbitter. Hence, likewise, they will avoid the necessity of those overgrown military establishments which, under any form of government, are inauspicious to liberty, and which are to be regarded as particularly hostile to republican liberty. In this sense it is, that your union ought to be considered as a main prop of your liberty, and that the love of one ought to endear to you the preservation of the other.

Ex. XCVIII.—*FAREWELL ADDRESS—CONTINUED.*

IN contemplating the causes which may disturb our union, it occurs as matter of serious concern, that any ground should have been furnished for characterizing parties by *geographical* discriminations; *northern* and *southern*—*Atlantic* and *western;* whence designing men may endeavor to excite a belief that there is a real difference of local interests and views. One of the expedients of party to acquire influence within particular districts, is to misrepresent the opinions and aims of other districts. You can not shield yourselves too much against the jealousies and heart-burnings which spring from these misrepresentations: they tend to render alien to each other those who ought to be bound together by fraternal affection. The inhabitants of our western country have lately had a useful lesson on this head; they have seen, in the negotiation by the executive, and in the unanimous ratification by the Senate of the treaty with Spain, and in the universal satisfaction at the event throughout the United States, a decisive proof how unfounded were the suspicions propagated among them of a policy in the general government and in the Atlantic States, unfriendly to their interests in regard to the Mississippi. They have been witnesses to the formation of two treaties, that with Great Britain and that with Spain, which secure to them everything they could desire, in respect to our foreign relations, towards confirming their prosperity. Will it not be their wisdom to rely for the preservation of these advantages on the union by which they were procured? will they not henceforth be deaf to these advisers, if such there are, who would sever them from their brethren, and connect them with aliens?

To the efficacy and permanency of your union, a government for the whole is indispensable. No alliances, however strict, between the parts can be an adequate substitute; they must inevitably experience the infractions and interruptions which all alliances, in all times, have experienced. Sensible of this momentous truth, you have improved upon your first essay, by the adoption of a constitution of government better calculated than your former for an intimate union, and for the efficacious management of your common concerns. This government, the offspring of our own choice, uninfluenced and unawed, adopted upon full investigation and mature deliberation, completely free in its principles, in the distribution of its powers uniting security with energy, and containing within itself a provision for its own amendment, has a just claim to your confidence and your support. Respect for its authority, compliance with its laws, acquiescence in its measures, are duties enjoined by the fundamental maxims of true liberty. The basis of our political system is the right of the people to make and to alter their constitutions of government. But the constitution which at any time exists, until changed by an explicit and authentic act of the whole people, is sacredly obligatory upon all. The very idea of the power and the right of the people to establish government, presupposes the duty of every individual to obey the established government.

All obstructions to the execution of the laws, all combinations and associations under whatever plausible character, with the real design to direct, control, counteract, or awe the regular deliberations and action of the constituted authorities, are destructive of this fundamental principle, and of fatal tendency. They serve to organize faction, to give it an artificial and extraordinary force, to put in the place of the delegated will of the nation the will of party, often a small but enterprising minority of the community; and, according to the alternate triumphs of different parties, to make the public administration the mirror of the ill-concerted and incongruous projects of faction, rather than the organ of consistent and wholesome plans digested by common councils, and modified by mutual interests.

Ex. XCIX.—*FAREWELL ADDRESS—CONTINUED.*

HARMONY, and a liberal intercourse with all nations, are recommended by policy, humanity, and interest. But even our commercial policy should hold an equal and impartial hand; neither seeking nor granting exclusive favors or preferences; consulting the natural course of things; diffusing and diversifying by gentle means the streams of commerce, but forcing nothing; establishing with powers so disposed,— in order to give trade a stable course, to define the rights of our merchants, and to enable the government to support them,—conventional rules of intercourse, the best that present circumstances and mutual opinion will permit, but temporary, and liable to be from time to time abandoned or varied as experience and circumstances shall dictate; constantly keeping in view, that it is folly in one nation to look for disinterested favors from another; that it must pay with a portion of its independence for whatever it may accept under that character; that by such acceptance, it may place itself in the condition of having given equivalents for nominal favors, and of being reproached with ingratitude for not giving more. There can be no greater error than to expect, or calculate upon real favors from nation to nation. It is an illusion which experience must cure, which a just pride ought to discard.

In offering to you, my countrymen, these counsels of an old and affectionate friend, I dare not hope they will make the strong and lasting impression I could wish; that they will control the usual current of the passions, or prevent our nation from running the course which has hitherto marked the destiny of nations; but if I may even flatter myself that they may be productive of some partial benefit, some occasional good,—that they may now and then recur to moderate the fury of party spirit, to warn against the mischiefs of foreign intrigue, to guard against the impostures of pretended patriotism,—this hope will be a full recompense for the solicitude for your welfare by which they have been dictated.

How far, in the discharge of my official duties, I have been guided by the principles which have been delineated, the public records and other evidences of my conduct must witness to you and to the world. To myself, the assurance of my own conscience is, that I have, at least, believed myself to be guided by them.

Though in reviewing the incidents of my administration, I am unconscious of intentional error, I am nevertheless too sensible of my defects not to think it probable that I may have committed many errors. Whatever they may be, I fervently beseech the Almighty to avert or mitigate the evils to which they may tend. I shall also carry with me the hope that my country will never cease to view them with indulgence; and that, after forty-five years of my life dedicated to its service, with an upright zeal, the faults of incompetent abilities will be consigned to oblivion, as myself must soon be to the mansions of rest.

Relying on its kindness in this as in other things, and actuated by that fervent love towards it which is so natural to a man who views in it the native soil of himself and his progenitors for several generations, I anticipate with pleasing expectation that retreat in which I promise myself to realize, without alloy, the sweet enjoyment of partaking, in the midst of my fellow-citizens, the benign influence of good laws under a free government—the ever favorite object of my heart, and the happy reward, as I trust, of our mutual cares, labors and dangers.

Ex. C.—*ADAMS AND LIBERTY.**

Ye sons of Columbia who bravely have fought
   For those rights, which unstained from your sires had descended,
May you long taste the blessings your valor has bought,
   And your sons reap the soil which your fathers defended.
       'Mid the reign of mild peace,
       May your nation increase,
With the glory of Rome and the wisdom of Greece;
And ne'er shall the sons of Columbia be slaves,
While the earth bears a plant, or the sea rolls its waves.

The fame of our arms, of our laws the mild sway,
   Had justly ennobled our nation in story,

---

* John Adams, second President of the United States, was inaugurated March 4, 1797, and this congratulatory ode is supposed to have been written at about that time.

Till the dark clouds of faction obscured our young day,
  And enveloped the sun of American glory.
      But let traitors be told,
      Who their country have sold,
And bartered their God for his image in gold,
      That ne'er will the sons, &c.,

Our mountains are crowned with imperial oak,
  Whose roots, like our liberties, ages have nourished;
But long e'er our nation submits to the yoke,
  Not a tree shall be left on the field where it flourished.
      Should invasion impend,
      Every grove would descend
From the hill-tops they shaded, our shores to defend.
      For ne'er shall the sons, &c.

Should the tempest of war overshadow our land,
  Its bolts could ne'er rend Freedom's temple asunder;
For, unmoved at its portal would Washington stand,
  And repulse, with his breast, the assaults of the thunder!
      His sword from the sleep
      Of its scabbard would leap,
And conduct, with its point, every flash to the deep!
      For ne'er shall the sons, &c.

Let fame to the world sound America's voice;
  No intrigues can her sons from their government sever;
Her pride is her Adams; her laws are his choice,
  And shall flourish, till Liberty slumbers forever.
      Then unite heart and hand,
      Like Leonidas' band,
And swear to the God of the ocean and land,
That ne'er shall the sons of Columbia be slaves,
While the earth bears a plant, or the sea rolls its waves.

Ex. CI.—*NECESSITY FOR PREPARATION FOR A WAR WITH FRANCE.**

Speech in Congress, May, 1787.

ROBERT GOODLOE HARPER.*

WHEN France shall at length be convinced that we are fully resolved to call forth all our resources, and exert all our strength to resist her encroachments and aggressions, she will soon desist from them. She need not be told what these resources are; she well knows their greatness and extent; she well knows that this country, if driven into a war, could soon become invulnerable to her attacks, and could throw a most formidable and prepondering weight into the scale of her adversary. She will not, therefore, drive us to this extremity, but will desist as soon as she finds us determined. Even if our means of injuring France, and of repelling her attacks, were less than they are, still they might be rendered all-sufficient by resolution and courage. It is in these that the strength of nations consists; not in fleets, nor armies, nor population, nor money, but in the "unconquerable will—the courage never to submit or yield."

These are the true sources of national greatness, and to use the words of a celebrated writer, " where these means are not wanting, all others will be found or created." It was by these means that Holland, in the days of her glory, triumphed over the mighty power of Spain. It is by these that in latter times, the Swiss, a people not half so numerous as we, and possessing few of our advantages, have honorably maintained their neutrality amid the shock of surrounding states, and against the haughty aggressions of France herself. It was this that made Rome the mistress of the world, and Athens the protectress of Greece. When was it that Rome attracted most strongly the admiration of mankind, and impressed the deepest sentiment of fear in the hearts of her enemies? It was when seventy thousand of her sons lay bleeding at Cannæ, and Hannibal, victorious over the Roman armies and twenty nations, was thundering at her gates. It was then that the young and heroic Scipio, having sworn on his sword, in the presence of the fathers of the country, not to despair of the republic, marched forth at the head of a people firmly determined to conquer or die; and

* Member of Congress from South Carolina.

that resolution secured them the victory. When did Athens appear the greatest and most formidable? It was when, giving up their houses and possessions to the flames of the enemy, and having transferred their wives, their children, their aged parents and the symbols of their religion on board of their fleet, they resolved to consider themselves as the republic, and their ships as their country. It was then they struck that terrible blow, under which the greatness of Persia sunk and expired.

These means, Sir, and many others, are in our power: let us resolve to use them, and act so as to convince France that we have taken the resolution, and there will be nothing to fear. The conviction will be to us instead of fleets and armies, and even more effectual. Seeing us thus prepared, she will not attack us. Then will she listen to our peaceable proposals; then will she accept the concessions we mean to offer. But should this offer not be thus supported, should it be attended by any circumstances from which she can discover weakness, distrust or division, then will she reject it with derision and scorn. And let it be remembered that when we give this vote, we vote not only on the peace of our country, but on what is far more important—its rights and its honor.

———•———

Ex. CII.—*INJUSTICE OF THE ALIEN AND SEDITION LAWS.*

Election Speech, delivered March, 1799.

JOHN RANDOLPH.*

AND what is the subject of alarm? What are the laws we have dared to pronounce upon as unconstitutional and tyrannical? The first is a law authorizing the President of the United States to order any alien he may judge dangerous, any unfortunate refugee that may happen to fall under his royal suspicion, forthwith to quit the country. It is true that the law says he must have *reasonable* grounds to sus-

---

* The biographer of Mr. Randolph does not profess to give here a literal transcript of his speech, but reports it from tradition; these were, however, the sentiments expressed by him on this occasion. As a result of this address Mr. Randolph obtained his first election to Congress, in which body he held a place for nearly thirty years. He was noted for his brilliant rhetoric and great powers of sarcasm, and was one of the warmest supporters of the Southern doctrine of "State Rights."

pect. Who is to judge of that reason but himself? Who can look into his breast and say what motives have dominion there? It is a mockery to give one man absolute power over the liberty of another, and then ask him, when the power is gone and can not be recalled, to exercise it reasonably! Power knows no other check but power.

Let the poor patriot who may have fallen under the frowns of Government because he dared assert the rights of his countrymen, seek refuge on our shores of boasted liberty; the moment he touches the soil of freedom, hoping here to find a period to all his persecutions, he is greeted, not with the smile of welcome, or the cheerful voice of freemen, but the stern demands of an officer of the law—the executor of a tyrant's will—who summons him to depart. What crime has he perpetrated? Vain inquiry! He is a *suspected* person. He is judged dangerous to the peace of the country; rebellious at home, he may be alike factious and seditious here. What remedy? What hope? He who condemns is judge; there is no appeal from his arbitrary will.

And what is that other law which so fully meets the approbation of my venerable friend? It is a law that makes it an act of sedition, punishable by fine and imprisonment, to utter or write a sentiment that any prejudiced judge or juror may think proper to construe into disrespect of the President of the United States. Is the man dreaming! do you exclaim? Is this a fancy picture he has drawn for our amusement? I am no fancy man, people of Virginia! I speak the truth. I deal only in stern realities! There is such a law on your Statute Book, in spite of your Constitution—in open contempt of those solemn guarantees that insure freedom of speech and of the press to every American citizen.

And yet the gentleman tells you we must wait until some infringement is made on our rights! Your Constitution broken, your citizens dragged to prison for daring to exercise the freedom of speech, armies levied, and yourselves threatened with immediate invasion for your audacious interference with the business of the Federal government—and you are told to wait for some infringement of your rights! How long are we to wait? Till the chains are fastened on us, and we can no longer help ourselves? But, the gentleman says, your course may lead to civil war, and where are your resources? I answer him in his own words, handed down by the tradition of the past generation, and engraven on the hearts of his grateful countrymen, " Shall we gather strength by irresolution and inaction? Shall we acquire the means of effectual resistance by lying supinely on our backs and hugging the delusive phantom of hope until our enemies have bound us hand and foot? Sir, we are not weak if we make a proper use of those means the God of nature hath placed in our power. The battle, Sir, is not to the strong alone; it is to the vigilant, the active, the brave."*

Ex. CIII.—*EULOGY ON WASHINGTON.*

Delivered February 8, 1800.

FISHER AMES.

It is natural that the gratitude of mankind should be drawn to their benefactors. A number of these have successively arisen, who were no less distinguished for the elevation of their virtues than the lustre of their talents. Of these, however, who were born, and who acted through life as if they were born, not for themselves, but for their country and the whole human race, how few, alas, are recorded in the long annals of ages, and how wide the intervals of time and space that divide them! In all this dreary length of way, they appear like five or six light-houses on as many thousand miles of coast; they gleam upon the surrounding darkness with an inextinguishable splendor, like stars seen through a mist; but they are seen like stars, to cheer, to guide and to save. Washington is now added to that small number. Already he attracts curiosity, like a newly discovered star, whose benignant light will travel on to the world's and time's farthest bounds. Already his name is hung up by history as conspicuously as if it sparkled in one of the constellations of the sky.

By commemorating his death, we are called this day to yield the homage that is due to virtue; to confess the common debt of mankind, as well as our own; and to pronounce for posterity, now dumb, that eulogium which they will delight to echo ten ages hence, when we are dumb.

I consider myself not merely in the midst of the citizens of this town, nor even of the State. In idea I gather around me the nation. In the vast and venerable congregation of the

---

* Patrick Henry.

patriots of all countries, and of all enlightened men, I would, if I could, raise my voice, and speak to mankind in a strain worthy of my audience, and as elevated as my subject. But you have assigned me a task that is impossible.

Oh, if I could perform it, if I could illustrate his principles in my discourse as he displayed them in his life; if I could paint his virtues as he practised them; if I could convert the fervid enthusiasm of my heart into the talent to transmit his fame as it ought to pass to posterity,—I should be the successful organ of your will, the minister of his virtues, and, may I dare to say, the humble partaker of his immortal glory. These are ambitious, deceiving hopes, and I reject them; for it is, perhaps, almost as difficult at once with judgment and feeling to praise great actions, as to perform them. A lavish and undistinguishing eulogium is not praise; and to discriminate such excellent qualities as were characteristic and peculiar to him, would be to raise a name, as he raised it, above envy, above parallel, perhaps, for that very reason, above emulation.

How great he appeared while he administered the government, how much greater when he retired from it; how he accepted the chief military command under his wise and upright successor; how his life was unspotted like his fame, and how his death was worthy of his life, are so many distinct subjects of instruction, and each of them singly more than enough for a eulogium. I leave the task, however, to history and to posterity; they will be faithful to it.

There has scarcely appeared a really great man whose character has been more admired in his life-time, or less correctly understood by his admirers. When it is comprehended, it is no easy task to delineate its excellences in such a manner as to give the portrait both interest and resemblance; for it requires thought and study to understand the true ground of his superiority over many others, whom he resembled in the principles of action, and even in the manner of acting. But perhaps he excels all the great men that ever lived in the steadiness of his adherence to his maxims of life, and in the uniformity of his conduct to the same maxims. These maxims, though wise, were yet not so remarkable for their wisdom as for their authority over his life; for if there were any errors in his judgment (and he discovered as few as any man), we know of no blemishes in his virtue.

He was the patriot without reproach; he loved his country well enough to hold his success in serving it an ample recompense. Thus far self-love and love of country coincided; but when his country needed sacrifices few could, or perhaps would be willing to make, he did not even hesitate. This was virtue in its most exalted character. More than once he put his fame at hazard, when he had reason to think it would be sacrificed, at least in this age. Two instances can not be denied; when the army was disbanded, and again when he stood, like Leonidas at the pass of Thermopylæ, to defend our independence against France.

Epaminondas is perhaps the brightest name of all antiquity. Our Washington resembled him in the purity and ardor of his patriotism; and, like him, he first exalted the glory of his country. There it is to be hoped the comparison ends; for Thebes fell with Epaminondas. But such comparisons cannot be pursued far, without departing from the similitude. For we shall find it as difficult to compare great men as great rivers; some we admire for the length and rapidity of their current, and the grandeur of their cataracts; others for the majestic silence and fulness of their streams; we can not bring them together to measure the difference of their waters. The unambitious life of Washington, declining fame, yet courted by it, seemed, like the Ohio, to choose its long way through solitudes, diffusing fertility; or, like his own Potomac, widening and deepening his channel as he approached the sea, and displaying most the usefulness and serenity of his greatness towards the end of his course. Such a citizen would do honor to any country. The constant veneration and affection of his country will show that it was worthy of such a citizen.

Ex. CIV.—*WASHINGTON A MODEL FOR THE FORMATION OF CHARACTER.*

WILLIAM WIRT.

LET your ambition, gentlemen, be to enroll your names among those over whose histories our hearts swell and our eyes overflow with admiration, delight, and sympathy, from infancy to old age; and the story of whose virtues, exploits and sufferings, will continue to produce the same effect throughout the world, at whatever distance of time they may be read. It is needless, and it would be endless, to name them. On the darker firmament of history, ancient and modern, they form a galaxy resplendent with their lustre. To go no further back, look for your model to the signers of our declaration of independence. You see revived in these men the spirit of ancient Rome in Rome's best day; for they were willing, with Curtius, to leap into the flaming gulf, which the oracle of their own wisdom had assured them could be closed in no other way.

There was one, however, whose name is not among those signers, but who must not, nay, can not, be forgotten; for, when a great and decided patriot is the theme, his name is not far off. Gentlemen, you need not go to past ages, nor to distant countries. You need not turn your eyes to ancient Greece, or Rome, or to modern Europe. You have, in your own Washington, a recent model, whom you have only to imitate to become immortal.

Nor must you suppose that he owed his greatness to the peculiar crisis which called out his virtues, and despair of such another crisis for the display of your own. His more than Roman virtues, his consummate prudence, his powerful intellect, and his dauntless decision and dignity of character, would have made him illustrious in any age. The crisis would have done nothing for him, had not his character stood ready to match it. Acquire his character, and fear not the recurrence of a crisis to show forth its glory. Look at the elements of commotion that are already at work in this vast republic, and threatening us with a moral earthquake that will convulse it to its foundation.

Look at the political degeneracy which pervades the country, and which has already borne us so far away from the golden age of the Revolution; look at all "the signs of the times," and you will see but little cause to indulge the hope that no crisis is likely to recur to give full scope for the exercise of the most heroic virtues. Hence it is, that I so anxiously hold up to you the model of Washington. Form yourselves on that noble model. Strive to acquire his modesty, his disinterestedness, his singleness of heart, his determined devotion to his country, his candor in deliberation, his accuracy of judgment, his invincible firmness of resolve, and then may you hope to be in your own age what he was in his,—"first in war, first in peace, and first in the hearts of your countrymen."

Commencing your career with this high standard of character, your course will be as steady as the needle to the pole.

Your end will always be virtuous, your means always noble. You will adorn as well as bless your country. You will exalt and illustrate the age in which you live. Your example will shake, like a tempest, that pestilential pool in which the virtues of our people are already beginning to stagnate, and restore the waters and the atmosphere to their revolutionary purity.

Ex. CV.—*WASHINGTON.*

ELIZA COOK.

LAND of the west! though passing brief the record of thine age,
Thou hast a name that darkens all on history's wide page!
Let all the blasts of fame ring out—thine shall be loudest far;
Let others boast their satellites—thou hast the planet star.

Thou hast a name whose characters of light shall ne'er depart;
'Tis stamped upon the dullest brain, and warms the coldest heart;
A war-cry fit for any land where Freedom's to be won;
Land of the West! it stands alone—it is thy Washington!

Rome had its Cæsar, great and brave; but stain was on his wreath;
He lived the heartless conqueror, and died the tyrant's death;
France had its eagle; but his wings, though lofty they might soar,
Were spread in false ambition's flight, and dipped in murderer's gore.

Those hero-gods, whose mighty sway would fain have chained the waves—
Who fleshed their blades with tiger zeal, to make a world of slaves—
Who, though their kindred barred the path, still fiercely waded on—
Oh! where shall be *their* glory by the side of Washington?

He fought, but not with love of strife; he struck but to defend;
And ere he turned a people's foe, he sought to be a friend.
He strove to keep his country's right by reason's gentle word,
And sighed when fell injustice threw the challenge, sword to sword.

He stood the firm, the calm, the wise—the patriot and sage;
He showed no deep avenging hate, no burst of despot rage.
He stood for liberty and truth, and dauntlessly led on,
Till shouts of victory gave forth the name of Washington.

No car of triumph bore him through a city filled with grief;
No groaning captives at the wheels proclaimed the victor chief;
He broke the gyves of slavery with strong and high disdain,
And cast no sceptre from the links when he had crushed the chain.

He saved his land, but did not lay his soldier trappings down
To change them for the regal vest, and don a kingly crown.
Fame was too earnest in her joy—too proud of such a son,
To let a robe and title mask a noble Washington.

Ex. CVI.—*EULOGIUM ON WASHINGTON.*

CHARLES PHILLIPS.*

It matters very little what immediate spot may be the birth-place of such a man as WASHINGTON. No people can claim, no country can appropriate him; the boon of Providence to the human race, his fame is eternity, and his residence creation. Though it was the defeat of our arms and the disgrace of our policy, I almost bless the convulsion in which he had his origin. If the heavens thundered and the earth rocked, yet, when the storm passed, how pure was the climate that it cleared; how bright in the brow of the firmament was the planet which it revealed to us! In the production of Washington it does really appear as if nature was endeavoring to improve upon herself, and that all the virtues of the ancient world were but so many studies preparatory to the patriot of the new.

* A celebrated Irish barrister.

Individual instances no doubt there were—splendid exemplifications of some single qualification; Cæsar was merciful, Scipio was continent, Hannibal was patient; but it was reserved for Washington to blend them all in one, and like the lovely *chef d'œuvre* of the Grecian artist, to exhibit in one glow of associated beauty, the pride of every model, and the perfection of every master. As a general, he marshalled the peasant into a veteran, and supplied by discipline the absence of experience; as a statesman, he enlarged the policy of the cabinet into the most comprehensive system of general advantage; and such was the wisdom of his views, and the philosophy of his counsels, that to the soldier and the statesman he almost added the character of the sage! A conqueror, he was untainted with the crime of blood; a revolutionist, he was free from any stain of treason; for aggression commenced the contest, and his country called him to the command.

Liberty unsheathed his sword, necessity stained, victory returned it. If he had paused here, history might have doubted what station to assign him; whether at the head of her citizens or her soldiers—her heroes or her patriots. But the last glorious act crowns his career and banishes all hesitation. Who, like Washington, after having emancipated a hemisphere, resigned its crown, and preferred the retirement of domestic life to the adoration of a land he might be almost said to have created?

> "How shall we rank thee upon glory's page,
> Thou more than soldier and just less than sage;
> All thou hast been reflects less fame on thee,
> Far less, than all thou hast forborne to be!"

Such, Sir, is the testimony of one not to be accused of partiality in his estimate of America. Happy, proud America! The lightnings of Heaven yielded to your philosophy! The temptations of earth could not seduce your patriotism!

Ex. CVII.—*GENIUS OF WASHINGTON.*

EDWIN P. WHIPPLE.

THIS illustrious man, at once the world's admiration and enigma, we are taught by a fine instinct to venerate, and by a wrong opinion to misjudge. The might of his character has taken strong hold upon the feelings of great masses of men; but in translating this universal sentiment into an intelligent form, the intellectual element of his wonderful nature is as much depressed as the moral element is exalted, and consequently we are apt to misunderstand both. How many times have we been told that he was not a man of genius, but a person of " excellent common sense," of " admirable judgment," of " rare virtues! " and, by a constant repetition of this, we have nearly succeeded in divorcing comprehension from his sense, insight from his judgment, force from his virtues, and life from the man.

He had no genius, it seems. Oh, no! genius, we must suppose, is the peculiar and shining attribute of some orator, whose tongue can spout patriotic speeches, or some versifier, whose muse can " Hail Columbia," but not of the man who supported states on his arm, and carried America in his brain. What is genius? Is it worth anything? Is splendid folly the measure of its inspiration? Is wisdom its base and summit,—that which it recedes from, or tends towards? And by what definition do you award the name to the creator of an epic, and deny it to the creator of a country? On what principle is it to be lavished on him who sculptures in perishing marble the image of possible excellence, and withheld from him who built up in himself a transcendent character, indestructible as the obligations of duty, and beautiful as her rewards?

Indeed, if by the genius of action you mean will enlightened by intelligence, and intelligence energized by will,—if force and insight be its characteristics, and influence its test,—and, especially, if great effects suppose a cause proportionably great, that is, a vital, causative mind,—then is Washington most assuredly a man of genius, and one whom no other American has equalled in the power of working morally and mentally on other minds. His genius, it is true, was of a peculiar kind; the genius of character, of thought and the objects of thought solidified and concentrated into active faculty. He belongs to that rare class of men,—rare as Homers and Miltons,—rare as Platos and Newtons,—who have impressed their characters upon nations without pampering national vices. Such men have natures broad enough to include all the facts of a people's practical life, and deep enough to discern the spiritual laws which underlie, animate, and govern those facts.

Washington, in short, had that greatness of character which is the highest expression and last result of greatness of mind; for there is no method of building up character except through mind. Indeed, character like his is not *built* up, stone upon stone, precept upon precept, but *grows* up, through an actual contact of thought with things; the assimilative mind transmuting the impalpable but potent spirit of public sentiment, and the life of visible facts, and the power of spiritual laws, into individual life and power, so that their mighty energies put on personality, as it were, and act through one centralizing human will. This process may not, if you please, make the great philosopher or the great poet; but it does make the great *man*,—the man in whom thought and judgment seem identical with volition,—the man whose vital expression is not in words, but deeds,—the man whose sublime ideas issue necessarily in sublime acts, not in sublime art. It was because Washington's character was thus composed of the inmost substance and power of facts and principles, that men instinctively felt the perfect reality of his comprehensive manhood. This reality enforced universal respect, married strength to repose, and threw into his face that commanding majesty, which made men of the speculative audacity of Jefferson, and the lucid genius of Hamilton recognize, with unwonted meekness, his awful superiority.

Ex. CVIII.—*INAUGURAL ADDRESS.*

Delivered before the Senate, March 4, 1801.

THOMAS JEFFERSON.

LET us reflect, fellow-citizens, that having banished from our land that religious intolerance under which mankind so long bled and suffered, we have yet gained little, if we countenance a political intolerance as despotic, as wicked, and capable of as bitter and bloody persecutions. During the throes and convulsions of the ancient world—during the agonizing spasms of infuriated man, seeking, through blood and slaughter, his long lost liberty—it is not wonderful that the agitation of the billows should reach even this distant and peaceful shore; that this should be more felt and feared by some, and less by others, and should divide opinions as to measures of safety; but every difference of opinion is not a difference of principle. We are all Republicans; we are all Federalists.

If there be any among us who would wish to dissolve this Union, or to change its republican form, let them stand undisturbed as monuments of the safety with which error of opinion may be tolerated, where reason is left free to combat it. I know, indeed, that some honest men fear that a republican government cannot be strong; but would the honest patriot, in the full tide of successful experiment, abandon a government which has so far kept us free and firm, on the theoretic and visionary fear that this government, the world's best hope, may by possibility want energy to preserve itself? I trust not. I believe this, on the contrary, the strongest government on earth. I believe it the only one where every man, at the call of the law, would fly to the standard of the law, and would meet invasions of the public order as his own personal concern. Sometimes it is said that man can not be trusted with the government of himself. Can he then be trusted with the government of others? Or have we found angels, in the form of kings, to govern him? Let history answer this question.

Let us then with courage and confidence pursue our own federal and republican principles. These principles form the bright constellation which has gone before us, and guided our steps through an age of revolution and reformation. The wisdom of our sages and blood of our heroes have been devoted to their attainment; they should be the creed of our political faith, the text of civic instruction, the touch-stone by which to try the services of those we trust; and, should we wander from them in moments of error or of alarm, let us hasten to retrace our steps, and to regain the road which alone leads to peace, liberty, and safety.

Ex. CIX.—*AGAINST THE REPEAL OF THE JUDICIARY ACT.*

Speech in Congress, 1802.

GOUVERNEUR MORRIS.*

MR. PRESIDENT, our situation is peculiar. At present our national compact can prevent a State from acting hostilely

* Mr. Morris was at this time U. S. Senator from New York. His public

towards the general interest. But let this compact be destroyed, and each State becomes instantaneously invested with absolute sovereignty. But what, I ask, will be the situation of these States, if, by the dissolution of our national compact, they be left to themselves? What is the probable result? We shall either be the victims of foreign intrigue, and, split into factions, fall under the domination of a foreign power; or else, after the misery and torment of civil war, become the subjects of a usurping military despot. What but this compact—what but this specific part of it, can save us from ruin?

The judicial power, that fortress of the Constitution, is now to be overturned. With honest Ajax, I would not only throw a shield before it—I would build around it a wall of brass. But I am too weak to defend the rampart against the host of assailants. I must call to my assistance their good sense, their patriotism, and their virtue. Do not, gentlemen, suffer the rage of passion to drive reason from her seat. If this law be indeed bad, let us join to remedy the defects. Has it been passed in a manner which wounded your pride or roused your resentment? Have, I conjure you, the magnanimity to pardon that offence. I entreat, I implore you, to sacrifice those angry passions to the interests of our country. Pour out this pride of opinion on the altar of patriotism. Let it be an expiatory libation for the weal of America. Do not, for God's sake, do not suffer that pride to plunge us all into the abyss of ruin.

Indeed, indeed, it will be of little, very little avail, whether one opinion or the other be right or wrong; it will heal no wounds; it will pay no debts; it will rebuild no ravaged towns. Do not rely on that popular will which has brought us frail beings into political existence. That opinion is but a changeable thing. It will soon change. This very measure will change it. You will be deceived. Do not, I beseech you, in reliance on a foundation so frail, commit the dignity, the harmony, the existence of our nation to the wild wind. Trust not your treasure to the waves.

services began with his election to the Provincial Congress of New York in 1775; he was afterward member of the Continental Congress, and of the Convention which framed the Constitution. He aided Robert Morris in those financial operations so important to the struggling country; and during Washington's administration was appointed Minister to France. His vast information, long political experience, and fervid eloquence, gave him a conspicuous place in the Senate, even among the brilliant lights so numerous in that body at the beginning of this century.

Throw not your compass and your charts into the ocean. Do not believe that its billows will waft you into port. Indeed, indeed, you will be deceived. Oh! cast not away this only anchor of our safety. I have seen its progress. I know the difficulties through which it was obtained. I stand in the presence of Almighty God and of the world. I declare to you, that if you lose this charter, never, no, never, will you get another! We are now, perhaps, arrived at the parting point. Here, even here, we stand on the brink of fate. Pause! Pause! For Heaven's sake, pause!

Ex. CX.—*NECESSITY OF AVOIDING A WAR WITH FRANCE.*

Speech in Congress, 1803.

DE WITT CLINTON.*

IF I were called upon to prescribe a course of policy most important for this country to pursue, it would be to avoid European connections and wars. The time must arrive when we will have to contend with some of the great powers of Europe, but let that period be put off as long as possible. As a young nation, pursuing industry in every channel, and adventuring commerce in every sea, it is highly important that we should not only have a pacific character, but that we should deserve it. If we manifest an unwarrantable ambition, and a rage for conquest, we unite all the great powers of Europe against us. The security of all the European possessions in our vicinity will eternally depend, not upon their strength, but upon our moderation and justice. Look at the Canadas; at the Spanish territories to the south; at the British, Spanish, French, Danish and Dutch West India Islands; at the vast countries to the west, as far as where

---

* Mr. Clinton was for two sessions in the U. S. Senate, but passed the rest of his political life in posts of honor and responsibility in his native State. Such was the value attached to his services by his fellow-citizens, that they never allowed him to be unemployed except when he declined an election. It was his public spirit and perseverance that carried through the construction of the Erie Canal, amid discouragement and opposition that would have overpowered a person of less firm determination. At the time of making the speech quoted above, he was comparatively a young man, and his cautious policy is in singular contrast with the impetuous war-temper of his colleague, Mr. Morris, many years his senior.

the Pacific rolls its waves. Consider well the consequences
that would result, if we were possessed by a spirit of conquest. Consider well the impression which a manifestation
of that spirit will make upon those who would be affected
by it.

If we are to rush at once into the territory of a neighboring nation with fire and sword, for the misconduct of a subordinate officer, will not our national character be greatly
injured? Will we not be classed with the robbers and destroyers of mankind? Will not the nations of Europe perceive in this conduct the germ of a lofty spirit and an enterprising ambition, which will level them to the earth, when
age has matured our strength, and expanded our powers of
annoyance, unless they combine to cripple us in our infancy?
May not the consequences be, that we must look out for a
naval force to protect our commerce—that a close alliance
will result—that we will be thrown at once into the ocean
of European politics, where every wave that rolls, and every
wind that blows, will agitate our bark? Is this a desirable
state of things? Will the people of this country be seduced
into it by all the colorings of rhetoric, and all the arts of
sophistry, by vehement appeals to their pride, and artful addresses to their cupidity? No, Sir! Three-fourths of the
American people—I assert it boldly and without fear of con-
tradiction—are opposed to this measure! And would you
take up arms with a mill-stone hanging around your neck?
How would you bear up, not only against the force of the
enemy, but against the irresistible current of public opinion?
The thing, Sir, is impossible; the measure is worse than
madness; it is wicked beyond the powers of description!

Ex. CXI.—*NECESSITY OF PREPARING FOR A WAR WITH FRANCE.*

Speech in Congress, 1803.

- GOUVERNEUR MORRIS.

MR. PRESIDENT: My object is peace. I could assign
many reasons to show that this declaration is sincere. But
can it be necessary to give the Senate any other assurance
than my word? Notwithstanding the acerbity of temper

which results from party strife, gentlemen will believe me on my word. I will not pretend, like my honorable colleague, to describe to you the waste, the ravages, and the horrors of war. I have not the same harmonious periods, nor the same musical tones; neither shall I boast of Christian charity, nor attempt to display that ingenuous glow of benevolence, so decorous to the cheek of youth, which gave a vivid tint to every sentence he uttered, and was, if possible, as impressive even as his eloquence. But though we possess not the same pomp of words, our hearts are not insensible to the woes of humanity. We can feel for the misery of plundered towns, the conflagration of defenceless villages, and the devastation of cultured fields.

Yes, Sir, we wish for peace; but how is that blessing to be preserved? In my opinion, there is nothing worth fighting for but national honor; for in the national honor is involved the national independence. I know that prudence may force a wise government to conceal the sense of indignity; but the insult should be engraven on tablets of brass with a pencil of steel. And when that time and change, which happen to all, shall bring forward the favorable moment, then let the avenging arm strike home. It is by avowing and maintaining this stern principle of honor, that peace can be preserved.

I have no hesitation in saying that you ought to have taken possession of New Orleans and the Floridas the instant your treaty was violated. You ought to do it now. Your rights are invaded, confidence in negotiation is in vain; there is therefore no alternative but force. You are exposed to imminent present danger; you have the prospect of great future advantage; you are justified by the clearest principles of right; you are urged by the strongest motives of policy; you are commanded by every sentiment of national dignity.

Look, Mr. President, at the conduct of America in her infant years. When there was no actual invasion of right, but only a claim to invade, she resisted the claim; she spurned the insult. Did we then hesitate? Did we then wait for foreign alliance? No; animated with the spirit, warmed by the soul of Freedom, we threw our oaths of allegiance in the face of our sovereign, and committed our fortunes and our fate to the God of battles. We were then subjects. We had not then attained to the dignity of an independent republic. We then had no rank among the nations of the earth. But we had the spirit which deserved that elevated station. And now that we have gained it, shall we fall from our honor?

Sir, I repeat to you that I wish for peace—real, lasting, honorable peace. To obtain and secure this blessing, let us, by a bold and decisive conduct, convince the powers of Europe that we are determined to defend our rights; that we will not submit to insult; that we will not bear degradation. This is the conduct which becomes a generous people. This conduct will command the respect of the world. I can not believe, with my honorable colleague, that three-fourths of America are opposed to vigorous measures. I can not believe that they will meanly refuse to pay the sums needful to vindicate their honor and support their independence. Sir, this is a libel on the people of America. They will disdain submission to the proudest sovereign of earth. They have not lost the spirit of '76. But, Sir, if they are so base as to barter their rights for gold, if they are so vile that they will not defend their honor, they are unworthy of the rank they enjoy, and it is no matter how soon they are parcelled out among better masters.

Ex. CXII.—*SONG.*

REMEMBER the glories of patriots brave,
    Though the days of the heroes are o'er;
Long lost to their country, and cold in their grave,
    They return to their kindred no more.
The stars of the field, which in victory poured
    Their beams on the battle, are set;
But enough of their glory remains on each sword
    To light us to victory yet!

Wollansac! when nature embellished the tint
    Of thy fields and thy mountains so fair,
Did she ever intend that a tyrant should print
    The footsteps of slavery there?
No! Freedom, whose smiles we shall never resign,
    Told those who invaded our plains,
That 'tis sweeter to bleed for an age at thy shrine,
    Than to sleep for a moment in chains.

Forget not the chieftains of Hampshire, who stood
    In the day of distress by our side;
Nor the heroes who nourished the fields with their blood,
    Nor the rights they secured as they died.
The sun that now blesses our eyes with his light,
    Saw the martyrs of liberty slain;
Oh, let him not blush, when he leaves us to-night,
    To find that they fell there in vain!

Ex. CXIII.—*JEFFERSON'S PURCHASE OF THE LOUISIANA TERRITORY, MADE IN 1803.*

HENRY S. RANDALL.

No conqueror who has trod the earth to fill it with desolation and mourning, ever conquered and permanently amalgamated with his native kingdom a remote approach to the same extent of territory secured by this peaceful purchase. But one kingdom in Europe equals the extent of one of its present states. Germany supports a population of thirty-seven millions of people. All Germany has a little more than the area of two-thirds of Nebraska; and, acre for acre, less tillable land. The Louisiana territory, as densely populated in proportion to its natural materials of sustentation as parts of Europe, would be capable of supporting from four to five hundred millions of people. The whole United States became capable, by this acquisition, of sustaining a larger population than ever occupied Europe.

This purchase secured, independently of territory, several prime national objects. It gave us that homogeneousness, unity and independence which is derived from the absolute control and disposition of our commerce, trade and industry, in every department, without the hindrance or meddling of any intervening nation between us and any natural element of industry, between us and the sea, or between us and the open market of the world. It gave us ocean boundaries on all exposed sides; it made us indisputably and forever (if our own Union is preserved), the controllers of the Western Hemisphere. It placed our national course, character, civilization and destiny solely in our own hands.

It gave us the certain sources of a not distant numerical strength to which that of the mightiest empires of the past or present is insignificant.

A Gallic Cæsar was leading his armies over shattered kingdoms. His armed foot shook the world. He decimated Europe. Millions on millions of mankind perished, and there was scarcely a human habitation from the Polar seas to the Mediterranean, where the voice of lamentation was not heard over kindred slaughtered to swell the conqueror's strength and "glory!" And the carnage and rapine of war are trifling evils compared with its demoralizations. The rolling tide of conquest subsided. France shrank back to her ancient limits. Napoleon died a repining captive on a rock of the ocean. The stupendous tragedy was played out, and no physical results were left behind but decrease, depopulation and universal loss.

A Republican President, on a distant continent, was also seeking to aggrandize his country. He led no armies. He shed not a solitary drop of human blood. He caused not a tear of human woe. He bent not one toiling back lower by governmental burdens. Strangest of political anomalies, (and ludicrous as strange to the representatives of the ideas of the tyrannical and bloody past,) he lightened the taxes while he was lightening the debts of a nation. And without interrupting either of these meliorations for an instant—without imposing a single new exaction on his people, he acquired, peaceably and permanently for his country, more extensive and fertile domains than ever for a moment owned the sway of Napoleon—more extensive ones than his gory plume ever floated over.

Which of these victors deserves to be termed "glorious?"

Ex. CXIV.—*WAR DISCOUNTENANCED.*

Speech in Congress, March, 1806.

JOHN RANDOLPH.

WHAT, Sir, is the question in dispute? The carrying trade. What part of it? The fair, the honest, and the useful trade, that is engaged in carrying our own productions to foreign markets, and bringing back their productions in exchange? No, Sir; it is that carrying trade which covers enemies' property, and carries the coffee, the sugar, and other West India products to the mother country. No, Sir; if this great agricultural nation is to be governed by Salem and Boston, New York and Philadelphia, Baltimore, Norfolk and Charleston, let gentlemen come out and say so; and let a committee of public safety be appointed from these towns to carry on the government. I, for one, will not mortgage my property and my liberty to carry on this trade. The nation said so seven years ago; I said so then, I say so now; it is not for the honest carrying trade of America, but for this mushroom, this fungus of war,—for a trade which, as soon as the nations of Europe are at peace, will cease to exist—it is for this that the spirit of avaricious traffic would plunge us into war.

But yet, Sir, I have a more cogent reason against going to war for the honor of the flag in the narrow seas, or any other maritime punctilio. It springs from my attachment to the principles of the government under which I live. I declare, in the face of day, that this government was not instituted for the purposes of offensive war. No; it was framed, to use its own language, for the common defence and general welfare, which are inconsistent with offensive war. As, in 1798, I was opposed to this species of warfare, because I believed it would raze the Constitution to its very foundation; so, in 1806, I am opposed to it on the very same grounds. No sooner do you put the Constitution to this use—to a test which it is by no means calculated to endure,—than its incompetency to such purposes becomes manifest and apparent to all. I fear that if you go into a foreign war, for a circuitous, unfair foreign trade, you will come out without your Constitution. We shall be told that our government is too free, or in other words, too weak and inefficient—much virtue, Sir, in terms;—that we must give the President power to call forth the resources of the nation—that is, to filch the last shilling from our pockets, or to drain the last drop of blood from our veins. I am against giving this power to any man, be he who he may. The American people must either withhold this power, or resign their liberties. There is no other alternative. Nothing but the most imperious necessity will justify such a grant; and is there a powerful enemy at our door? You may begin with a First Consul. From that chrysalis state he soon becomes an emperor. You have your choice. It depends upon your election whether you will be a free, happy and united people at home, or the light of your executive majesty shall beam across the ocean in one general blaze of the public liberty.

Ex. CXV.—*JUSTICE DEMANDED FOR THE SOLDIERS OF THE REVOLUTION.*

P. SPRAGUE.

Sir: the present relief for the soldiers of the Revolution is not sufficient. The act should have embraced all, without any discrimination, except of services. But that act, partly by subsequent laws, and partly by illiberal rules of construction, has been narrowed far within its original scope. I am constrained to say, that, in the practical execution of these laws, the whole beneficent spirit of our institutions seems to have been reversed. Instead of presuming every man to be upright and true, until the contrary appears, every applicant seems to be presupposed to be false and perjured. Instead of bestowing these hard-earned rewards with alacrity, they appear to have been refused, or yielded with reluctance; and to send away the war-worn veteran, bowed down with the infirmities of age, empty from your door, seems to have been deemed an act of merit.

So rigid has been the construction and application of the existing law, that cases most strictly within its provisions of meritorious service and abject poverty, have been excluded from its benefits. Yet gentlemen tell us, that this law, so administered, is too liberal; that it goes too far, and they would repeal it. They would take back even the little which they have given! And is this possible? Look abroad upon this wide-extended land, upon its wealth, its happiness, its hopes; and then turn to the aged soldier, who gave you all, and see him descend in neglect and poverty to the tomb!! The time is short.

A few years, and these remnants of a former age will no longer be seen. Then we shall indulge in unavailing regrets for our present apathy; for how can the ingenuous mind look upon the grave of an injured benefactor? How poignant the reflection, that the time for reparation and atonement has gone forever! In what bitterness of soul shall we look back upon the infatuation which shall have cast aside an opportunity which can never return, to give peace to our consciences!

We shall then endeavor to stifle our convictions, by empty honors to their bones. We shall raise high the monument, and trumpet loud their deeds, but it will be all in vain. It can not warm the hearts which shall have sunk cold and comfortless to the earth. This is no illusion. How often do we see in our public gazettes a pompous display of honors to the memory of some veteran patriot, who was suffered to linger out his latter days in unregarded penury!

"How proud we can press to the funeral array
Of him whom we shunned in his sickness and sorrow;
And bailiffs may seize his last blanket to-day,
Whose pall shall be borne up by heroes to-morrow."

We are profuse in our expressions of gratitude to the soldiers of the revolution. We can speak long and loud in their praise, but when asked to bestow something substantial upon them, we hesitate and palter. To them we owe everything, even the soil which we tread, and the air of freedom which we breathe. Let us not turn them houseless from habitations which they erected, and refuse them even a pittance from the exuberant fruits of their own labors.

Ex. CXVI.—*PENSIONERS' MUSTER, AUG. 3, 1807.*

They once marched in glory—their banners were streaming,
With the glance of the sunbeam their armor was gleaming;
Then hope swelled their bosoms; then firm was their tread—
And round them the garlands of victory were spread.

Then little they dreamed that the country they saved—
That the country for whom every danger they braved,
Would forget their desert when old age should come on,
And leave them forsaken—their comforts all gone.

They now march in glory—still memory sheds
The brightest of halos around their gray heads;
Though faltering the footstep, though rayless the eye,
Remembrance still dwells on the days long gone by.

Yes; saviours and sires! though the pittance be small
Which your country awards, and that pittance your all;
Though the cold hand of poverty press on your frames,
Yet your children shall bless you, and boast of your names.

And when life with its toil and afflictions shall cease,
Oh! then may you hail the bright angel of peace;
Then freemen shall weep o'er the veteran's grave,
And around it the laurel and cypress shall wave.

Ex. CXVII.—*REMONSTRANCE AGAINST THE WAR OF* 1812–15.

Speech in Congress, Dec. 10, 1811.

JOHN RANDOLPH.

I KNOW not how gentlemen calling themselves republicans can advocate such a war. What was their doctrine in 1798 and '9, when the command of the army—that highest of all possible trusts in any government, be the form what it may,—was reposed in the bosom of the father of his country; in the sanctuary of a nation's love; the only hope that never came in vain! Republicans were then unwilling to trust a standing army even to his hands, who had given proof that he was above all human temptation. Where now is the revolutionary hero to whom you are about to confide this sacred trust? To whom will you confide the charge of leading the flower of our youth to the heights of Abraham? When Washington himself was at the head, did you show such reluctance, feel such scruples; and are you now nothing loth, fearless of every consequence?

Imputations of British influence have been uttered against the opponents of the war. Against whom are these charges brought? Against men who, in the war of the Revolution, were in the councils of the nation, or fighting the battles of your country! Strange that we should have no objection to any other people or government, civilized or savage, in the whole world, than the British! The great autocrat of all the Russias receives the homage of our high consideration. The dey of Algiers and his divan of pirates are very civil, good sort of people, with whom we find no difficulty in maintaining the relations of peace and amity. "Turks,

Jews and Infidels," barbarians and savages of every clime and color, are welcome to our arms. With chiefs of banditti, negro or mulatto, we can treat and can trade. Name, however, but England, and all our antipathies are up in arms against her.

Against whom ? Against those whose blood runs in our veins; in common with whom we claim Shakspeare, and Newton, and Chatham for our countrymen; whose form of government is the freest on earth, our own only excepted; from whom every valuable principle in our own institutions has been borrowed—representation, jury trial, voting the supplies, writ of *habeas corpus*, our whole civil and criminal jurisprudence; against our fellow Protestants, identical in blood, in language, in religion with ourselves. In what school did the worthies of our land, the Washingtons, Henrys, Hancocks, Franklins, Rutledges of America learn those principles of civil liberty which were so nobly asserted by their wisdom and valor? American resistance to British usurpation has not been more warmly cherished by these great men and their compatriots, than by Chatham and his illustrious associates in the British Parliament. I acknowledge the influence of a Shakspeare and a Milton upon my imagination, of a Locke upon my understanding, of a Sydney upon my political principles, of a Chatham upon qualities which I would to God I possessed in common with that illustrious man! of a Tillotson, a Sherlock, a Porteus, upon my religion. This is a British influence which I can never shake off.

Before this miserable force of ten thousand men is raised to take Canada, I beg gentlemen to look at the state of defence at home; to count the cost of the enterprise before it is set on foot, not when it may be too late—when the best blood of the country may be spilt, and nought but empty coffers left to defray the expense. Once more, I beseech gentlemen, before they run their heads against this post, Quebec, to count the cost.

Ex. CXVIII.—*REASONS FOR PROSECUTING THE WAR.*

Speech in Congress, Dec. 12, 1811.

JOHN C. CALHOUN.*

Mr. Speaker: There are many reasons why this country should never resort to war but for causes the most urgent and necessary. It is sufficient that, under a government like ours, none but such will justify it in the eye of the nation; and were I not satisfied that such is our present cause, I certainly would be no advocate of the proposition now before the house.

Sir, I consider the war, should it ensue, justifiable and necessary by facts undoubted and universally admitted. The extent, duration, and character of the injuries received; the failure of those peaceful means hitherto resorted to for the redress of our wrongs, is my proof that it is necessary. Why should I mention the impressment of our seamen; depredation on every branch of our commerce, including the direct export trade, continued for years, and made under laws which professedly undertake to regulate our trade with other nations; negotiation resorted to, time after time, till it has become hopeless; the restrictive system persisted in, to avoid war, and in the vain expectation of returning justice? The evil still grows, and in each succeeding year swells in extent and pretension beyond the preceding. The question, even in the opinion and admission of our opponents in this House, is reduced to this single point: which shall we do, abandon or defend our own commercial and maritime rights, and the personal liberties of our citizens employed in exerting them? Sir, which alternative this House ought to embrace, it is not for me to say. I hope the decision is made already by a higher authority than the voice of any man. It

---

* Mr. Calhoun had taken his seat in the House of Representatives for the first time about a month previous to the date of this speech, and had thus but just entered upon that long and influential public career which terminated only with his death, in March, 1850. His *début* was made at a critical period in our history, when the crisis was just approaching which was to decide the question of a war with Great Britain or submission to her power; he warmly espoused the war policy, and soon acquired that commanding position in political life which he ever afterwards retained. In after years his pernicious doctrine of "State Rights" was destined to work great injury to his country, and finally to plunge the Southern States into rebellion against the Federal government. Few men have left their mark more decidedly on the history of this country.

is not for the human tongue to instil the sense of independence and honor. This is the work of nature—a generous nature, that disdains tame submission to wrongs.

The first argument of the gentleman from Virginia which I shall notice, is the unprepared state of the country. Whatever weight this argument might have in a question of immediate war, it surely has little in that of preparation for it. If our country is unprepared, let us remedy the evil as soon as possible. Let the gentleman submit his plan; and if it is a reasonable one, I doubt not it will be supported by the House. We are next told of the expenses of the war, and that the people will not pay taxes. Why not? Is it a want of capacity? What! with one million tons of shipping, a trade of near one hundred million dollars, manufactures of one hundred and fifty million dollars, and agriculture of twice that amount, shall we be told that the country wants capacity to raise and support ten or fifteen thousand additional regulars?

No; it has the ability; that is admitted; but will it have the disposition? Shall we then utter this libel on the nation? Where will be found proof of a fact so disgraceful? Is not the course a just and necessary one? If taxes should become necessary, I do not hesitate to say the people will pay cheerfully. I know of only one principle to make a nation great—to produce in this country not merely the form, but the whole spirit of union; and that is, to protect every citizen in the lawful pursuit of his business. He will then feel that he is backed by his government—that its arm is his arm, and he will rejoice in its increased strength and prosperity. This is the road that all great nations have trod. Protection and patriotism are reciprocal.

The gentleman has not failed to touch on the calamity of war—that fruitful source of declamation by which pity becomes the advocate of cowardice; but I know not what we have to do with that subject. If the gentleman desires to repress the gallant ardor of our countrymen by such topics, let me inform him that true courage regards only the cause, that it is just and necessary, and that it despises the pain and danger of war. If he really wishes to promote the cause of humanity, let his eloquence be addressed to Lord Wellesley or Mr. Percival, and not to the American Congress. Tell them, if they persist in such daring insult and injury to a neutral nation, that, however inclined to peace, it will be bound in honor and interest to resist; that their patience and benevolence, however great, will be exhausted; that the calamity of war will ensue, and that they, in the opinion of wounded humanity, will be answerable for all its devastation and misery. Let melting pity, a regard to the interests of humanity, stay the hand of injustice, and my life on it, the gentleman will not find it difficult to call off his countrymen from the bloody scenes of war.

Again, the gentleman is at a loss to account for what he calls our hatred of England. He asks, How can we hate the country of Locke, of Newton, Hampden and Chatham; having the same language, and customs as ourselves, and descending from a common ancestry? Sir, the laws of human affection are uniform. If we have so much to attach us to that country, powerful indeed must be the cause that has overpowered it.

Ex. CXIX.—*THE STAR-SPANGLED BANNER.*

FRANCIS SCOTT KEY.

Oh! say, can you see, by the dawn's early light,
  What so proudly we hailed at the twilight's last gleaming?
Whose broad stripes and bright stars through the perilous
    night,
  O'er the ramparts we watched were so gallantly streaming;
And the rocket's red glare, the bombs bursting in air,
Gave proof through the night that our flag was still there.
  Oh! say, does that star-spangled banner yet wave
  O'er the land of the free and the home of the brave?

On the shore, dimly seen through the mists of the deep,
  Where the foe's haughty host in dread silence reposes,
What is that which the breeze, o'er the towering steep
  As it fitfully blows, half conceals, half discloses?
Now it catches the gleam of the morning's first beam,
In full glory reflected now shines on the stream.
  'Tis the star-spangled banner; oh! long may it wave
  O'er the land of the free and the home of the brave.

And where is that band, who so vauntingly swore
  That the havoc of war and the battle's confusion

A home and a country should leave us no more?
  Their blood has washed out their foul footsteps' pollution;
No refuge could save the hireling and slave,
From the terror of death and the gloom of the grave:
  And the star-spangled banner in triumph shall wave
  O'er the land of the free and the home of the brave.

Oh! thus be it ever, when freemen shall stand
  Between their loved home and the war's desolation;
Blest with victory and peace, may the heaven-rescued land
  Praise the power that has made and preserved us a nation.
Then conquer we must, for our cause it is just,
And this be our motto, In God is our trust.
  And the star-spangled banner in triumph shall wave
  O'er the land of the free and the home of the brave.

Ex. CXX.—*ON THE CONDUCT OF THE WAR OF* 1812-15.

HENRY CLAY.*

WHEN the administration was striving, by the operation of peaceful measures, to bring Great Britain back to a sense of justice, the gentlemen of the opposition were for old-fashioned war. And, now they have got old-fashioned war, their sensibilities are cruelly shocked, and all their sympathies lavished upon the harmless inhabitants of the ad-

---

* Mr. Clay is well known to have been one of the most successful of American orators, invariably captivating by his manner of delivery and style of composition, even when his hearers were not convinced by his reasoning. It may be well for young aspirants to distinction in public speaking to know what he regarded as the secret of his power. "I owe my success in life," he said, "to one single fact; namely, that at an early age I commenced, and continued for some years, the practice of daily reading and speaking the contents of some historical or scientific book." Acting on this hint, who need despair of achieving the same result?

Henry Clay was in active public life for fifty years; probably a longer time than any other American statesman has been. His name is often united with those of Calhoun and Webster, all having been distinguished as orators and statesmen, all passing their lives in the public service, and all dying within the space of about two years—1850-52. This triple loss was deeply felt by the nation, who knew that in the course of events it must be long before another such illustrious trio should arise to thread the tangled ways of political life together. A beautiful tribute to their memory will be found in its historical order in this book.

joining provinces. What does a state of war present? The united energies of one people arrayed against the combined energies of another; a conflict in which each party aims to inflict all the injury it can, by sea and land, upon the territories, property and citizens of the other,—subject only to the rules of mitigated war, practised by civilized nations. The gentlemen would not touch the continental provinces of the enemy; nor, I presume, for the same reason, her possessions in the West Indies. The same humane spirit would spare the seamen and soldiers of the enemy. The sacred person of his Majesty must not be attacked, for the learned gentlemen are quite familiar with the maxim that the King can do no wrong. Indeed, Sir, I know of no person upon whom we may make war but the author of the Orders in Council, or the Board of Admiralty, who authorize and regulate the principle of impressment!

The disasters of the war admonish us, we are told, of the necessity of terminating the contest. If our achievements by land have been less splendid than those of our intrepid seamen by water, it is not because the American soldier is less brave. On the one element, organization, discipline, and a thorough knowledge of their duties exist on the part of the officers and their men. On the other, almost everything is yet to be acquired. We have, however, the consolation that our country abounds with the richest materials, and that in no instance, when engaged in action, have our arms been tarnished.

An honorable peace is attainable only by an efficient war. My plan would be, to call out the ample resources of the country, give them a judicious direction, prosecute the war with the utmost vigor, strike wherever we can reach the enemy, at sea or on land, and negotiate the terms of a peace at Quebec or at Halifax. We are told that England is a proud and lofty nation, which, disdaining to wait for danger, meets it half way. Haughty as she is, we once triumphed over her; and if we do not listen to the counsels of timidity and despair, we shall again prevail. In such a cause, with the aid of Providence, we must come out crowned with success; but if we fail, let us fail like men,—lash ourselves to our gallant tars and expire together in one common struggle, fighting for FREE TRADE and SEAMEN'S RIGHTS!

Ex. CXXI.—*RIGHT OF OPPOSITION.*

Speech in Congress, 1814.

DANIEL WEBSTER.*

ALL the evils which afflict the country are imputed to opposition. It is said to be owing to opposition that the war became necessary, and owing to opposition, also, that it has been prosecuted with no better success. This, Sir, is no new strain. It has been sung a thousand times. It is the constant tune of every weak and wicked administration. What minister ever yet acknowledged that the evils which fell on his country were the necessary consequences of his own incapacity, his own folly, or his own corruption? What possessor of political power ever yet failed to charge the mischiefs resulting from his own measures upon those who had uniformly opposed those measures?

The people of the United States may well remember the administration of Lord North. He lost America to his country, yet he could find pretences for throwing the odium upon his opponents. He could throw it upon those who had forewarned him of consequences, and who had opposed him, at every stage of his disastrous policy, with all the force of truth, reason and talent. It was not his own weakness, his own ambition, his own love of arbitrary power, that disaffected the colonies. It was not the Tea Act, the Stamp Act, the Boston Port Bill, that severed the empire of Britain. Oh, no! It was owing to no fault of Administration. It was

---

* This speech, apart from its intrinsic interest, is worthy of special notice as being the first formal one uttered by Daniel Webster on the floor of the House of Representatives, where he was destined so often to hold captive his entranced audience with those weighty sentences which, to use the words of a historian, "fell with all the force and sure aim of a trip-hammer." Many of his subsequent efforts are more brilliant, but the effect of this is said to have been "to demolish the pretences of the administration orators that it was the opposition who were to blame for the present state of affairs." He continues in an earnest appeal to Congress to make the American Navy their main dependence in the existing contest: "If the war must continue, go to the ocean. If you are seriously contending for maritime rights, go to the theatre where alone those rights can be defended. In protecting naval interests by naval means, you will arm yourselves with the whole power of national sentiment, and may command the whole abundance of national resources." Thus did his far-seeing wisdom point out the true stronghold of our national glory, which the government was so slow to acknowledge and to take advantage of.

the work of Opposition. It was the impertinent boldness of Chatham, the idle declamation of Fox, the unseasonable sarcasm of Barré. These men, and men like them, would not join the minister in his American war. They would not give the name and character of wisdom to what they believed to be the extreme of folly. They would not pronounce those measures just and honorable which their principles led them to condemn. They foresaw the end of the minister's war, and pointed it out plainly, both to him and to the country. He persisted in his course, and the result is in history.

Important as I deem it, Sir, to discuss, on all proper occasions, the policy of the measures at present pursued, it is still more important to maintain the right of such discussion in its full and just extent. Sentiments lately sprung up, and now growing popular, render it necessary to be explicit on this point. It is the ancient and constitutional right of this people to canvass public measures, and the merits of public men. It is a home-bred right, a fireside privilege. It has ever been enjoyed in every house, cottage and cabin, in the nation. It is not to be drawn into controversy. It is as undoubted as the right of breathing the air and of walking on the earth. Belonging to private life as a right, it belongs to public life as a duty; and it is the last duty which those whose representative I am shall find me to abandon. This high constitutional privilege I shall defend and exercise within this House, and without this House, and in all places; in time of war, in time of peace, and at all times. Living, I will assert it, dying, I will assert it; and should I leave no other legacy to my children, by the blessing of God I will leave them the inheritance of free principles, and the example of a manly, independent and constitutional defence of them!

Ex. CXXII.—*SONG.*

JAMES GATES PERCIVAL.

YE sons of sires who fought and bled
  For liberty and glory,
Whose fame shall ever wider spread
  Till Time is bent and hoary—
Awake to meet the invading foe!
  Rouse at the call of danger!

> Beat down again his standard low,
> And backward hurl the stranger!
>
> They knew no fear, those sires of old—
> 'Mid swords and bayonets clashing,
> Still high they bore their banner's fold,
> Its stars like lightnings flashing.
> Be like those sires! With freeborn might
> Renew the deeds of story!
> Who lives, shall win a wreath of light—
> Who falls, shall sleep in glory!

Ex. CXXIII.—*ADDRESS TO THE ARMY AT NEW ORLEANS, DECEMBER 18, 1814.*

ANDREW JACKSON.*

FELLOW CITIZENS AND SOLDIERS:—The general commanding in chief would not do justice to the noble ardor that has animated you in the hour of danger, he would not do justice to his own feelings, if he suffered the example you have shown to pass without public notice. Inhabitants of an opulent commercial town, you have, by a spontaneous effort, shaken off the habits which are created by wealth, and shown that you are resolved to deserve the blessings of fortune, by bravely defending them. Long strangers to the perils of war, you have emboldened yourselves to face them with the cool countenance of veterans;—with motives of disunion that might have operated on some minds, you have forgotten the differences of language and prejudice of national pride,

---

* This address was read at the close of a military review held about three weeks before the battle of New Orleans, which virtually closed the war of 1812-15. It is supposed to have been penned by Edward Livingston, an eminent New York lawyer, then residing in Louisiana, and a valued friend and supporter of General Jackson. The biographer of the latter remarks: "This address was Jackson's spirit in Livingston's language. The manuscript, in the handwriting of Edward Livingston, still exists."

General Jackson, with many striking peculiarities of manner and character, was the idol of his army and the nation. He was successful in war, and conducted the Administration as President for eight years with such inflexible vigor and determination as commanded the respect alike of friends and enemies. Had it not been for his promptness and decision, the Rebellion of 1861 would have begun in 1833, when an attempt was made by South Carolina, under the name of Nullification, to resist the government of the United States.

and united with a cordiality that does honor to your understanding as well as to your patriotism.

Natives of the United States! They are the oppressors of your infant political existence with whom you are to contend—they are the men your fathers fought and conquered, whom you are now to oppose.

Descendants of Frenchmen! Natives of France! They are English;—the hereditary, the eternal enemies of your ancient country—the invaders of that you have adopted—who are your foes.

Spaniards! remember the conduct of your allies at St. Sebastian's, and recently at Pensacola; and rejoice that you have an opportunity of avenging the brutal injuries inflicted by men who dishonor the human race.

Citizens of Louisiana! the General commanding in chief rejoices to see the spirit that animates you, not only for your honor, but for your safety; for whatever had been your conduct or wishes, his duty would have led, and will now lead him, to confound the citizen unmindful of his rights with the enemy he ceases to oppose. Now, leading men who know their rights and who are determined to defend them, he salutes you as brethren in arms, and has now a new motive to exert all his faculties, which shall be strained to the utmost in your defence. Continue with the energy you have begun with, and he promises you not only safety, but victory over the insolent enemy who insulted you by an affected doubt of your attachment to the Constitution of your country.

Soldiers! The President of the United States shall be informed of your conduct on the present occasion, and the voice of the Representatives of the American nation shall applaud your valor, as your General now praises your ardor. The enemy is near. His sails cover the lakes. But the brave are united; and if he finds us contending among ourselves, it will be for the prize of valor, and fame, its noblest reward.

Ex. CXXIV.—*RETROSPECTIVE VIEW OF THE WAR OF* 1812-15.

HENRY CLAY.

WE are asked, What have we gained by the war? I have shown that we have lost nothing in rights, territory, or honor; nothing for which we ought to have contended, according to the principles of the gentlemen on the other side, or according to our own. Have we gained nothing by the war? Let any man look at the degraded condition of this country before the war, the scorn of the universe, the contempt of ourselves, and tell me if we have gained nothing by the war? What is our present situation? Respectability and character abroad, security and confidence at home. If we have not obtained, in the opinion of some, the full measure of retribution, our character and constitution are placed on a solid basis never to be shaken.

The glory acquired by our gallant tars, by our Jacksons and our Browns on the land,—is that nothing? True, we had our vicissitudes; there were humiliating events which the patriot can not review without deep regret; but the great account, when it comes to be balanced, will be found vastly in our favor. Is there a man who would obliterate from the proud pages of our history the brilliant achievements of Jackson, Brown and Scott, and the host of heroes on land and sea, whom I can not enumerate? Is there a man who could not desire a participation in the national glory acquired by the war? Yes, *national glory*, which, however the expression may be condemned by some, must be cherished by every genuine patriot.

What do I mean by national glory? Glory such as Hull, Jackson and Perry have acquired. And are gentlemen insensible to their deeds—to the value of them in animating the country in the hour of peril hereafter? Did the battle of Thermopylæ preserve Greece but once? While the Mississippi continues to bear the tributes of the iron mountains and the Alleghanies to her Delta, and to the Gulf of Mexico, the eighth of January shall be remembered, and the glory of that day shall stimulate future patriots, and nerve the arms of unborn freemen in driving the presumptuous invader from our country's soil.

Gentlemen may boast of their insensibility to feelings inspired by the contemplation of such events. But I would ask, does the recollection of Bunker Hill, Saratoga and Yorktown afford them no pleasure? Every act of noble sacrifice to the country, every instance of patriotic devotion to her cause, has its beneficial influence. A nation's character is the sum of its splendid deeds; they constitute one common patrimony, the nation's inheritance. They awe foreign powers; they arouse and animate our own people. I love true glory. It is this sentiment which ought to be cherished; and in spite of cavils, and sneers, and attempts to put it down, it will finally conduct this nation to that height to which God and nature have destined it.

Ex. CXXV.—*THE AMERICAN FLAG.*

JOSEPH RODMAN DRAKE.

When Freedom, from her mountain height,
   Unfurled her standard to the air,
She tore the azure robe of night,
   And set the stars of glory there!
She mingled with its gorgeous dyes
The milky baldric of the skies,
And striped its pure celestial white
With streakings of the morning light;
Then from his mansion in the sun,
She called her eagle-bearer down,
And gave into his mighty hand
The symbol of her chosen land!

Majestic monarch of the cloud!
   Who rear'st aloft thy regal form,
To hear the tempest trumping loud,
And see the lightning-lances driven
   When stride the warriors of the storm,
And rolls the thunder-drum of heaven!
Child of the sun! to thee 'tis given
   To guard the banner of the free;
To hover in the sulphur smoke,
To ward away the battle-stroke,
And bid its blendings shine afar,
Like rainbows on the cloud of war—
   The harbingers of victory.

Flag of the brave! thy folds shall fly,
The sign of hope and triumph high!
When speaks the signal trumpet tone,
And the long line comes gleaming on,
(Ere yet the life-blood, warm and wet,
Hath dimmed the glistening bayonet,)

Each soldier's eye shall brightly turn
To where thy meteor glories burn,
And as his springing steps advance,
Catch war and vengeance from the glance!
And when the cannon's mouthings loud
Heave in wild wreaths the battle shroud,
And gory sabres rise and fall,
Like shoots of flame on midnight's pall,
There shall thy victor glances glow,
    And cowering foes shall sink beneath
Each gallant arm, that strikes below
    That lovely messenger of death.

Flag of the seas! on ocean's wave
Thy stars shall glitter o'er the brave,
When Death, careering on the gale,
Sweeps darkly round the bellied sail,
And frightened waves rush wildly back,
Before the broadside's reeling rack;
The dying wanderer of the sea,
Shall look at once to heaven and thee,
And smile to see thy splendors fly
In triumph o'er his closing eye.

Flag of the free heart's hope and home,
    By angel hands to valor given!
Thy stars have lit the welkin dome,
    And all thy hues were born in heaven.
Forever float that standard sheet!
    Where breathes the foe but falls before us,
With Freedom's soil beneath our feet,
    And Freedom's banner floating o'er us?—

Ex. CXXVI.—*THE MISSOURI COMPROMISE.**

Speech in Congress, February, 1819.

JAMES TALLMADGE.

Mr. Speaker: My hold on life is probably as frail as that of any man who now hears me, but while that hold lasts,

---

* We often hear of the "Missouri Compromise," but all do not fully understand what it was. The following is a brief explanation of it:

my life shall be devoted to the freedom of man. If blood is necessary to extinguish any fire which I have assisted to kindle, while I regret the necessity, I shall not hesitate to contribute my own. The violence which gentlemen have resorted to on this subject will not move my purpose, nor drive me from my ground. I have the fortune and honor to stand here as the representative of freemen who possess intelligence to know their rights, and who have the spirit to maintain them. I know the will of my constituents, and, regardless of consequences, I will avow it. As their representative, I will proclaim their hatred to slavery in every shape. As their representative here will I hold my stand, till this floor, with the National Constitution which supports it, shall sink beneath me. If I am doomed to fall, I shall at least have the painful consolation of falling as a fragment of the ruins of my country.

Missouri applied to Congress for admission as a State in March, 1818; nothing material was done at that session; at the next session, (1819), the bill for the admission of Missouri was taken up for consideration, and an amendment in the following words was proposed: "And provided, that the introduction of slavery or involuntary servitude be prohibited, except for the punishment of crime whereof the party has been duly convicted; and that all children, born within the said State after the admission thereof into the Union, shall be declared free at the age of twenty-five." After much excited discussion, the bill with *that proviso* failed to pass at that session; at the next session, (1820), the bill being again before Congress, the following section was *by way of compromise* proposed in lieu of the above-mentioned "proviso," namely: "Be it further enacted that, in all the territory ceded by France to the United States under the name of Louisiana, *which lies north of thirty-six degrees thirty minutes north latitude*, except only such part thereof as is included within the limits of the State contemplated by this act, *slavery and involuntary servitude, otherwise than in the punishment of crime, whereof the party shall have been duly convicted, shall be, and is hereby, forever prohibited.* But any person escaping into the same, from whom labor or service is lawfully claimed in any State or Territory of the United States, such fugitive may be lawfully reclaimed and conveyed to the person claiming his or her labor or service as aforesaid." After long and animated debate, the bill passed at that session with *the section just mentioned* as a part of it. This is what has since been known as "*the Missouri Compromise.*"

The "repeal" of the Missouri Compromise is also frequently mentioned. A few words will explain this expression:

At the session of Congress in 1854, a bill for the organization of the Territory of Kansas was introduced, and after protracted and most earnest discussion, in that bill a section was inserted declaring "inoperative" (in other words *repealing*) the section just quoted from the Missouri Bill; and thus the "*Missouri Compromise*" was "*repealed.*"

The students of American history will find, in the debates in Congress on the bills above mentioned, a vast fund of interesting and valuable information.

If it is not safe now to discuss slavery on this floor, if it can not now come before us as a proper subject for general legislation, what will be the result when it is spread through your widely-extended domain? Its present threatening aspect and the violence of its supporters, so far from inducing me to yield to its progress, prompt me to resist its march. Now is the time! The extension of the evil must now be prevented, or the opportunity will be lost forever!

Look down the long vista of futurity! See your empire, in extent unequalled, in advantageous situation without a parallel, occupying all the valuable part of our continent. Behold this extended empire inhabited by the hardy sons of America,—freemen knowing their rights and inheriting the will to maintain them; owners of the soil on which they live, and interested in the institutions which they labor to uphold; with two oceans laving your shores and tributary to your purposes, bearing on their bosoms the commerce of your people,—compared to yours, the governments of Europe dwindle into insignificance, and the world has no parallel. But reverse the scene. People this fair domain with the slaves of your planters. Spread slavery, that bane of man, that abomination of heaven, over your extended empire! You prepare its dissolution; you turn its accumulated strength into positive weakness; you cherish a cancer in your breast; you put a viper in your bosom; you place a vulture on your heart. Your enemies will learn the source and the cause of your weakness. As often as external dangers shall threaten, or internal commotions await you, you will realize that by your own procurement you have placed amid your families and in the bosom of your country, a population at once the greatest cause of individual danger and of national weakness. With this defect, your government must crumble to pieces, and your people become the scoff of the world.

But we are told that any attempt to legislate upon this subject is a violation of that faith and mutual confidence upon which our Union was formed and our Constitution adopted. If the restriction were attempted to be enforced against any of the slave-holding States, parties in the adoption of the Constitution, this argument might seem plausible. But it can have no application to a new district of country recently acquired, never contemplated in the formation of the government, and not embraced in the mutual concessions and declared faith upon which the Constitution was agreed to.

As an evil brought upon us without our fault and before the formation of our government, through the sin of that nation from which we revolted, we must of necessity legislate upon this subject; and it is our business so to legislate as never to encourage, but always to restrict it.

You boast of the freedom of your institutions and your laws. You have proclaimed in the Declaration of Independence that all men are created equal; that they are endowed by their Creator with certain inalienable rights; that among these are life, liberty and the pursuit of happiness. And yet you have slaves in your country! The enemies of your government point to your inconsistencies, and blazon your alleged defects. Confine slavery to the original slave-holding States, where you found it at the formation of your government, and you stand acquitted of these imputations. Allow it to pass into territories whence you have the lawful power to exclude it, and you take upon yourselves all these charges of inconsistency.

Ex. CXXVII.—*OUR COUNTRY.*

WILLIAM JEWETT PABODIE.

Our country!—'tis a glorious land,
 With broad arms stretched from shore to shore;
The proud Pacific chafes her strand,
 She hears the dark Atlantic roar;
And nurtured on her ample breast
 How many a goodly prospect lies,
In nature's wildest grandeur dressed,
 Enamelled with her loveliest dyes!

Rich prairies, decked with flowers of gold,
 Like sunlit oceans roll afar;
Broad lakes her azure heavens behold,
 Reflecting clear each trembling star;
And mighty rivers, mountain-born,
 Go sweeping onward, dark and deep,
Through forests, where the bounding fawn
 Beneath their sheltering branches leap.

And, cradled 'mid her clustering hills,
 Sweet vales in dreamlike beauty hide,

Where love the air with music fills,
  And calm content and peace abide.
For Plenty here her fulness pours
  In rich profusion o'er the land,
And, sent to seize her generous stores,
  There prowls no tyrant's hireling band.

Great God! we thank thee for this home,
  This bounteous birth-right of the free,
Where wanderers from afar may come
  And breathe the air of liberty!
Still may her flowers untrampled spring,
  Her harvests wave, her cities rise;
And yet, till time shall fold her wing,
  Remain earth's loveliest paradise!

Ex. CXXVIII.—*LIBERTY AND GREATNESS.*

HUGH S. LEGARÉ.*

THE name of Republic is inscribed upon the most imperishable monuments of the species, and it is probable that it will continue to be associated, as it has been in all past ages, with whatever is heroic in character, sublime in genius, elegant and brilliant in the cultivation of arts and letters. It would not have been difficult to prove that the base hirelings who, in this age of legitimacy and downfall, have so industriously inculcated a contrary doctrine, have been compelled to falsify history and abuse reason. I might have "called up antiquity from the old schools of Greece," to show that these apostles of despotism would have passed at Athens for barbarians and slaves. I might have asked triumphantly, what land had ever been visited with the influences of liberty, that did not flourish like the spring? What people had ever worshipped at her altars, without kindling with a loftier spirit, and putting forth more noble energies? Where she had ever acted, that her deeds had not been heroic? Where she

---

* Pronounced *Legree*. Mr. Legaré was a citizen of South Carolina, distinguished for his legal attainments, which procured him the position of Attorney-General of the United States, and for his brilliancy as a writer. He was strongly opposed to Mr. Calhoun's scheme of "nullification."

had ever spoken, that her eloquence had not been triumphant and sublime? It might have been demonstrated that a state of society in which nothing is obtained by patronage, nothing is yielded to the accidents of birth and fortune, where those who are already distinguished must exert themselves lest they be speedily eclipsed by their inferiors, and these inferiors are, by every motive, stimulated to exert themselves that they may become distinguished, and where, the lists being open to the whole world without any partiality or exclusion, the champion who bears off the prize must have tasked his prowess to the very uttermost, and proved himself the first of a thousand competitors, is necessarily more favorable to a bold, vigorous and manly way of thinking and acting than any other. I should have asked with Longinus, Who but a republican could have spoken the philippics of Demosthenes? and what has the patronage of despotism ever done to be compared with the spontaneous productions of the Attic, the Roman and the Tuscan muse?

With respect to ourselves, would it not be enough to say that we live under a form of government and in a state of society to which the world has never yet exhibited a parallel? Is it then *nothing* to be free? How many nations, in the whole annals of human kind, have proved themselves worthy of being so? Is it nothing that we are republicans? Were all men as enlightened, as brave, as *proud* as they ought to be, would they suffer themselves to be insulted with any other title? Is it nothing that so many independent sovereignties should be held together in such a confederation as ours? What does history teach us of the difficulty of instituting and maintaining such a polity, and of the glory that of consequence ought to be given to those who enjoy its advantages in so much perfection and on so grand a scale? For can anything be more striking and sublime than the idea of an IMPERIAL REPUBLIC, spreading over an extent of territory more immense than the empire of the Cæsars in the accumulated conquests of a thousand years; without prefects or proconsuls or publicans; founded in the maxims of common sense; employing within itself no arms but those of reason, and known to its subjects only by the blessings it bestows or perpetuates, yet capable of directing, against a foreign foe, all the energies of a military despotism; a republic, in which men are completely insignificant, and *principles* and *laws* exercise, throughout its vast dominions, a peaceful and irresistible sway, blending in one divine harmony such various habits and conflicting opinions, and mingling in our institutions the light of philosophy with all that is dazzling in the associations of heroic achievement, and extended domination, and deep-seated and formidable power?

Ex. CXXIX.—*THE AMERICAN REVOLUTION.*

JOHN QUINCY ADAMS.*

At the opening of the American revolution, Great Britain had been victorious in her long and bloody conflict with France. She had expelled her rival totally from the continent over which, bounded herself by the Mississippi, she was thence to hold divided empire only with Spain. She had acquired undisputed control over the Indian tribes, still tenanting the forests unexplored by European man. She had established an uncontested monopoly of the commerce of all her colonies. But forgetting all the warnings of preceding ages—forgetting the lessons written in the blood of her own children, through centuries of departed time—she undertook to tax the people of the colonies *without their consent.*

Resistance—instantaneous, unconcerted, sympathetic, inflexible resistance—like an electric shock startled and roused the people of all the English colonies on this continent.

This was the first signal of the North American Union. The struggle was for chartered rights, for English liberties, for the cause of Algernon Sidney and John Hampden, for trial by jury, for habeas corpus and Magna Charta.

But the English lawyers had decided that parliament was omnipotent; and parliament in their omnipotence, instead of trial by jury and the habeas corpus, enacted admiralty courts in England to try Americans for offences charged against them as committed in America; instead of the privileges of Magna Charta, nullified the charter itself of Massachusetts Bay; shut up the port of Boston; sent armies and navies to keep the peace, and teach the colonies that John Hampden was a rebel, and Algernon Sidney a traitor.

* Sixth President of the United States. Mr. Adams, like his father, occupied many positions of trust and distinction, including that of ambassador at several European courts. His son, Charles Francis Adams, our present minister to England, is the third of his family who has represented our country at the court of St. James.

English liberties had failed them. From the omnipotence of parliament the colonists appealed to the rights of man and the omnipotence of the God of battles. *Union! union!* was the instinctive and simultaneous cry throughout the land. Their Congress, assembled at Philadelphia, once—twice had petitioned the king; had remonstrated to parliament; had addressed the people of Britain for the rights of Englishmen—in vain. Fleets and armies, the blood of Lexington, and the fires of Charleston and Falmouth, had been the answer to petition, remonstrance and address.

Independence was declared. The colonies were transformed into States. Their inhabitants were proclaimed to be *one people*, renouncing all allegiance to the British crown; all claims to chartered rights as Englishmen. Therefore their charter was the Declaration of Independence. Their rights, the natural rights of mankind. Their government, such as should be instituted by themselves, *under the solemn mutual pledges of perpetual union*, founded on the self-evident truths proclaimed in the Declaration.

The Declaration of Independence was issued in the excruciating agonies of a civil war, and by that war independence was to be maintained. Six long years the war raged with unabated fury, and the Union was yet no more than a mutual pledge of faith, and a mutual participation of common sufferings and common dangers.

At last, the omnipotence of the British parliament was vanquished. The independence of the United States was not granted, but recognized. The nation had assumed that separate and equal station to which the laws of nature and of nature's God entitled it among the powers of the earth.

Ex. CXXX.—*ODE COMPOSED AFTER LISTENING TO THE ORATION, OF WHICH THE ABOVE FORMS A PART.*

" The ark of our covenant is the Declaration of Independence ; our Mount Ebal, the Articles of Confederation ; our Gerizim, the Constitution."
J. Q. ADAMS.

WILLIAM CUTTER.

PRIESTS of this holy land,
  Bear on the hallowed ark,
Blest symbol of the God at hand,
  Our guide through deserts dark.

There, by God's finger graven
  Is our eternal creed,
Drawn from the liturgy of heaven,
  In Freedom's hour of need.

Escaped from that dread curse
  That lowered o'er Ebal's brow,
Threatening with stern and dark reverse
  The shrine at which we bow,—
Oh! shun with pious awe
  Corruption's least approach,
Nor on that sacred fount of law
  Let aught profane encroach.

Round Gerizim's fair hill
  Where first our Union rose,
In peace and glory clustered still,
  Our growing tribes repose.
There may our children rest,
  Till Time himself shall die;
Still with that heavenly presence blest,
  Our ARK OF LIBERTY.

Ex. CXXXI.—*THE EXAMPLE OF AMERICA.*

FRANCIS JEFFREY.[*]

How absurd are the sophisms and predictions by which the advocates of existing abuses have, at all times, endeavored to create a jealousy and apprehension of reform! You can not touch the most corrupt and imbecile government without involving society in disorders at once frightful and contemptible, and reducing all things to the level of an insecure, and ignoble, and bloody equality! Such are the reasonings by which we are now to be persuaded that liberty is incompatible with private happiness or national prosperity. To these we need not now answer in words, or by reference to past and questionable examples; but we put them down

---

[*] Afterwards Lord Jeffrey; a brilliant British essayist and reviewer.

at once, and trample them contemptuously to the earth, by a short appeal to the *existence and condition of America!* What is the country of the universe, I would now ask, in which property is most sacred, or industry most sure of its reward? Where is the authority of law most omnipotent? Where are intelligence and wealth most widely diffused, and most rapidly progressive? Where, but in America?—in America, who laid the foundation of her Republican Constitution in a violent radical sanguinary Revolution; America, with her fundamental Democracy, made more unmanageable, and apparently more hazardous, by being broken up into I do not know how many confederated and independent Democracies; America, with universal suffrage, and yearly elections, with a free and unlicensed press, without an established Priesthood, an hereditary Nobility or a permanent Executive,—with all that is combustible, in short, and pregnant with danger on the hypothesis of Tyranny, and without one of the checks or safeguards by which alone, they contend, the benefits or the very being of society can be maintained!

There is something at once audacious and ridiculous in maintaining such doctrines, in the face of such experience. Nor can anything be founded on the novelty of these institutions, or the pretence that they have not yet been fairly put to their trial. America has gone on prospering under them for forty years, and has exhibited a picture of uninterrupted, rapid, unprecedented advances in wealth, population, intelligence and concord; while all the arbitrary governments of the Old World have been overrun with bankruptcies, conspiracies, rebellions and revolutions; and are at this moment trembling in the consciousness of their insecurity, and vainly endeavoring to repress irrepressible discontents by confederated violence and terror.

Ex. CXXXII.—*THE SHIP OF STATE.*

H. W. LONGFELLOW.

SAIL on, sail on, O Ship of State!
Sail on, O Union, strong and great!
Humanity, with all its fears,
With all the hopes of future years,

Is hanging breathless on thy fate!
We know what Master laid thy keel,
What Workmen wrought thy ribs of steel,
Who made each mast, and sail, and rope;
What anvils rang, what hammers beat,
In what a forge and what a heat
Were forged the anchors of thy hope!
Fear not each sudden sound and shock,—
'Tis of the wave, and not the rock;
'Tis but the flapping of the sail,
And not a rent made by the gale!
In spite of rock and tempest roar,
In spite of false lights on the shore,
Sail on, nor fear to breast the sea!
Our hearts, our hopes, are all with thee.
Our hearts, our hopes, our prayers, our tears,
Our faith triumphant o'er our fears,
Are all with thee, are all with thee!

CXXXIII.—*BUNKER HILL MONUMENT.*

From an Address delivered at the laying of its corner-stone, June 17, 1825.

DANIEL WEBSTER.

WE come, as Americans, to mark a spot which must ever be dear to us and our posterity. We wish that whosoever in all coming time shall turn his eye hither, may behold that the place is not undistinguished where the first great battle of the Revolution was fought. We wish that this structure may proclaim the magnitude and importance of that event to every class and every age. We wish that infancy may learn the purpose of its erection from maternal lips, and that weary and withered age may behold it and be solaced by the recollections which it suggests. We wish that labor may look up here, and be proud in the midst of its toil. We wish that in those days of disaster which, as they come upon all nations, must be expected to come upon us also, desponding patriotism may turn its eyes hitherward, and be assured that the foundations of our national power still stand strong. We wish that this column, rising toward Heaven among the pointed spires of so many temples dedicated to God, may contribute also to produce, in all minds, a pious feeling of dependence and gratitude. We wish, finally, that the last object on the sight of him who leaves his native shore, and the first to gladden his who revisits it, may be something which shall remind him of the liberty and the glory of his country. Let it rise till it meet the sun in its coming; let the earliest light of the morning gild it, and parting day linger and play on its summit.

We hold still among us some of those who were active agents in the scenes of 1775, and who are now here from every quarter of New England, to visit once more, and under circumstances so affecting, this renowned theatre of their courage and patriotism.

Venerable men! you have come down to us from a former generation. You are now where you stood, fifty years ago this very hour, with your brothers and your neighbors, shoulder to shoulder, in the strife for your country. Behold, how altered! You hear now no roar of hostile cannon, you see no mixed volumes of smoke and flame rising from burning Charlestown. The ground strewed with the dead and the dying; the impetuous charge, the steady and successful repulse; the loud call to repeated assault; the summoning of all that is manly to repeated resistance; a thousand bosoms freely and fearlessly bared in an instant to whatever of terror there may be in war and death;—all these you have witnessed, but you witness them no more. All is peace. The heights of yonder metropolis, its towers and roofs, which you then saw filled with wives and children and countrymen in distress and terror, and looking with unutterable emotions for the issue of the combat, have presented you to-day with the sight of its whole happy population, come out to welcome and greet you with a universal jubilee. All is peace; and God has granted you the sight of your country's happiness ere you slumber in the grave forever. He has allowed you to behold and to partake the reward of your patriotic toils; and he has allowed us, your sons and countrymen, to meet you here, and in the name of the present generation, in the name of your country, in the name of liberty to thank you! May the Father of all mercies smile upon your remaining years, and bless them! And when you shall here have exchanged your embraces; when you shall once more have pressed the hands which have been so often extended to give succor in adversity, or grasped in the exultation of victory; then look abroad into this lovely land which your young valor defended, and mark the happiness with which it is filled; yea, look abroad into the whole earth, and see what a name you have contributed to give to your country, and what a praise you have added to freedom, and then rejoice in the sympathy and gratitude which beam upon your last days from the improved condition of mankind.

Ex. CXXXIV.—*ODE FOR THE FOURTH OF JULY.*

CHARLES SPRAGUE.

To the sages who spoke, to the heroes who bled,
  To the day and the deed, strike the harp-strings of glory!
Let the song of the ransomed remember the dead,
  And the tongue of the eloquent hallow the story.
     O'er the bones of the bold
     Be that story long told,
And on Fame's golden tablets their triumphs unrolled,
Who on Freedom's green hills Freedom's banner unfurled,
And the beacon-fire raised that gave light to the world.

They are gone—mighty men! and they sleep in their fame;
  Shall we ever forget them? Oh, never! no, never!
Let our sons learn from us to embalm each great name,
  And the anthem send down—Independence forever!
     Wake, wake, heart and tongue!
     Keep the theme ever young;
Let their deeds through the long line of ages be sung,
Who on Freedom's green hills Freedom's banner unfurled,
And the beacon-fire raised that gave light to the world.

Ex. CXXXV.—*PARTING ADDRESS TO LA FAYETTE, SEPTEMBER 7th, 1825.**

JOHN QUINCY ADAMS.

GENERAL: The ship is now prepared for your reception, and equipped for sea. From the moment of her departure

---

* We hope that no American student is ignorant of the debt of gratitude

the prayers of millions will ascend to Heaven that her passage may be prosperous, and your return to the bosom of your family as propitious to your happiness as your visit to the scene of your youthful glory has been to that of the American people.

Go, then, our beloved friend; return to the land of brilliant genius, of generous sentiment, of heroic valor; to that beautiful France, the nursing mother of the twelfth Louis and the fourth Henry; the native soil of Bayard and Coligni, of Turenne and Catinat, of Fenelon and D'Auguesseau. In that illustrious catalogue of names which she claims as of her children, and with honest pride holds up to the admiration of other nations, the name of La Fayette has already for centuries been enrolled. And it shall henceforth burnish into brighter fame; for if in after days a Frenchman shall be called to indicate the character of his nation by that of one individual, during the age in which we live, the blood of lofty patriotism shall mantle in his cheek, the fire of conscious virtue shall sparkle in his eye, and he shall pronounce the name of La Fayette. Yet we too, and our children, in life and after death, shall claim you for our own. You are ours by that more than patriotic self-devotion with which you flew to the aid of our fathers at the crisis of our fate. Ours by that long series of years in which you have cherished us in your regard. Ours by that unshaken sentiment of gratitude for your services which is a precious portion of our inheritance. Ours by that tie of love, stronger than death, which has linked your name for the endless ages of time with the name of Washington.

At the painful moment of parting from you, we take comfort in the thought that wherever you may be, to the last pulsation of your heart, our country will be ever present to your affections; and a cheering consolation assures

owed by our country to the Marquis de La Fayette—a French nobleman who volunteered his assistance in the struggle for freedom, in the days when our prospects looked darkest and most hopeless. He purchased and fitted out a vessel for the American naval service at his own expense, and on arriving in this country was at once appointed Major General, and served as aide to Gen. Washington, with whom he was on terms of the closest intimacy. In 1824–5 he revisited the United States, passing through each of the twenty-four States and all the principal cities, and was everywhere received with heartfelt enthusiasm. As his own immense fortune had been confiscated and lost in the French Revolution, Congress voted him during this visit a grant of $200,000 and a township of land, in recognition of his services in our Revolutionary War, which had been given without pay or reward.

us that we are not called to sorrow most of all that we shall see your face no more. We shall indulge the pleasing anticipation of beholding our friend again. In the mean time, speaking in the name of the whole people of the United States, and at a loss only for language to give utterance to that feeling of attachment with which the heart of the nation beats, as the heart of one man,—I bid you a reluctant and affectionate farewell.

Ex. CXXXVI.—*REPLY TO PRESIDENT ADAMS.*

LA FAYETTE.

AMIDST all my obligations to the general government, and particularly to you, Sir, its respected Chief Magistrate, I have most thankfully to acknowledge the opportunity given me, at this solemn and painful moment, to present the people of the United States with a parting tribute of profound, inexpressible gratitude.

To have been, in the infant and critical days of these States, adopted by them as a favorite son,—to have participated in the toils and perils of our unspotted struggle for independence, freedom and equal rights—to have received at every stage of the Revolution and during forty years after that period, from the people of the United States and their representatives at home and abroad, continual marks of their confidence and kindness, has been the pride, the encouragement, the support of a long and eventful life.

But how could I find words to acknowledge that series of welcomes, those unbounded and universal displays of public affection, which have marked each step, each hour, of a twelve months' progress through the twenty-four States, and which, while they overwhelm my heart with grateful delight, have most satisfactorily evinced the concurrence of the people in the kind testimonies, in the immense favors bestowed on me by the several branches of their representatives, in every part and at the central seat of the confederacy?

Yet gratifications still higher await me. In the wonders of creation and improvement that have met my enchanted eye, in the unparalleled and self-felt happiness of the people, in their rapid prosperity and ensured security, public and private, in a practice of good order, the appendage of true freedom, and a national good sense, the final arbiter of all difficulties, I have had proudly to recognize a result of the republican principles for which we fought, and a glorious demonstration of the superiority over degrading aristocracy or despotism, of popular institutions founded on the plain rights of man, where the local rights of every section are preserved under a constitutional bond of union. The cherishing of that union between the States, as it has been the farewell entreaty of our great paternal Washington, and will ever be the dying prayer of every American patriot, so it has become the sacred pledge of the emancipation of the world, an object in which I am happy to observe that the American people show themselves every day more anxiously interested.

In conclusion I can only say, God bless you, Sir, and all who surround us. God bless the American people, each of their States, and the Federal government. Accept this patriotic farewell of an overflowing heart; such will be its last throb when it ceases to beat.

Ex. CXXXVII.—*NEW ENGLAND AND THE UNION.*

S. S. PRENTISS.

GLORIOUS New England! thou art still true to thy ancient fame, and worthy of thy ancestral honors. We have assembled in this far distant land to celebrate thy birthday. A thousand fond associations throng upon us, roused by the spirit of the hour. On thy pleasant valleys rest, like sweet dews of morning, the gentle recollections of our early life. Around thy hills and mountains cling, like gathering mists, the mighty memories of the Revolution. And, far away in the horizon of thy past, gleam, like thy own bright northern lights, the awful virtues of thy pilgrim sires!

But while we devote this day to the remembrance of our native land, we forget not that in which our happy lot is cast. We exult in the reflection, that though we count by thousands the miles that separate us from our birthplace, still our country is the same. We are no exiles, meeting upon the banks of a foreign river to swell its waters with our homesick tears. Here floats the same banner that rustled over our boyish heads, except that its mighty folds are wider, and its glittering stars increased in number.

The sons of New England are found in every State of the broad republic! In the East, the South, and the unbounded West, their blood mingles freely with every kindred current. We have but changed our chamber in the paternal mansion. In all its rooms we are at home, and all who inhabit it are our brothers. To us the Union has but one domestic hearth. Its households gods are all the same. Upon us, then, peculiarly devolves the duty of feeding the fires upon that kindly hearth; of guarding with pious care those sacred household gods.

We can not do with less than the whole Union. To us it admits of no division. In the veins of our children flow Northern and Southern blood. How shall it be separated? Who shall put asunder the best affections of the heart, the noblest instincts of our nature? We love the land of our adoption; so do we that of our birth. Let us ever be true to both; and ever exert ourselves in maintaining the unity of our country, the integrity of the republic.

Accursed, then, be the hand put forth to loosen the golden cord of union! Thrice accursed the traitorous lips that shall propose its severance! But no! the Union *can not be dissolved.*' Its fortunes are too brilliant to be marred; its destinies too powerful to be resisted. And when, a century hence, this city shall have filled her golden horns—when within her broad-armed port shall be gathered the products of the industry of freemen,—when galleries of art and halls of learning shall have made classic this mart of trade,—then may the sons of the Pilgrims, still wandering from the bleak hills of the North, stand upon the banks of the Great River and exclaim, with mingled pride and wonder, Lo! this is our country. When did the world ever behold so great and glorious a republic?

Ex. CXXXVIII.—*NEW ENGLAND'S DEAD.*

ISAAC MCLELLAN.

New England's dead! New England's dead!
    On every hill they lie;
On every field of strife, made red
    By bloody victory.

Each valley where the battle poured
    Its red and awful tide,
Beheld the brave New England sword
    With slaughter deeply dyed.
Their bones are on the northern hill,
    And on the southern plain;
By brook and river, lake and rill,
    And by the roaring main.

The land is holy where they fought,
    And holy where they fell;
For by their blood that land was bought—
    The land they loved so well.
Then glory to that gallant band,
The honored saviours of the land.
Oh, few and weak their numbers were,—
    A handful of brave men;
But to their God they gave their prayer,
    And rushed to battle then:
The God of battles heard their cry,
And sent to them the victory.

They left the ploughshare in the mould,
Their flocks and herds without a fold,
The sickle in the unshorn grain,
The corn, half-garnered, on the plain,
And mustered in their simple dress,
For wrongs to seek a stern redress;
To right those wrongs, come weal, come woe;
To perish, or o'ercome their foe.

And where are ye, oh fearless men?
    And where are ye to-day?
I call:—the hills reply again
    That ye have passed away.
That on old Bunker's lonely height,
    In Trenton and on Monmouth's ground,
The grass grows green, the harvest bright,
    Above each soldier's mound!

The bugle's wild and warlike blast
    Shall muster them no more;
An army now might thunder past,
    And they not heed its roar.

The starry flag 'neath which they fought
In many a bloody day,
From their old graves shall rouse them not,
For they have passed away.

Ex. CXXXIX.—*APPEAL TO THE REPUBLIC.*

JOSEPH STORY.*

WHEN we reflect on what has been, and is now, is it possible not to feel a profound sense of the responsibleness of this republic to all future ages? What vast motives press upon us for lofty efforts! What brilliant prospects invite our enthusiasm! What solemn warnings at once demand our vigilance, and moderate our confidence!

We stand the latest, and, if we fail, probably the last experiment of self-government by the people. We have begun it under circumstances of the most auspicious nature. We are in the vigor of youth. Our growth has never been checked by the oppressions of tyranny. Our constitutions have never been enfeebled by the vices or luxuries of the old world. Such as we are, we have been from the beginning; simple, hardy, intelligent, accustomed to self-government and self-respect.

The Atlantic rolls between us and any formidable foe. Within our own territory, stretching through many degrees of latitude and longitude, we have the choice of many products, and many means of independence. The government is mild. The press is free. Religion is free. Knowledge reaches, or may reach, every home. What fairer prospect of success could be presented? What means more adequate to accomplish the sublime end? What more is necessary than for the people to preserve what they themselves have created?

Already has the age caught the spirit of our institutions. It has already ascended the Andes, and snuffed the breezes of both oceans. It has infused itself into the life-blood of Europe, and warmed the sunny plains of France, and the low lands of Holland. It has touched the philosophy of Ger-

* Judge of the Supreme Court of the United States; a distinguished jurist and writer on jurisprudence. Judge Story was a native of Massachusetts.

many and the North, and, moving onward to the South, has opened to Greece the lessons of her better days.

Can it be that America, under such circumstances, can betray herself? that she is to be added to the catalogue of republics, the inscription of whose ruins is, "They were, but they are not!" Forbid it, my countrymen; forbid it, Heaven!

I call upon you, fathers, by the shades of your ancestors, by the dear ashes which repose in this precious soil, by all you are, and all you hope to be; resist every project of disunion; resist every encroachment upon your liberties; resist every attempt to fetter your consciences, or smother your public schools, or extinguish your system of public instruction.

I call upon you, mothers, by that which never fails in woman—the love of your offspring; teach them, as they climb your knees or lean upon your bosom, the blessing of liberty. Swear them at the altar, as with their baptismal vows, to be true to their country, and never to forget or forsake her.

I call upon you, young men, to remember whose sons you are—whose inheritance you possess. Life can never be too short, which brings nothing but disgrace and oppression. Death can never come too soon, if necessary in defence of the liberties of your country.

I call upon you, old men, for your counsel, your prayers and your benedictions. May your gray hairs not go down in sorrow to the grave, with the recollection that you have lived in vain. May your last sun not sink in the west upon a nation of slaves.

No! I read in the destiny of my country far better hopes, far brighter visions. We who are now assembled here, must soon be gathered to the congregation of other days. The time for our departure is at hand, to make way for our children upon the theatre of life. May God speed them and theirs. May he who at the distance of another century shall stand here to celebrate this day, still look round upon a free, happy and virtuous people. May he have reason to exult as we do! May he, with all the enthusiasm of truth as well as of poetry, exclaim that here is still his country—

"Zealous, yet modest; innocent, though free;
Patient of toil; serene amidst alarms;
Inflexible in faith; invincible in arms."

Ex. CXL.—*NATIONAL RECOLLECTIONS THE FOUNDATION OF NATIONAL CHARACTER.*

EDWARD EVERETT.*

How is the spirit of a free people to be formed, and animated, and cheered, but out of the store-house of its historic recollections? Are we to be eternally ringing the changes upon Marathon and Thermopylæ; and going back to read, in obscure texts of Greek and Latin, of the exemplars of patriotic virtue? I thank God that we can find them nearer home, in our own country, on our own soil; that strains of the noblest sentiment that ever swelled in the breast of man are breathing to us out of every page of our country's history, in the native eloquence of our mother tongue; that the colonial and provincial councils of America exhibit to us models of the spirit and character which gave Greece and Rome their name and their praise among nations. Here we ought to go for our instruction; the lesson is plain, it is clear, it is applicable. When we go to ancient history, we are bewildered with the difference of manners and institutions. We are willing to pay our tribute of applause to the memory of Leonidas, who fell nobly for his country in the face of his foe. But when we trace him to his home, we are confounded at the reflection, that the same Spartan heroism to which he sacrificed himself at Thermopylæ, would have led him to tear his own child, if it happened to be a sickly babe, the very object for which all that is kind and good in man rises up to plead, from the bosom of its mother, and carry it out to be eaten by the wolves of Taygetus. We feel a glow of admiration at the heroism displayed at Marathon, by the ten thousand champions of invaded Greece; but we can not forget that the tenth part of the number were slaves, unchained from the work-shops and door-posts of their masters, to go out and fight the battles of freedom. I do not mean that these examples are to destroy the interest with

---

* For many years Mr. Everett was best known among us as the statesman, the orator and the man of letters; but during the latter part of his life he added to these titles the far nobler one of a disinterested patriot. He contributed nearly one hundred thousand dollars, the proceeds of lectures and other literary labors, towards purchasing Washington's estate of Mount Vernon, together with the family tomb upon it, as a gift to the nation; and throughout the war of the Rebellion devoted his best energies and efforts to the advancement of the Union cause. He died in 1864, deeply lamented.

which we read the history of ancient times; they possibly increase that interest by the very contrast they exhibit. But they do warn us, if we need the warning, to seek our great practical lessons of patriotism at home; out of the exploits and sacrifices of which our own country is the theatre; out of the characters of our own fathers. Them we know, the high-souled, natural, unaffected citizen heroes. We know what happy firesides they left for the cheerless camp. We know with what pacific habits they dared the perils of the field. There is no mystery, no romance, no madness, under the name of chivalry, about them. It is all resolute, manly resistance, for conscience and liberty's sake, not merely of an overwhelming power, but of all the force of long-rooted habits and native love of order and peace.

Above all, their blood calls to us from the soil which we tread; it beats in our veins; it cries to us not merely in the thrilling words of one of the first victims in this cause: "My sons, scorn to be slaves!" but it cries with a still more moving eloquence, "My sons, forget not your fathers!"

Ex. CXLI.—*THE YOUNG AMERICAN.*

ALEXANDER H. EVERETT.*

Scion of a mighty stock!
Hands of iron—heart of oak—
Follow with unflinching tread
Where thy noble fathers led!

Craft and subtle treachery,
Gallant youth! are not for thee;
Follow then in words and deeds
Where the God within thee leads.

Honesty, with steady eye,
Truth and pure simplicity,
Love that gently winneth hearts,
These shall be thy only arts.

* An elder brother of Edward Everett. He was an accomplished man and able writer, and filled many diplomatic situations.

Prudent in the council train,
Dauntless on the battle plain,
Ready at the country's need
For her glorious cause to bleed.

Let thy noble motto be
GOD, OUR COUNTRY, LIBERTY!
Planted on Religion's rock,
Thou shalt stand in every shock.

Laugh at danger far or near!
Spurn at baseness, spurn at fear!
Still, with persevering might,
Spread the truth and do the right!

So shall Peace, a charming guest,
Dove-like in thy bosom rest;
So shall Honor's steady blaze
Beam upon thy closing days.

Happy if celestial favor
Smile upon thy high endeavor;
Happy if it be thy call
In the holy cause to fall.

Ex. CXLII.—*THE SWORD AND THE STAFF.*

Speech in Congress on the Presentation of these Memorials.

JOHN QUINCY ADAMS.

THE Sword of Washington! The Staff of Franklin! Oh, Sir, what associations are linked in adamant with these names! Washington, whose sword was never drawn but in the cause of his country, and never sheathed when wielded in his country's defence! Franklin, the philosopher of the thunderbolt, the printing-press, and the ploughshare! What names are these in the scanty catalogue of the benefactors of human kind! Washington and Franklin! What other two men whose lives belong to the eighteenth century of Christendom, have left a deeper impression of themselves upon the age in which they lived, and upon all after time?

Washington, the warrior and the legislator! In war,

contending by the wager of battle for the independence of his country, and for the freedom of the human race,—ever manifesting amid its horrors, by precept and by example, his reverence for the laws of peace and for the tenderest sympathies of humanity;—in peace, soothing the ferocious spirit of discord among his own countrymen into harmony and union, and giving to that very sword, now presented to his country, a charm more potent than that attributed in ancient times to the lyre of Orpheus.

Franklin! the mechanic of his own fortune; teaching in early youth, under the shackles of indigence, the way to wealth, and in the shade of obscurity, the path to greatness; in the maturity of manhood, disarming the thunder of its terrors, the lightning of its fatal blast, and wresting from the tyrant's hand the still more afflictive sceptre of oppression; while descending into the vale of years, traversing the Atlantic Ocean, braving in the dead of winter the battle and the breeze, bearing in his hand the Charter of Independence, which he had contributed to form, and tendering, from the self-created nation to the mightiest monarchs of Europe, the olive-branch of peace, the mercurial wand of commerce, and the amulet of protection and safety to the man of peace, on the pathless ocean, from the inexorable cruelty and merciless rapacity of war.

And, finally, in the last stage of life, with fourscore winters upon his head, under the torture of an incurable disease, returning to his native land; closing his days as the chief magistrate of his adopted commonwealth, after contributing by his counsels, under the Presidency of Washington, and recording his name, under the sanction of devout prayer invoked by him to God, to that Constitution under the authority of which we are here assembled as the representatives of the North American people, to receive, in their name and for them, these venerable relics of the wise, the valiant and the good founders of our great confederated republic,—these sacred symbols of our golden age. May they be deposited among the archives of our government! And may every American who shall hereafter behold them, ejaculate a mingled offering of praise to that Supreme Ruler of the Universe by whose tender mercies our Union has been hitherto preserved through all the vicissitudes and revolutions of this turbulent world; and of prayer for the continuance of these blessings by the dispensations of Providence, to our beloved country, from age to age till time shall be no more!

Ex. CXLIII.—CONSEQUENCES OF AMERICAN INDEPENDENCE.

VIRGIL MAXCY.

In a full persuasion of the excellency of our government, let us shun those vices which tend to its subversion, and cultivate those virtues which will render it permanent, and transmit it in full vigor to all succeeding ages. Let not the haggard forms of intemperance and luxury ever lift up their destroying visages in this happy country. Let economy, frugality, moderation, and justice at home and abroad, mark the conduct of all our citizens. Let it be our constant care to diffuse knowledge and goodness through all ranks of society. The people of this country will never be uneasy under its present form of government, provided they have sufficient information to judge of its excellence. No nation under heaven enjoys so much happiness as the Americans. Convince them of this, and will they not shudder at the thought of subverting their political constitution, of suffering it to degenerate into aristocracy or monarchy? Let a sense of our happy situation awaken in us the warmest sensations of gratitude to the Supreme Being. Let us consider Him as the author of all our blessings, acknowledging Him as our beneficent parent, protector and friend. The predominant tendency of His providences towards us as a nation, evinces His benevolent designs. Every part of His conduct speaks in a language plain and intelligible. Let us open our ears, let us attend, let us be wise.

While we celebrate the anniversary of our independence, let us not pass over in silence the defenders of our country. Where are those brave Americans whose lives were cloven down in the tempest of battle? Are they not bending from their bright abodes? A voice from the altar cries, "These are they who loved their country—these are they who died for liberty!" We now reap the fruit of their agony and toil. Let their memory be eternally embalmed in our bosoms. Let the infants of all posterity prattle their fame, and drop tears of courage for their fate.

The consequences of American independence will soon reach to the extremities of the world. The shining car of Freedom will soon roll over the necks of kings, and bear off the oppressed to scenes of liberty and peace. The clamors of war will cease under the whole heaven. The tree of liberty will shoot its top up to the sun. Its boughs will hang over the ends of the world, and wearied nations will lie down and rest under its shade.

Here in America stands the asylum for the distressed and persecuted of all nations. The vast temple of Freedom rises majestically fair. Founded on a rock, it will remain unshaken by the force of tyrants, undiminished by the flight of time. Long streams of light emanate through its portals, and chase the darkness from distant nations. Its turrets will swell into the heavens, rising above every tempest; and the pillar of divine glory, descending from God, will rest for ever on its summit.

Ex. CXLIV.—*DEVOTION TO COUNTRY.*

ALFRED B. STREET.

Hail to this planting of Liberty's tree!
Hail to the charter declaring us free!
Millions of voices are chanting its praises,
   Millions of worshippers bend at its shrine,
Wherever the sun of America blazes,
   Wherever the stars of our bright banner shine.

Sing to the heroes who breasted the flood,
That swelling, rolled o'er them—a deluge of blood.
Fearless they clung to the ark of the nation,
   And dashed on 'mid lightning, and thunder and blast,
Till Peace, like the dove, brought her branch of salvation,
   And Liberty's mount was their refuge at last.

Bright is the beautiful land of our birth,
The home of the homeless all over the earth:
Oh, then, let us ever, with fondest devotion,
   The freedom our fathers bequeathed us, watch o'er,
Till the Angel shall stand on the earth and the ocean,
   And shout 'mid earth's ruins that Time is no more.

Ex. CXLV.—*AMERICAN HISTORY.*

GULIAN C. VERPLANCK.

The study of the history of most other nations fills the mind with sentiments not unlike those which the American traveller feels on entering the venerable and lofty cathedral of some proud old city of Europe. Its solemn grandeur, its vastness, its obscurity, strike awe to his heart. From the richly painted windows, filled with sacred emblems and strange antique forms, a dim religious light falls around. A thousand recollections of romance and poetry and legendary story, come thronging in upon him. He is surrounded by the tombs of the mighty dead, rich with the labors of ancient art, and emblazoned with the pomp of heraldry.

What names does he read upon them? Those of princes and nobles who are now remembered only for their vices, and of sovereigns at whose death no tears were shed, and whose memories lived not an hour in the affections of their people. There, too, he sees other names, long familiar to him for their guilty or ambiguous fame. There rest the blood-stained warrior of fortune,—the orator who was ever the apologist of tyranny,—great scholars, who were the pensioned flatterers of power, and poets who profaned the high gift of genius to pamper the vices of a corrupted court.

Our own history, on the contrary, like that poetical temple of fame reared by the imagination of Chaucer, and decorated by the taste of Pope, is almost exclusively dedicated to the memory of the truly great. Or rather, like the Pantheon of Rome, it stands in calm and severe beauty amid the ruins of ancient magnificence and "the toys of modern state." Within, no idle ornament encumbers its bold simplicity. The pure light of heaven enters from above, and sheds an equal and serene radiance around. As the eye wanders about its extent, it beholds the unadorned monuments of brave and good men who have bled or toiled for their country, or it rests on votive tablets inscribed with the names of the best benefactors of mankind.

We have been repeatedly told, and sometimes, too, in a tone of affected impartiality, that the highest praise which can fairly be given to the American mind, is that of possessing an enlightened selfishness; that if the philosophy and talents of this country, with all their effects, were forever swept into oblivion, the loss would be felt only by ourselves;

and that if to the accuracy of this general charge, the labors of Franklin present an illustrious, it is still but a solitary, exception.

The answer may be given confidently and triumphantly. Is it nothing for the universal good of mankind to have carried into successful operation a system of self-government uniting personal liberty, freedom of opinion and equality of rights, with national power and dignity such as had before existed only in the Utopian dreams of philosophers? Is it nothing in moral science to have anticipated, in sober reality, numerous plans of reform in civil and criminal jurisprudence, which are but now received as plausible theories by the politicians and economists of Europe? Is it nothing to have been able to call forth on every emergency, either in war or peace, a body of talents always equal to the difficulty? Is it nothing to have given the world examples of disinterested patriotism, of political wisdom, of public virtue; of learning, eloquence and valor, never exerted, save for some praiseworthy end? It is sufficient to have briefly suggested these considerations; every mind would anticipate me in filling up the details.

No—land of Liberty! thy children have no cause to blush for thee. What though the arts have reared few monuments among us, and scarce a trace of the Muse's footstep is found in the paths of our forests, or along the banks of our rivers—yet our soil has been consecrated by the blood of heroes, and by great and holy deeds of peace. Its wide extent has become one vast temple and hallowed asylum, sanctified by the prayers and blessings of the persecuted of every sect, and the wretched of all nations.

Land of Refuge! Land of Benedictions! Those prayers still arise and they still are heard: "May peace be within thy walls, and plenteousness within thy palaces!" "May there be no decay, no leading into captivity, and no complaining in thy streets!" "May truth flourish out of the earth, and righteousness look down from Heaven!"

Ex. CXLVI.—*ENNOBLING RECOLLECTIONS OF THE REVOLUTION.*

ROBERT Y. HAYNE.*

It has been usual, on occasions like the present, to give a history of the wrongs endured by our fathers. But we have prouder and more ennobling recollections connected with our revolution. They are to be found in the spirit displayed by our fathers when all their petitions had been slighted, their remonstrances despised, and their appeals to the generous sympathies of their brethren utterly disregarded. Yes, my friends, theirs was that pure and lofty spirit of devoted patriotism which never quailed beneath oppression, which braved all dangers, trampled upon difficulties, and in "the times which tried men's souls" taught them to be faithful to their principles, and to their country true; and which induced them in the very spirit of that Brutus whose mantle has fallen, in our own day, upon the shoulders of one so well able to wear it, to swear on the altar of liberty to give themselves up wholly to their country. There is one characteristic, however, of the American revolution, which constituting as it does its living principle, its proud distinction, and its crowning glory, can not be passed over in silence. It is this—that our revolution had its origin, not so much in the weight of actual oppression, as in the great principle, the sacred duty, of resistance to the exercise of unauthorized power. Other nations have been driven to rebellion by the iron hand of despotism, the insupportable weight of oppression, which leaving men nothing worth living for, has taken away the fear of death itself, and caused them to rush upon the spears of their enemies, or to break their chains upon the heads of their oppressors. But it was a tax of three pence a pound upon tea, imposed without right, which was considered by our ancestors as a burden too grievous to be borne. And why? Because they were men "who felt oppression's lightest finger as a mountain weight," and, in the fine language of that just and beautiful tribute paid to their character by one "whose praises will wear well"—they "judged of the grievance by the badness of the principle, they augured misgovernment at a distance, and snuffed the approach of tyranny in every tainted breeze—because they were men

* U. S. Senator from South Carolina.

who in the darkest hour could say to their oppressors, 'We have counted the cost, and find nothing so deplorable as voluntary slavery;' and who were ready to exclaim with the orator of Virginia, 'give me liberty or give me death!'" Theirs was the same spirit which inspired the immortal Hampden to resist, at the peril of his life, the imposition of ship-money; not because, as remarked by Burke, "the payment of twenty shillings would have ruined his fortune, but because the payment of half twenty shillings or the principle on which it was demanded, would have made him a slave." It was the spirit of liberty which still abides on the earth, and whose home is in the bosoms of the brave; which but yesterday, in "beautiful France," restored their violated charter; which even now burns brightly on the towers of Belgium, and has rescued Poland from the tyrant's grasp; making their sons—aye, and their daughters too—the wonder and the admiration of the world,—the pride and glory of the human race!

Ex. CXLVII.—*ODE.*

ANNE C. LYNCH.

Our patriot sires are gone;
   The conqueror Death lays low
Those veterans one by one
   Who braved each other foe;
Though on them rests Death's sable pall,
Yet o'er their deeds no shade shall fall.

No; ye of deathless fame!
   Ye shall not sleep unsung
While freedom hath a name,
   Or gratitude a tongue;
Yet shall your names and deeds sublime
Shine brighter through the mists of Time.

Oh, keep your armor bright,
   Sons of those mighty dead,
And guard ye well the right
   For which such blood was shed!
Your starry flag should only wave
O'er Freedom's home, or o'er your grave.

Ex. CXLVIII.—*BOND OF UNION BETWEEN NORTH AND SOUTH.**

Speech in Congress, Jan. 26, 1830.

DANIEL WEBSTER.

MR. PRESIDENT: The eulogium pronounced by the honorable gentleman on the character of the State of South Carolina, for her Revolutionary and other merits, meets my hearty concurrence. I shall not acknowledge that the honorable member goes before me in regard for whatever of distinguished talent, or distinguished character, South Carolina has produced. I claim part of the honor; I partake in the pride of her great names. I claim them for countrymen, one and all; the Laurenses, the Rutledges, the Pinckneys, the Sumters, the Marions,—Americans all, whose fame is no more to be hemmed in by State lines than their talents and patriotism were capable of being circumscribed within the same narrow limits.

In their day and generation they served and honored the country, and the whole country; and their renown is of the treasures of the whole country. Him whose honored name the gentleman himself bears,—does he esteem me less capable of gratitude for his patriotism, or sympathy for his sufferings, than if his eyes had first opened upon the light of Massachusetts instead of South Carolina? Sir, does he suppose it in his power to exhibit a South Carolina name so bright as to produce envy in my bosom? No, Sir; increased gratification and delight rather. I thank God that, if I am gifted with little of the spirit which is able to raise mortals to the skies, I have yet none, as I trust, of that other spirit which would drag angels down.

When I shall be found, Sir, in my place here in the

---

* This and the following extract are taken from Webster's "Reply to Hayne," which has been pronounced the most celebrated parliamentary speech ever delivered. Robert Y. Hayne, Senator from South Carolina, took occasion while speaking ostensibly on a bill relating to the public lands, to use contemptuous language towards Massachusetts and the New England States in general, and to advance the doctrine of "nullification," or the right of a State to resist the operation of any law which she considered unconstitutional or opposed to her interests, and declare it null and void. Mr. Webster's reply was a complete refutation of every point in his opponent's argument, and justly ranks as a masterpiece of parliamentary eloquence. From this splendid speech we can give only short extracts; but every American student who has access to Webster's writings should study it thoroughly as a whole. It is called in the collection of his published works, "Second Speech on Foot's Resolutions."

Senate or elsewhere, to sneer at public merit because it happens to spring up beyond the little limits of my own State or neighborhood; when I refuse, for such cause, or for any cause, the homage due to American talent, to elevated patriotism, to sincere devotion to liberty and the country; or if I see an uncommon endowment of Heaven, if I see extraordinary capacity and virtue in any son of the South, and if, moved by local prejudice or gangrened by State jealousy I get up here to abate the tithe of a hair from his just character and just fame, may my tongue cleave to the roof of my mouth!

Sir, let me refer to pleasing recollections, let me indulge in refreshing remembrance of the past; let me remind you that, in early times, no States cherished greater harmony, both of principle and feeling, than Massachusetts and South Carolina. Would to God that harmony might again return! Shoulder to shoulder they went through the Revolution, hand in hand they stood round the administration of Washington, and felt his great arm lean on them for support. Unkind feeling, if it exist, alienation and distrust are the growth, unnatural to such soils, of false principles since sown. They are weeds, the seeds of which that same great arm never scattered.

Mr. President, I shall enter on no encomium on Massachusetts. She needs none. There she is; behold her, and judge for yourselves. There is her history; the world knows it by heart. The past, at least, is secure. There is Boston, and Concord, and Lexington, and Bunker Hill; and there they will remain forever. The bones of her sons, falling in the great struggle for Independence, now lie mingled with the soil of every State from New England to Georgia; and there they will lie forever. And, Sir, where America raised its first voice, and where its youth was nurtured and sustained, there it still lives, in the strength of its manhood and full of its original spirit. If discord and disunion shall wound it, if party strife and blind ambition shall hawk at and tear it, if folly and madness, if uneasiness under salutary and necessary restraint, shall succeed in separating it from that Union by which alone its existence is made sure, it will stand, in the end, by the side of that cradle in which its infancy was rocked; it will stretch forth its arm with whatever of vigor it may still retain over the friends who gather round it; and it will fall at last, if fall it must, amidst the proudest monuments of its own glory, and on the very spot of its origin.

Ex. CXLIX.—*THE UNION MUST BE PRESERVED.*

Speech in Congress, January 26, 1830.

DANIEL WEBSTER.

MR. PRESIDENT: I have thus stated the reasons of my dissent to the doctrines which have been advanced and maintained. I am conscious of having detained you and the Senate much too long. I was drawn into the debate with no previous deliberation, such as is suited to the discussion of so grave and important a subject. But it is a subject of which my heart is full, and I have not been willing to suppress the utterance of its spontaneous sentiments. I can not, even now, persuade myself to relinquish it without expressing once more my deep conviction that, since it respects nothing less than the union of the States, it is of most vital and essential importance to the public happiness.

I profess, sir, in my career hitherto, to have kept steadily in view the prosperity and the honor of the whole country, and the preservation of the Federal Union. I have not allowed myself to look beyond the union, to see what might be hidden in the dark recess behind. I have not coolly weighed the chances of preserving liberty, when the bonds that unite us together shall be broken asunder. I have not accustomed myself to hang over the precipice of disunion, to see whether, with my short sight, I can fathom the depths of the abyss below; nor could I regard him as a safe counsellor in the affairs of this government, whose thoughts should be mainly bent on considering, not how the Union should be preserved, but how tolerable might be the condition of the people when it shall be broken up and destroyed.

While the union lasts, we have high, exciting, gratifying prospects spread out before us, for us and our children. Beyond that, I seek not to penetrate the veil. God grant, that in my day at least, the curtain may not rise! God grant that on my vision never may be opened what lies behind! When my eyes shall be turned to behold, for the last time, the sun in heaven, may I not see him shining on the broken and dishonored fragments of a once glorious union; on States dissevered, discordant, belligerent; on a land rent with civil feuds, or drenched, it may be, in fraternal blood! Let their last feeble and lingering glance rather behold the gorgeous ensign of the republic, now known and honored throughout the earth, still full high advanced, its arms and trophies streaming in their original lustre, not a star obscured, not a stripe erased or polluted, bearing for its motto no such miserable interrogatory as *What is all this worth?* or those other words of delusion and folly, *Liberty first, and union afterward;* but everywhere spread all over in characters of living light, blazing on all its ample folds as they float over the sea, and over the land, and in every wind under the whole heavens, that other sentiment, dear to every true American heart: LIBERTY AND UNION, NOW AND FOREVER, ONE AND INSEPARABLE.

Ex. CL.—*UNION AND LIBERTY.*

THOMAS S. GRIMKE.*

HAIL, our country's natal morn!
Hail, our spreading kindred born!
Hail, thou banner, not yet torn,
    Waving o'er the free!
While this day in festal throng
Millions swell the patriot song,
Shall not we thy notes prolong,
    Hallowed jubilee?

Who would sever Freedom's shrine?
Who would draw th' invidious line?
Though, by birth, one spot be mine,
    Dear is all the rest!
Dear to me the South's fair land,
Dear the central mountain band,
Dear New England's rocky strand,
    Dear the prairied West!

By our altars pure and free,
By our law's deep-rooted tree,
By the Past's dread memory,
    By our WASHINGTON!—

---

* A patriotic son of South Carolina. This poem was written July 4th, 1832, in the midst of the excitement attending the discussion of "nullification." Mr. Grimké, with many others of his fellow-citizens, strongly opposed this doctrine, and used all the eloquence of his tongue and pen in favor of maintaining the authority of the general government in contradistinction to what were called "State Rights."

By our common kindred tongue,
By our hopes, bright, buoyant, young,
By the ties of country strong—
    We will still be one!

Fathers, have ye bled in vain?
Ages, must ye droop again?
Maker! shall we rashly stain
    Blessings sent by Thee?
No! Receive our solemn vow,
While before Thy throne we bow,
Ever to maintain, as now,
    Union and Liberty!

Ex. CLI.—*APPEAL TO THE PEOPLE OF SOUTH CAROLINA.**

December 11th, 1832.

ANDREW JACKSON.

FELLOW-CITIZENS OF MY NATIVE STATE: Contemplate the condition of that country of which you form an important part. Consider its government, uniting in one bond of common interest and general protection so many different States, giving to all their inhabitants the proud title of American citizens, protecting their commerce, securing their literature and their arts, facilitating their intercommunication, defending their frontiers, and making their name respected in the remotest parts of the earth. Consider the extent of its territory, its increasing and happy population, its advance in arts which render life agreeable, and the sciences which elevate the mind.

See education spreading the light of religion, humanity, and general information into every cottage in this wide extent of our Territories and States. Behold it as the asylum

---

* This earnest appeal is the conclusion of a proclamation to the people of South Carolina, in which President Jackson stated his determination to enforce the U. S. Revenue Laws, notwithstanding the action of the S. C. Convention, which had just declared them null and void in that State. He agreed with the Convention in thinking that the Tariff Bill, which was the point in dispute, ought to be modified, but insisted that while the laws stood they should be obeyed. The matter was finally settled by a compromise, but not until after the passage of a bill by Congress enabling the President to maintain the supremacy of the law by force, if necessary.

where the wretched and the oppressed find a refuge and support. Look on this picture of happiness and honor, and say, "We, too, are citizens of America!" Carolina is one of these proud States. Her arms have defended, her best blood has cemented, this happy union! And then add, if you can without horror and remorse, "This happy union we will dissolve,—this picture of peace and prosperity we will deface,—this free intercourse we will interrupt,—these fertile fields we will deluge with blood,—the protection of that glorious flag we renounce,—the very name of Americans we discard!" And for what, mistaken men, for what do you throw away these inestimable blessings—for what would you exchange your share in the advantages and honor of the Union? For the dream of a separate independence—a dream interrupted by bloody conflicts with your neighbors, and a vile dependence on a foreign power. If your leaders could succeed in establishing a separation, what would be your situation? Do our neighboring republics, every day suffering some new revolution, or contending with a new insurrection,—do they excite your envy? But the dictates of a high duty oblige me solemnly to announce that you can not succeed.

The laws of the United States must be executed. I have no discretionary power on the subject; my duty is emphatically pronounced in the Constitution. Those who told you that they might peaceably prevent their execution, deceived you; they could not have been deceived themselves. They knew that a forcible opposition could alone prevent the execution of the laws, and they knew that such opposition must be repelled. Their object is disunion, but be not deceived by names; disunion by armed force is *treason.* Are you really ready to incur its guilt? If you are, on the heads of the instigators of the act be the dreadful consequences; on their heads be the dishonor, but on yours may fall the punishment; on your unhappy State will inevitably fall all the evils of the conflict you force upon the government of your country. Its enemies have beheld our prosperity with a vexation they could not conceal; it was a standing refutation of their slavish doctrines, and they will point to our discord with the triumph of malignant joy.

But it is yet in your power to disappoint them. There is yet time to show that the descendants of the Pinckneys, the Sumters, the Rutledges, and of the thousand other names which adorn the pages of your Revolutionary history, will not abandon that Union to support which so many of them fought, and bled, and died. I adjure you, as you honor their memory,—as you love the cause of freedom to which they dedicated their lives,—as you prize the peace of your country, the lives of its best citizens, and your own fair fame,—to retrace your steps. Snatch from the archives of your State the disorganizing edict of its convention; bid its members to reassemble and promulgate the decided expressions of your will to remain in the path which alone can conduct you to safety, prosperity and honor; tell them that compared to disunion all evils are light, because that brings with it an accumulation of all; declare that you will never take the field, unless the star-spangled banner of your country shall float over you,—that you will not be stigmatized when dead, and dishonored and scorned while you live, as the authors of the first attack on the constitution of your country; its destroyers you cannot be.

Fellow citizens, the momentous case is before you. On your individual support of the government depends the decision of the great question it involves, whether our sacred Union will be preserved, and the blessing it secures to us as one people shall be perpetuated. No one can doubt that the unanimity with which that decision will be expressed will be such as to inspire new confidence in Republican institutions, and that the prudence, the wisdom and the courage which it will bring to their defence, will transmit them unimpaired and invigorated to our children.

May the Great Ruler of nations grant that the signal blessings with which he has favored ours may not, by the madness of party or personal ambition, be disregarded and lost, and may His wise Providence bring those who have produced this crisis to see their folly before they feel the misery of civil strife; and inspire a returning veneration for that Union which, if we may dare to penetrate, His designs, He has chosen as the only means of attaining the high destinies to which we may reasonably aspire.

Ex. CLII.—*INDIAN'S FAREWELL SPEECH.*

BLACK HAWK.*

You have taken me prisoner, with all my warriors. I am much grieved; for I expected, if I did not defeat you, to hold out much longer and give you more trouble before I surrendered. I tried hard to bring you into ambush, but your last general understood Indian fighting. I determined to rush on you, and fight you face to face. I fought hard. But your guns were well aimed. The bullets flew like birds in the air, and whizzed by our ears like the wind through the trees in winter.

My warriors fell around me; it began to look dismal. I saw my evil day at hand. The sun rose dim on us in the morning, and at night it sank in a dark cloud, and looked like a ball of fire. That was the last sun that shone on Black Hawk. His heart is dead, and no longer beats quick in his bosom. He is now a prisoner to the white men; they will do with him as they wish. But he can stand torture, and is not afraid of death. He is no coward. Black Hawk is an Indian.

He has done nothing of which an Indian ought to be ashamed. He has fought for his countrymen, against white men who came year after year to cheat them and take away their lands. You know the cause of our making war. It is known to all white men. They ought to be ashamed of it. The white men despise the Indians, and drive them from their homes. They smile in the face of the poor Indian to cheat him; they shake him by the hand to gain his confidence, to make him drunk, and to deceive him. We told them to let us alone, and keep away from us; but they followed on, and beset our paths, and coiled themselves among us like the snake. They poisoned us by their touch.

We called a great council, and built a large fire. The spirit of our fathers arose and spoke to us to avenge our wrongs or die. We set up the war-whoop, and dug up the tomahawk; our knives were ready, and the heart of Black Hawk swelled high in his bosom when he led his warriors to

---

* Black Hawk was an Indian Chief, commanding several tribes on the upper Mississippi, who in 1832 ravaged large portions of the western country, breaking up settlements and killing whole families. Generals Scott and Atkinson were sent to defend the frontier, and succeeded in scattering the hostile tribes and taking many prisoners, among whom was the dreaded chief.

battle. He is satisfied. He will go to the world of spirits contented. He has done his duty. His father will meet him there and commend him.

Black Hawk is a true Indian, and disdains to cry like a woman. He feels for his wife, his children and his friends. But he does not care for himself. He cares for the nation and the Indians. They will suffer. He laments their fate.

Farewell my nation! Black Hawk tried to save you and avenge your wrongs. He drank the blood of some of the whites. He has been taken prisoner, and his plans are stopped. He can do no more. He is near his end. His sun is setting, and he will rise no more. Farewell to Black Hawk!

Ex. CLIII.—*FARWELL ADDRESS TO THE PEOPLE OF THE UNITED STATES,* 1837.

ANDREW JACKSON.

FELLOW-CITIZENS: We have now lived almost fifty years under the Constitution framed by the patriots and sages of the Revolution. We have had our seasons of peace and of war, with all the evils which precede or follow a state of hostility with powerful nations. We encountered these trials with our Constitution yet in its infancy, and under the disadvantages which a new and untried government must always feel when it is called upon to put forth its whole strength, without the lights of experience to guide it, or the weight of precedents to justify its measures. But we have passed triumphantly through all these difficulties. Our Constitution is no longer a doubtful experiment, and at the end of nearly half a century, we find that it has preserved unimpaired the liberties of the people, secured the rights of property, and that our country has improved and is flourishing beyond any former example in the history of nations.

The progress of the United States, under our free and happy institutions, has surpassed the most sanguine hopes of the founders of the Republic. Our growth has been rapid beyond all former example, in numbers, in wealth, in knowledge, and in all the useful arts which contribute to the comfort and convenience of man; and from the earliest ages of history to the present day, there never have been thirteen millions of people associated together in one political body who enjoyed so much freedom and happiness as the people of these United States. You have no longer any cause to fear danger from abroad; your strength and power are well known throughout the civilized world, as well as the high and gallant bearing of your sons. It is from within, among yourselves; from cupidity, from corruption, from disappointed ambition and inordinate thirst for power, that factions will be formed and liberty endangered. It is against such designs, whatever disguise the actors may assume, that you have especially to guard yourselves. You have the highest of human trusts committed to your care. Providence has showered on this favored land blessings without number, and has chosen you as the guardians of freedom to preserve it for the benefit of the human race. May He who holds in his hands the destinies of nations make you worthy of the favors He has bestowed, and enable you, with pure hearts and pure hands, and sleepless vigilance, to guard and defend, to the end of time, the great charge He has committed to your keeping.

My own race is nearly run; advanced age and failing health warn me that before long I must pass beyond the reach of human events, and cease to feel the vicissitudes of human affairs. I thank God that my life has been spent in a land of liberty, and that He has given me a heart to love my country with the affection of a son. And, filled with gratitude for your constant and unwavering kindness, I bid you a last and affectionate farewell.

Ex. CLIV.—*THE UNITED STATES FLAG.*

WILLIAM ROSS WALLACE.

FLAG of the valiant and the tried,
Where Marion fought and Warren died!
Flag of the mountain and the lake,
  Of rivers rolling to the sea,
In that broad grandeur fit to make
  The symbols of eternity!
Oh, fairest flag! oh, dearest land!
  Who shall your banded children sever?
God of our fathers! here we stand,
A true, a free, a fearless band,

Heart pressed to heart, hand linked to hand,
  And swear that flag shall float forever!

Still glorious banner of the free,
The nations turn with hope to thee!
And when thy mighty shadow falls
Along the armory's trophied walls,
  The ancient trumpets long for breath;
The dinted sabres fiercely start
  To vengeance from each clanging sheath,
As if they sought some traitor's heart!

Oh, sacred banner of the brave!
  Oh, standard of ten thousand ships!
Oh, guardian of Mount Vernon's grave,
  Come! let us press thee to our lips!
There is a heaving of the rocks,—
New England feels the patriot shocks;
There is a heaving of the lakes,—
New York, with all the West, awakes;
And lo! on high, the glorious shade
  Of Washington lights all the gloom,
And points unto these words, arrayed
  In fire around his tomb:

"Americans! your fathers shed
  Their blood to rear the Union's fane;
For this that peerless banner spread
  On many a gory plain!
Americans! let no one dare,
  On mountain, valley, prairie, flood,
By hurling down that temple there,
  To desecrate that blood!
The Right shall live, while faction dies;
  All traitors draw a fleeting breath!
But patriots drink, from God's own eyes,
  Truth's light that conquers Death!"

Then, dearest flag and dearest land,
  Who shall your banded children sever?
God of our fathers! here we stand,
A true, a free, a fearless band,
Heart pressed to heart, hand linked in hand,
  And swear that flag shall float forever!

Ex. CLV.—*SECESSION DOCTRINES COMBATED.*

Speech in Congress, March 12, 1838.

DANIEL WEBSTER.

MR. PRESIDENT: The honorable member from Carolina * habitually indulges in charges of usurpation and oppression against the government of his country. He daily denounces its important measures in the language in which our Revolutionary fathers spoke of the oppressions of the mother country. Not merely against executive usurpation, either real or supposed, does he utter these sentiments, but against laws of Congress passed by large majorities; laws sanctioned for a course of years by the people. These laws he proclaims every hour to be but a series of acts of oppression. He speaks of them as if it were an admitted fact that such is their true character. This is the language he uses, these are the sentiments he expresses, to the rising generation around him. Are they sentiments and language which are likely to impress our children with the love of union, to enlarge their patriotism, or to teach them and to make them feel that their destiny has made them common citizens of one great Republic!

A principal object in his late political movements, the gentleman tells us, was to unite the entire South; and against whom, or against what, does he wish to unite the entire South? Is not this the very essence of local feeling and local regard? Is it not the acknowledgment of a wish and object to create political strength, by uniting political opinions geographically? While the gentleman wishes to unite the entire South, I pray to know, Sir, if he expects me to turn towards the polar star, and, acting on the same principle, to utter a cry of Rally! to the whole North? Heaven forbid! To the day of my death neither he nor others shall hear such a cry from me.

Finally, the honorable member declares that he shall now march off, under the banner of State rights! March off from whom? March off from what? We have been contending for great principles. We have been struggling to maintain the liberty and to restore the prosperity of the country; we have made these struggles here, in the national councils, with the old flag—the true American flag, the eagle and the stars

---

* John C. Calhoun.

and stripes—waving over the chamber in which we sit. He now tells us, however, that he marches off under the State-rights banner!

Let him go. I remain. I am where I have ever been, and ever mean to be. Here, standing on the platform of the general Constitution,—a platform broad enough, and firm enough, to uphold every interest of the whole country,—I shall still be found. Intrusted with some part in the administration of that Constitution, I intend to act in its spirit, and in the spirit of those who framed it. Yes, Sir. I would act as if our fathers, who formed it for us, and who bequeathed it to us, were looking on me,—as if I could see their venerable forms bending down to behold us from the abodes above! I would act, too, as if the eye of posterity was gazing on me.

Standing thus, as if in the full gaze of our ancestors and our posterity, having received this inheritance from the former to be transmitted to the latter, and feeling that, if I am born for any good in my day and generation, it is for the good of the whole country,—no local policy, no local feeling, no temporary impulse, shall induce me to yield my foothold on the constitution and the Union. I move off under no banner not known to the whole American people, and to their Constitution and laws. No, Sir! These walls, these columns,

"Fly
From their firm base as soon as I."

I came into public life, Sir, in the service of the United States. On that broad altar my earliest and all my public vows have been made. I propose to serve no other master. So far as depends on any agency of mine, they shall continue *united* States; united in interest and in affection; united in everything in regard to which the Constitution has decreed their union; united in war, for the common defence, the common renown, and the common glory; and united, compacted, knit firmly together, in peace, for the common prosperity and happiness of ourselves and our children!

Ex. CLVI.—*THE BIRTH-DAY OF WASHINGTON.*

RUFUS CHOATE.

THE birth-day of the "Father of his Country!" May it ever be freshly remembered by American hearts! May it ever reawaken in them a filial veneration for his memory; ever rekindle the fires of patriotic regard to the country which he loved so well; to which he gave his youthful vigor and his youthful energy during the perilous period of the early Indian warfare; to which he devoted his life, in the maturity of his powers, in the field; to which again he offered the counsels of his wisdom and his experience, as President of the Convention that framed our Constitution; which he guided and directed while in the chair of state, and for which the last prayer of his earthly supplication was offered up when the moment came for him so well, so grandly and so calmly, to die.

He was the first man of the time in which he grew. His memory is first and most sacred in our love; and ever hereafter, till the last drop of blood shall freeze in the last American heart, his name shall be a spell of power and might. "First in the hearts of his countrymen!" Yes, first! He has our first and most fervent love. Undoubtedly there were brave and wise and good men before his day, in every colony. But the American Nation, as a nation, I do not reckon to have begun before 1774. And the first love of that young America was Washington. The first word she lisped was his name. Her earliest breath spoke it. It is still her proud ejaculation; and it will be the last gasp of her expiring life!

Yes! others of our great men have been appreciated—many admired by all. But him we love. About and around him we call up no discordant and dissatisfied elements,—no sectional prejudice nor bias,—no party, no creed, no dogma of politics. None of these shall assail him. When the storm of battle blows darkest and rages highest, the memory of Washington shall nerve every American arm, and cheer every American heart. It shall re-illumine that Promethean fire, that sublime flame of patriotism, that devoted love of country, which his words have commended, which his example has consecrated.

> Where may the wearied eye repose,
>   When gazing on the great,
> Where neither guilty glory glows,
>   Nor despicable state?

> Yes, one—the first, the last, the best,
> The Cincinnatus of the West,
>   Whom Envy dared not hate,
>   Bequeathed the name of Washington,
> To make man blush there was but one."

Ex. CLVII.—"*E PLURIBUS UNUM.*"

JOHN PIERPONT.

The harp of the minstrel with melody rings,
  When the muses have taught him to touch and to tune it;
But though it may have a full octave of strings,
  To both maker and minstrel, the harp is a unit.
        So the power that creates
        Our Republic of States,
Into harmony brings them at different dates;
And the thirteen or thirty, the Union once done,
Are " E Pluribus Unum "—of many made one.

The science that weighs in her balance the spheres,
  And has watched them since first the Chaldean began it,
Now and then, as she counts them and measures their years,
  Brings into our system, and names, a new planet.
        Yet the old and new stars,
        Venus, Neptune and Mars,
As they drive round the sun their invisible cars,
Whether faster or slower their races they run,
Are "E Pluribus Unum "—of many made one.

Of that system of spheres, should but one fly the track,
  Or with others conspire for a general dispersion,
By the great central orb they would all be brought back,
  And each held in her place by a wholesome coercion.
        Should one daughter of light
        Be indulged in her flight,
They would all be engulfed by old Chaos and Night.
So must none of our sisters be suffered to run;
For, " E Pluribus Unum "—we all go, if one.

Let the demon of discord our melody mar,
  Or Treason's red hand rend our Union asunder;

Break one string from our harp, or extinguish one star,
  The whole system's ablaze with its lightning and thunder.
    Let the discord be hushed!
    Let the traitors be crushed,
Though Legion their name, all with victory flushed!
  For aye must our motto stand, fronting the sun: -
"E Pluribus Unum,"—though many, we're one!

Ex. CLVIII.—*REMONSTRANCE AGAINST THE WAR WITH MEXICO.*—1847.

THOMAS CORWIN.*

SIR: while the American president can command the army, thank God I can command the purse. He shall have no funds from me in the prosecution of such a war. That I conceive to be the duty of a senator. If it is my duty to grant whatever the president demands, for what am I here? Have an American Senate and House of Representatives nothing to do but to obey the bidding of the President, as the army he commands is compelled to obey under penalty of death? No, your Senate and House of Representatives were never elected for such purpose as that. They have been modelled on the good old plan of English liberty, and are intended to represent the English House of Commons, who curbed the proud power of the king in olden time, by witholding supplies if they did not approve the war. It was on this very proposition of controlling the executive power of England by witholding the money supplies, that the House of Orange came in; and by their accession to the throne commenced a new epoch in the history of England, distinguishing it from the old reign of the Tudors and Plantagenets and those who preceded it. Then it was that Parliament specified the purpose of appropriation, and since 1688 it has been impossible for a king of England to involve the people of England in a war, which your president, under your republican institutions, and with your republican constitution, has yet managed to do. He commands this army, and you must not withhold their supplies. He involves your country in wasteful and exterminating war against a nation with whom we have no cause of complaint, but Congress may say nothing!

* U. S. Senator from Ohio.

Sir, I scarcely understand the meaning of all this myself. If we are to vindicate our rights by battles, in bloody fields of war, let us do it. If that is not the plan, then let us call back our armies into our own territory, and propose a treaty with Mexico, based upon the proposition that money is better for her and land is better for us. Thus we can treat Mexico like an equal, and do honor to ourselves. But what is it you ask? You have taken from Mexico one-fourth of her territory, and you now propose to run a line comprehending about another third; and for what? What has Mexico got from you for parting with two-thirds of her domain? She has given you ample redress for every injury of which you have complained. She has submitted to the award of your commissioners, and, up to the time of the rupture with Texas, faithfully paid it. And for all that she has lost, what requital do we, her strong, rich, robust neighbor, make? Do we send our missionaries there to point the way to Heaven? Or do we send schoolmasters to pour daylight into her dark places, to aid her infant strength to conquer freedom, and reap the fruit of the independence herself alone had won? No, no; none of this do we. But we send regiments, storm towns, and our colonels prate of liberty in the midst of the solitudes their ravages have made. They proclaim the empty forms of social compact, to a people bleeding and maimed with wounds received in defending their hearthstones against the invasion of these very men who shoot them down and then exhort them to be free. Oh, Mr. President, are you not the light of the earth, if not its salt?

What, Sir, is the territory which you propose to wrest from Mexico? It is consecrated to the heart of the Mexican by many a well-fought battle with his old Castilian master. His Bunker Hills, and Saratogas, and Yorktowns, are there! The Mexican can say: "There I bled for liberty, and shall I surrender that consecrated home of my affections to the Anglo-Saxon invaders? What do they want with it? They have Texas already. They have possessed themselves of the territory between the Nueces and the Rio Grande. What else do they want? To what shall I point my children as memorials of that independence which I bequeath to them, when those battle-fields shall have passed from my possession?"

Sir, had one come and demanded Bunker Hill of the people of Massachusetts,—had England's lion ever showed himself there,—is there a man over thirteen and under ninety who would not have been ready to meet him; is there a river on this continent that would not have run red with blood; is there a field but would have been piled high with the unburied bones of slaughtered Americans, before these consecrated battle-fields of liberty should have been wrested from us?

Ex. CLIX.—*INJUSTICE OF THE WAR AGAINST MEXICO.*

JOHN M. BERRIEN.*

Sir: there is a responsibility direct, immediate, which may not be disregarded, which we are compelled to recognize. He is recreant from all the duties of an American senator, of an American citizen, who will not obey its behests. It is our responsibility to our immediate constituents—to the American people. To them we must render an account of the origin of this war, of the manner in which it is conducted, of the purposes for which it is prosecuted. That people, Sir, are awake to these inquiries. The excitement of feeling produced by the first intelligence from the Rio Grande, has given place to reflection. In the fervor of that feeling, they did not stop to inquire into the indignity offered to Mexico by the occupation of a disputed territory—of a territory which we had ourselves admitted to be the subject of negotiation—of the erection of a fort on the eastern bank of the Rio Grande, and the pointing of our cannon on the town of Matamoras. All this was forgotten in the excitement of the moment. American blood had been shed, and it must be avenged. They are calmer now; that feeling has been appeased. Whatever indignity was offered by Mexican officers to American arms, has been washed out by Mexican blood, which flowed so copiously at Palo Alto, at Resaca de la Palma, and at Monterey. Great God! Is not this sufficient atonement to Christian men? Sir, the indignity has been expiated; and now the inquiries are, with what views is this war still prosecuted? With what object has our army been pushed into the heart of Mexico? What do you expect to gain, which it may consist with your honor, or even with your interest, to receive? For what practical purposes, for what

* U. S. Senator from Georgia.

attainable objects, to what end, useful and honorable to the United States, is that army maintained there, and still urged onward, at such an expense of blood and treasure—loading us with a national debt, to be redeemed by a burdensome taxation, and involving a wanton sacrifice of the lives of our patriotic citizens who have flocked to the national standard? Will you go before the American people, gallant, generous, noble-minded as you know they are, and tell them the national honor has been redeemed, the shed blood of our people has been avenged by the gallantry of our army,—and that now we are fighting to despoil a stricken foe of such portion of her territory as may indemnify us for the expense of vindicating our honor? Believe me, they will reject the appeal with scorn and indignation. The inquiries I have presented will be reiterated in your ears; not perhaps by politicians—certainly not by party presses—assuredly not by those ardent spirits who, tired of the dull pursuits of civil life, seek military glory at whatever cost;—but they will be made by the patriotic yeomanry, by the merchant, the mechanic, the manufacturer, by men of all occupations—by the moral, religious, conservative portion of our countrymen, constituting in numbers a portion of the American people whose voice may not be disregarded. Mr. President, in the bustle of the public mart, in the quiet retirement of the domestic fireside, these inquiries and these reflections now press upon the minds of our countrymen with a force and intensity which I have no power to express, and I pray senators to receive, in the spirit in which it is offered, the warning which I give them, that they and that I must answer them.

Ex. CLX.—*CIVIL WAR DEPRECATED.**

Speech in Congress, Feb. 1850.

HENRY CLAY.

IF there be any who want civil war—who want to see the blood of any portion of our countrymen spilt—I am not one

* From Mr. Clay's speech urging the passage of his "Compromise Bill," or series of resolutions intended to allay the irritation on the subject of slavery which was threatening to divide the Union. His main propositions were, that

of them. I wish to see war of no kind; but above all, I do not desire to see a civil war. When war begins, whether civil or foreign, no human foresight is competent to foresee when, or how, or where it is to terminate. But when a civil war shall be lighted up in the bosom of our own happy land, and armies are marching, and commanders are winning their victories, and fleets are in motion on our coasts—tell me if you can, tell me if any human being can tell, its duration? God alone knows where such a war will end.

I do not desire to see the lustre of one single star dimmed of that glorious confederacy which constitutes our political sun; still less do I wish to see it blotted out, and its light obliterated forever. Has not the State of South Carolina been one of the members of this Union in "days that tried men's souls?" Have not her ancestors fought by the side of our ancestors? Have we not, conjointly, won together many a glorious battle? If we had to go into a civil war with such a State, how would it terminate? Whenever it should have terminated, what would be her condition? If she should ever return to the Union, what would be the condition of her feelings and affections? What the state of her heart and of the heart of her people? She has been with us before, when our ancestors mingled in the throng of battle; and as I hope our posterity will mingle with hers, for ages and centuries to come, in the the united defence of liberty, and for the honor and glory of the Union, I do not wish to see her degraded or defaced as a member of this confederacy.

In conclusion, allow me to entreat and implore each individual member of this body to bring into the consideration of this measure which I have had the honor of proposing, the same love of country which, if I know myself, has actuated me, and the same desire of restoring harmony to the Union which has prompted this effort. If we can forget for a moment— but that would be asking too much of human nature—if we

---

California should be admitted into the Union without restrictions with respect to slavery; that no provision should be made by law for the exclusion of slavery from any of the territory recently acquired from Mexico; that it was inexpedient to abolish it in the District of Columbia, under existing circumstances; that Congress had no power to prohibit or obstruct trade in slaves between the slaveholding States, though it might be prohibited within the District as far as concerned slaves brought from other places; and that more effectual provision ought to made by law for the restitution of fugitive slaves to their masters. After a long and stormy contest, bills were passed in accordance with these propositions, California having in the mean time adopted a State constitution excluding slavery from her limits.

could suppress, for one moment, party feelings and party causes,—and as I stand here before my God, I declare I have looked beyond these considerations, and regarded only the vast interests of this united people,—I should hope that under such feelings and with such dispositions, we may advantageously proceed to the consideration of this bill, and heal, before they are yet bleeding, the wounds of our distracted country.

Ex. CLXI.—*IMPOSSIBILITY OF PEACEABLE SECESSION.*

Speech on Mr. Clay's resolutions, March 7th, 1850.

DANIEL WEBSTER.

PEACEABLE secession! Sir, your eyes and mine are never destined to see that miracle. The dismemberment of this vast country without convulsions! The breaking up of the fountains of the great deep without ruffling the surface! Who is so foolish—I beg everybody's pardon—as to expect to see any such thing? Sir, he who sees the States now revolving in harmony around a common centre, and expects to see them quit their places and fly off without convulsion, may look the next hour to see the heavenly bodies rush from their spheres, and jostle against each other in the realms of space, without causing the crush of the universe. There can be no such thing as peaceable secession. It is an utter impossibility. Is the great Constitution under which we live, covering this whole country,—is it to be thawed and melted away by secession, as the snows on the mountain melt under the influence of a vernal sun, disappear almost unobserved, and run off? No, Sir! I will not state what might produce the disruption of the Union; but I see, as plainly as I see the sun in heaven, what that disruption itself must produce; I see that it must produce war, and such a war as I will not describe, *in its twofold character.*

Peaceable secession! The concurrent agreement of all the members of this great Republic to separate! Why, what would be the result? Where is the line to be drawn? What States are to secede? What is to remain American? What am I to be? An American no longer? Heaven forbid! Where is the flag of the Republic to remain?

Where is the eagle still to tower?—or is he to cower and shrink, and fall to the ground? Why, Sir, our ancestors—our fathers and our grandfathers, those of them that are yet living among us, with prolonged lives—would rebuke and reproach us, and our children and grandchildren would cry out shame upon us, if we of this generation should dishonor these ensigns of the power of the Government and the harmony of the Union, which is every day felt among us with so much joy and gratitude. What is to become of the army? What is to become of the navy? What is to become of the public lands? How is any one of thirty States to defend itself?

And now, Mr. President, instead of speaking of the possibility or utility of secession, instead of dwelling in these caverns of darkness, instead of groping with these ideas of all that is horrid and horrible, let us come out into the light of day; let us enjoy the fresh air of Liberty and Union; let us cherish those hopes which belong to us; let us devote ourselves to those great objects that are fit for our consideration and our action; let us raise our conceptions to the magnitude and the importance of the duties that devolve upon us; let our comprehension be as broad as the country for which we act, our aspirations as high as its certain destiny; let us not be pigmies in a case that calls for men. Let us make our generation one of the strongest and brightest links in that golden chain which is destined, I fondly believe, to grapple the people of all the States to this constitution for ages to come.

Ex. CLXII.—*ON THE ADMISSION OF CALIFORNIA INTO THE UNION.*

Speech in Congress, March 11th, 1850.

WILLIAM H. SEWARD.[*]

SIR: when the founders of the Republic of the South come to draw those fearful lines, they will indicate what portions of the continent are to be broken off from their connection with the Atlantic through the St. Lawrence, the Hudson,

[*] At that time U. S. Senator from New York.

the Delaware, the Potomac and the Mississippi; what portion of this people are to be denied the use of the lakes, the railroads and the canals, now constituting common and customary avenues of travel, trade and social intercourse; what families and kindred are to be separated and converted into enemies; and what States are to feel the horrors of perpetual border warfare, aggravated by interminable horrors of servile insurrection. When those portentous lines shall be drawn, they will disclose what portion of this people is to retain the army and the navy and the flag of so many victories; and on the other hand, what portion of the people is to be subjected to new and onerous imposts, direct taxes and forced loans and conscriptions, to maintain an opposing army, an opposing navy, and the new and hateful banner of sedition. Then the projectors of the new republic of the South will meet the question—and they may well prepare now to answer it—What is all this for? What intolerable wrong, what unfraternal injustice have rendered these calamities unavoidable? The answer will be: All this is done to secure the institution of African Slavery.

I have heard somewhat here, and almost for the first time in my life, of divided allegiance—of allegiance to the South and to the Union—of allegiance to States severally and to the Union. But for all this I know only one country and one sovereign—the United States of America and the American people. And such as is my allegiance, is the loyalty of every other citizen of the United States. As I speak he will speak when his time arrives. He knows no other country and no other sovereign. He has life, liberty, property, and precious affections and hopes for himself and his posterity, treasured up in the ark of the Union. He knows as well and feels as strongly as I do, that this government is his own government; that he is a part of it; that it was established for him and that it is maintained by him; that it is the only truly wise, just, free and equal government that has ever existed; that no other government could be so wise, just, free and equal; and that it is safer and more beneficent than any which time or change could bring into its place.

Ex. CLXIII.—*LIBERTY TRIUMPHANT.*

Address delivered on laying the corner-stone of the new wing of the Capitol at Washington, July 4th, 1851.

DANIEL WEBSTER.

ON the Fourth of July, 1776, the representatives of the United States of America, in Congress assembled, declared that these United Colonies are, and of right ought to be, free and independent States. This declaration, made by most patriotic and resolute men, trusting in the justice of their cause and the protection of Heaven, and yet made not without deep solicitude and anxiety,—has now stood for seventy-five years, and still stands. It was sealed in blood. It has met dangers, and overcome them; it has had enemies, and conquered them; it has had detractors, and abashed them all; it has had doubting friends, but it has cleared all doubts away; and now, to-day, raising its august form higher than the clouds, twenty millions of people contemplate it with hallowed love, and the world beholds it, and the consequences which have followed from it, with profound admiration.

This anniversary animates, and gladdens, and unites, all American hearts. On other days of the year we may be party men, indulging in controversies more or less important to the public good; we may have likes and dislikes, and we may maintain our political differences, often with warm and sometimes with angry feelings. But to-day we are Americans all; and all nothing but Americans. Every man's heart swells within him as he remembers that seventy-five years have rolled away and that the great inheritance of liberty is still his; his, undiminished and unimpaired; his, in all its original glory; his to enjoy, his to protect, and his to transmit to future generations.

If Washington was now among us,—if he could draw around him the shades of the great public men of his own days—patriots and warriors, orators and statesmen—and were to address us in their presence, would he not say to us: "Ye men of this generation, I rejoice and thank God for being able to see that our labors, and toils, and sacrifices were not in vain. You are prosperous,—you are happy,—you are grateful. The fire of liberty burns brightly and steadily in your hearts, while duty and law restrain it from bursting forth in wild and destructive conflagration. Cherish liberty as you love it; cherish its securities as you wish to preserve it. Maintain the Constitution which we labored so painfully to establish, and which has been to you such a source of inestimable blessings. Preserve the Union of the States, cemented as it was by our prayers, our tears and our blood. Be true to God, to your country, and to your duty. So shall the whole Eastern world follow the morning sun, to contemplate you as a nation; so shall all generations honor you as they honor us; and so shall the Almighty Power which so graciously protected us, and which now protects you, shower its everlasting blessings upon you and your posterity!"

Great father of your country! we heed your words; we feel their force, as if you now uttered them with lips of flesh and blood. Your example teaches us, your affectionate addresses teach us, your public life teaches us, the value of the blessings of the Union. Those blessings our fathers have tasted, and we have tasted, and still taste. Nor do we intend that those who come after us shall be denied the same high fruition. Our honor, as well as our happiness, is concerned. We can not, we dare not, we will not, betray our sacred trust. We will not filch from posterity the treasure placed in our hands to be transmitted to future generations. The bow that gilds the clouds in the heavens, the pillars that uphold the firmament, may disappear and fall away in the hour appointed by the will of God; but, until that day comes, or so long as our lives may last, no ruthless hand shall undermine that bright arch of Union and Liberty which spans the continent from Washington to California!

Ex. CLXIV.—*A FOURTH OF JULY ADDRESS ON SECESSION.**

FRANCIS LIEBER.

I ASK, will any one who desires secession for the sake of bringing about a Southern Confederacy, honestly aver that he would insist upon a provision in the new constitution securing the full right of secession whenever it may be desired by any member of the expected Confederacy?

* In the year 1850, after the admission of California as a free State, secession was urged by a strong party in South Carolina; but when a convention

To secede, then, requires revolution. Revolution for what? To remedy certain evils. And how are they to be remedied? It is a rule laid down among all the authorities of international law and ethics, that to be justified in going to war it is not sufficient that right be on our side. We must also have a fair prospect of success in our favor. This rule applies with far greater force to revolutions. The Jews who rose against Vespasian had all the right, I dare say, on their side; but their undertaking was not a warrantable one for all that. We, however, should we have sufficient right on our side for plunging into a revolution—for letting loose a civil war? Does the system against which we should rise contain within its own bosom no peaceful, lawful remedies?

We are often told that our forefathers plunged into a revolution, why should not we? Even if the two cases were comparable, which they are obviously not, I would ask, on the other hand, Are we to have a revolution every fifty years? Give me the Muscovite Czar rather than live under such a government, if government it could be called. I am a good swimmer, but I should not like to spend my life in whirlpools. And does the question of right or wrong, of truth and justice, go for nothing in revolutions?

Nor would the probability of success be in our favor, since it is certain that secession can not take place without war, and this war must end in one or the other of two ways. It must either kindle a general conflagration, or we must suffer, single-handed, the consequences of our rashness—bitter if we succeed in lopping ourselves off from the trunk, bitter if we can not succeed. Unsuccessful revolutions are not only misfortunes, they become stigmas. And what if the conflagration becomes general? Let us remember that it is a rule which pervades all history, because it pervades every house, that the enmity of contending parties is implacable and venomous in the same degree as they have previously stood near each other, or as nature intended the relation of good will to exist between them. It is the secret of all civil and religious wars;

was held in Charleston, it was found that the so-called Co-operationists—that is to say, those who were in favor of secession, indeed, but only conjointly with other States,—were in the majority. The Union-men of the State, desirous of doing, on their part, whatever might be in their power to strengthen the Union feeling, resolved, in 1851, to celebrate, by a mass-meeting at Greenville, S. C., the Fourth of July, a day already then frequently spoken of with little respect. Dr. Lieber, the author of the above address, was at that time Professor of History and Political Economy in the South Carolina College at Columbia.

it is the secret of divided families; it is the explanation of unrelenting hatred between those who once were bosom friends. Our war would be the repetition of the Peloponnesian War, or of the German Thirty Years' War, with still greater bitterness between the enemies, because it would be far more unnatural. It would shed the dismal glare of barbarism on the nineteenth century. Have they that long for separation forgotten that England, at first behind Germany, France, Italy, and Spain, rapidly outstripped all, because earlier united, without permitting the crown to absorb the people's rights? The separation of the South from the North would speedily produce a manifold disrupture, and bring us back to a heptarchy, which was no government of seven, but a state of things where many worried all. If there be a book which I would recommend, before all others, to read at this juncture, that book is Thucydides. It reads as if it had been written to make *us* pause; as if the orators introduced there had spoken expressly for our benefit; as if the fallacies of our days had all been used and exposed at that early time; and as if in that book a very mirror was held up for our admonition. Or we may peruse the history of cumbered, ailing Germany, deprived of unity, dignity, strength, wealth, peace, and liberty, because her unfortunate princes have pursued, with never-ceasing eagerness, what is called in that country *particularism*—that is, hostility of the parts to the whole of Germany, and after the downfall of Napoleon preferred the salvation of their petty sovereignties, conferred upon them by Napoleon, to the grandeur, peace, and strength of their common country. The history of Germany, the battlefield of Europe for these three centuries, will tell you what idol we should worship, were we to toss our blessings to the winds, and were we to deprive mankind of the proud example inviting to imitation.

I, for one, dare not do anything toward the disruption of the Union. Situated, as we are, between Europe and Asia, on a fresh continent, I see the finger of God in it. I believe our destiny to be a high, a great, and a solemn one, before which the discussions now agitating us shrink into much smaller dimensions than they appear if we pay exclusive attention to them. I have come to this country, and pledged a voluntary oath to be faithful to it, and I will keep this oath. This is my country from the choice of manhood, and not by chance of birth. In my position, as a servant of the state, in a public institution of education, I have imposed upon myself the duty of using my influence with the young neither one way nor the other in this discussion. I have scrupulously and conscientiously adhered to it in all my teaching and intercourse. There is not a man or a youth that can gainsay this. But I am a man and a citizen, and as such I have a right, or the duty, as the case may be, to speak my mind and my inmost convictions on solemn occasions before my fellow-citizens, and I have thus not hesitated to make these remarks. Take them, gentlemen, for what they may be worth. They are, at any rate, sincere and fervent; and, whatever judgment others may pass upon them, or whatever attacks may be levelled against them, no one will be able to say that they can have been made to promote any individual advantages. God save the commonwealth! God save the common land!

Ex. CLXV.—*ELEGY.*

On the death of Clay, Calhoun and Webster.—1850-52.

THOMAS BUCHANAN READ.

THE great are falling from us; to the dust
   Our flag droops midway, full of many sighs;
A nation's glory and a people's trust
   Lie in the ample pall where WEBSTER lies.

The great are falling from us, one by one,
   As fell the patriarchs of the forest trees;
The wind shall seek them vainly, and the sun
   Gaze on their vacant place for centuries.

Lo! Carolina mourns her steadfast pine,
   That like a mainmast towered above her realm;
And Ashland hears no more the voice divine
   From out the branches of her graceful elm;

And Marshfield's giant oak, whose stormy brow
   Oft turned the ocean-tempest from the West,
Lies on the shore it guarded long; and now
   Our startled eagle knows not where to rest.

Ex. CLXVI.—*THE AMERICAN SAILOR.*

R. F. STOCKTON.

LOOK to your history—that part of it which the world knows by heart—and you will find on its brightest page the glorious achievements of the American sailor. He, at least, has never disgraced his country; he has always been ready to serve her; he always has served her faithfully and effectually. He has often been weighed in the balance and never found wanting. The only fault ever found with him is that he sometimes fights ahead of his orders. The world has no match for him, man for man, and he asks no odds, he cares for no odds, when the cause of humanity or the glory of his country calls him to fight. Who, in the darkest days of our Revolution, carried your flag into the very chops of the British channel, bearded the lion in his den, and woke the echoes of old Albion's hills by the thunders of his cannon, and the shouts of his triumph? It was the American sailor. And the names of John Paul Jones and the Bon Homme Richard will go down the annals of time forever. Who struck the first blow that humbled the Barbary flag, which for a hundred years had been the terror of Christendom— drove it from the Mediterranean, and put an end to the infamous tribute it had been accustomed to extort? It was the American sailor. And the name of Decatur and his gallant companions will be as lasting as monumental brass. In your war of 1812, when your arms on shore were covered by disaster—when Winchester had been defeated, when the army of the Northwest had surrendered, and when the gloom of despondency hung like a cloud over the land, who first relit the fires of national glory, and made the welkin ring with the shouts of victory? It was the American sailor. And the names of Hull and the Constitution will be remembered as long as we have anything left worth remembering. That was no small event. The wand of Mexican prowess was broken on the Rio Grande. The wand of British invincibility was broken when the flag of the Guerrière came down. That one event was worth more to the Republic than all the money which has ever been expended for the navy. Since that day, the navy has had no stain upon its escutcheon, but has been cherished as your pride and glory. And the American sailor has established a reputation throughout the world—in peace and in war, in storm and in battle—for heroism and prowess unsurpassed. He shrinks from no danger, dreads no foe, and yields to no superior. No shoals are too dangerous, no seas too boisterous, no climate too rigorous for him. The burning sun of the tropics can not make him effeminate, nor can the eternal winter of the polar seas paralyze his energies. Foster, cherish, develop these characteristics, by a generous and paternal government. Excite his emulation and stimulate his ambition; inspire him with love and confidence for your service, and there is no achievement so arduous, no conflict so desperate, in which his actions will not shed glory upon his country And when the final struggle comes, as come it will, for the empire of the seas, you may rest with entire confidence in the persuasion that victory will be yours.

Ex. CLXVII.—*OLD IRONSIDES.**

OLIVER WENDELL HOLMES.

Aye! tear her tattered ensign down!
  Long has it waved on high,
And many an eye has danced to see
  That banner in the sky.
Beneath it rang the battle-shout,
  And burst the cannon's roar;
The meteor of the ocean air
  Shall sweep the clouds no more.

Her deck,—once red with heroes' blood,
  Where knelt the vanquished foe,
When winds were hurrying o'er the flood,
  And waves were white below,—
No more shall feel the victor's tread,
  Or know the conquered knee;
The harpies of the shore shall pluck
  The eagle of the sea!

Oh! better that her shattered hulk
  Should sink beneath the wave;

* The United States frigate Constitution, employed in the war of 1812-15.

Her thunders shook the mighty deep
  And there should be her grave.
Nail to the mast her holy flag,
  Set every threadbare sail,
And give her to the God of storms,
  The lightning and the gale!

Ex. CLXVIII.—*EIGHTY YEARS AGO.*

CHARLES SPRAGUE.

EIGHTY years have rolled away
Since that high, heroic day,
When our fathers, in the fray,
  Struck the conquering blow!
Praise to them—the bold who spoke;
Praise to them—the brave who broke
Stern oppression's galling yoke,
  Eighty years ago!

Pour the wine of sacrifice,
Let the grateful anthem rise;
Shall we e'er resign the prize?
  Never, never! No!
Hearts and hands shall guard those rights,
Bought on Freedom's battle heights,
Where he fixed his signal lights,
  Eighty years ago!

Swear it! by the mighty dead—
Those who counselled, those who led;
By the blood your fathers shed,
  By your mothers' woe;
Swear it by the living few,
Those whose breasts were scarred for you,
When to Freedom's ranks they flew,
  Eighty years ago!

By the joys that cluster round,
By our vales with plenty crowned,
By our hill-tops—holy ground,
  Rescued from the foe,

Where of old the Indian strayed,
Where of old the Pilgrim prayed,
Where the Patriot drew his blade,
    Eighty years ago!

Should again the war trump peal,
There shall Indian firmness seal
Pilgrim faith and patriot zeal,
    Prompt to strike the blow;
There shall Valor's work be done;
Like the sire shall be the son,
Where the fight was waged and won,
    Eighty years ago!

Ex. CLXIX.—*REASONS FOR CELEBRATING THE FOURTH OF JULY.*

From an address delivered at Chicago, July 10, 1858.

ABRAHAM LINCOLN.

WE are now a mighty nation; we are thirty or about thirty millions of people, and we own and inhabit about one-fifteenth part of the dry land of the whole earth. We run our memory back over the pages of history for about eighty-two years, and we discover that we were then a very small people in point of numbers, vastly inferior to what we are now, with a vastly smaller extent of country, with vastly less of everything we deem desirable among men; we look upon the change as exceedingly advantageous to us and our posterity, and we fix upon something that happened a long way back as in some way or other being connected with this rise of prosperity. We find a race of men living in that day whom we claim as our fathers and grandfathers; they were iron men; they fought for the principle they were contending for; and we understand that by what they then did it has followed that the degree of prosperity we now enjoy has come to us. We hold an annual celebration to remind ourselves of all the good done in this process of time; of how it was done and who did it, and how we are historically connected with it, and we go from these meetings in better humor with ourselves; we feel more attached the one to the other, and more firmly bound to the country we inhabit. In every way we are better men for these celebrations. But after we have done all this, we have not yet reached the whole. There is something else connected with it. We have besides these, men among us descended by blood from our ancestors, who are not descendants of these men of the Revolution, they are men who have come from Europe—German, Irish, French and Scandinavian—who have come from Europe themselves, or whose ancestors have settled here, finding themselves our equals in all things. If they look back through this history to trace their connection with those days by blood, they find they have none; they can not carry themselves back into that glorious epoch and make themselves feel that they are part of us, but when they look through that old Declaration of Independence they find that those old men say: " We hold these truths to be self-evident, that all men are created equal;" and then they feel that the moral sentiment taught in that day evinces their relation to those men; that it is the father of all moral principle in them, and that they have a right to claim it as though they were blood of the blood and flesh of the flesh of the men who wrote that Declaration; and so they are. That is the electric cord in our Declaration which links the hearts of patriotic and liberty-loving men together; that will link those patriotic hearts as long as the love of freedom exists in the minds of men throughout the world.

CLXX.—*THE FOURTH OF JULY.*

J. PIERPONT.

Day of glory! welcome day!
Freedom's banners greet thy ray;
See! how cheerfully they play
   With thy morning breeze,
On the rocks where pilgrims kneeled,
On the heights where squadrons wheeled,
When a tyrant's thunder pealed
   O'er the trembling seas.

God of armies! Did thy " stars
In their courses" smite his cars,

Blast his arms and wrest his bars
    From the heaving tide?
On our standard, lo! they burn,
And when days like this return,
Sparkle o'er the soldier's urn
    Who for freedom died.

God of peace! whose spirit fills
All the echoes of our hills,
All the murmurs of our rills,
    Now the storm is o'er;
Oh, let freemen be our sons;
And let future WASHINGTONS
Rise, to lead their valiant ones,
    Till there's war no more.

By the patriot's hallowed rest,
By the warrior's gory breast,
Never let our graves be pressed
    By a despot's throne;
By the Pilgrims' toils and cares,
By their battles and their prayers,
By their ashes—let our heirs
    Bow to Thee alone.

Ex. CLXXI.—*THE CRISIS.*

JOHN GREENLEAF WHITTIER.

THE crisis presses on us; face to face with us it stands,
With solemn lips of question, like the Sphynx in Egypt's
    sands!
This day we fashion Destiny; our web of fate we spin;
This day for all hereafter choose we holiness or sin;
Even now from starry Gerizim, or Ebal's cloudy crown,
We call the dews of blessing, or the bolts of cursing down!

By all for which the martyrs bore their agony and shame;
By all the warning words of truth with which the Prophets
    came;
By the future which awaits us; by all the hopes which cast

Their faint and trembling beams across the blackness of the Past,
And in the awful name of Him who for earth's freedom died;
O, ye people! O, my brothers! let us choose the righteous side!

So shall the hardy pioneer go joyful on his way,
To wed Penobscot's waters to San Francisco's bay;
To make the rugged places smooth, and sow the vales with grain,
And bear, with Liberty and Law, the Bible in his train;
The mighty West shall bless the East, and sea shall answer sea,
And mountain unto mountain call, PRAISE GOD, FOR WE ARE FREE!

Ex. CLXXII.—*SECESSION AS VIEWED BY A VIRGINIAN.*

Speech in the House of Delegates of Virginia, March 30th, 1861.

JOSEPH SEGAR.

FOR what, Mr. Speaker, are we plunging into the dark abyss of disunion? In God's name, tell me! I vow I do not know, nor have I ever heard one sensible or respectable reason assigned for this harsh resort. We shall lose everything; gain nothing but war, blood, carnage, famine, starvation, social desolation, wretchedness in all its aspects, ruin in all its forms. We shall gain a taxation, to be levied by the new government, that will eat out the substance of the people, and make them "poor indeed." We shall gain alienation and distrust in all the dear relations of life. We shall gain ill-blood between father and son, and brother and brother, and neighbor and neighbor. Bereaved widowhood and helpless orphanage we shall gain to our heart's content. Lamentation, and mourning, and agonized hearts we shall gain in every corner where "wild war's deadly blast" shall blow. We shall gain the prostration—most lamentable calamity will it be—of that great system of internal development, which the statesmen of Virginia have looked to as the basis of all her future progress and grandeur, and the great hope of her speedy regeneration and redemption. We shall gain

repudiation, not that Virginia will ever be reluctant to redeem her engagements, but that she will be disabled by the heavy burdens of secession and war. We shall gain the blockade of our ports, and entire exclusion from the commerce, and markets, and storehouses of the world. We shall gain the hardest times the people of this once happy country have known since the War of Independence. I know not, indeed, of one single interest of Virginia that will not be wrecked by disunion. And, entertaining these views, I do shrink with horror from the very idea of the secession of the State. I can never assent to the fatal measure. No! I am for the Union yet. Call me submissionist, or traitor, or what else you will, I am for the Union while Hope's light flickers in the socket. In Daniel Webster's immortal words, give me "Liberty and Union—now and forever—one and inseparable."

Ex. CLXXIII.—*FALSE PROPHETS.*

EMELINE S. SMITH.

Who said that the stars on our banner were dim—
    That their glory had faded away?
Look up, and behold! how bright, through each fold,
    They are flashing and smiling to-day.
Some wandering meteors only have paled—
    They shot from their places on high;
But the fixed and the true still illumine the blue,
    And will while the Ages go by!

Who said the fair temple, so patiently reared
    By heroes, at Liberty's call,
Was built insecure—that it could not endure—
    And was tott'ring e'en now to its fall?
False, false, every word; for that fame is upheld
    By the stoutest of hearts and of hands;
Some columns unsound may have gone to the ground,
    But proudly the temple yet stands.

Ex. CLXXIV.—*SHALL WE GIVE UP THE UNION?*

Speech Delivered at New York, May 20, 1861.

DANIEL S. DICKINSON.

SHALL we then surrender to turbulence, and faction, and rebellion, and give up the Union with all its elements of good, all its holy memories, all its hallowed associations, all its blood-bought history?

> No! let the eagle change his plume,
> The leaf its hue, the flower its bloom—

But do not give up the Union. Preserve it to "flourish in immortal youth," until it is dissolved amid "the wreck of matter and the crash of worlds." Let the patriot and statesman stand by it to the last, whether assailed by foreign or domestic foes, and if he perishes in the conflict, let him fall like Rienzi, the last of the Tribunes, upon the same stand where he has preached liberty and equality to his countrymen.

Preserve it in the name of the Fathers of the Revolution—preserve it for its great elements of good—preserve it in the sacred name of liberty—preserve it for the faithful and devoted lovers of the Constitution in the rebellious States—those who are persecuted for its support, and are dying in its defence. Rebellion can lay down its arms to Government—Government can not surrender to rebellion.

Give up the Union!—" this fair and fertile plain, to batten on that moor!" Divide the Atlantic so that its tides shall beat in sections, that some spurious Neptune may rule in an ocean of his own—draw a line upon the sun's disc, that it may cast its beams upon earth in divisions—let the moon, like Bottom in the play, show but half its face—separate the constellation of the Pleiades and sunder the bands of Orion—but retain the Union!

Give up the Union, with its glorious flag—its stars and stripes, full of proud and pleasing and honorable recollections, for the spurious invention with no antecedents but the history of a violated Constitution and of lawless ambition! No! let us stand by the emblem of our fathers:

> "Flag of the free heart's hope and home,
> By angel hands to valor given,
> Thy stars have lit the welkin dome,
> And all thy hues were born in Heaven."

Give up the Union? Never! The Union shall endure, and its praises shall be heard, when its friends and its foes, those who support and those who assail, those who bared their bosoms in its defence, and those who aim their daggers at its heart, shall all sleep in the dust together. Its name shall be heard with veneration amid the roar of Pacific's waves, away upon the rivers of the North and East, where liberty is divided from monarchy, and be wafted in gentle breezes upon the Rio Grande. It shall rustle in the harvest and wave in the standing corn, on the extended prairies of the West, and be heard in the bleating folds and lowing herds upon a thousand hills. It shall be with those who delve in mines, and shall hum in the manufactories of New England, and in the cotton-gins of the South. It shall be proclaimed by the stars and stripes in every sea of the earth, as the American Union, one and indivisible; upon the great thoroughfares, wherever steam drives and engines throb and shriek, its greatness and perpetuity shall be hailed with gladness. It shall be lisped in the earliest words, and ring in the merry voices of childhood, and swell to heaven upon the song of maidens. It shall live in the stern resolve of manhood, and rise to the mercy-seat upon woman's gentle, availing prayer. Holy men shall invoke its perpetuity at the altars of religion, and it shall be whispered in the last accents of expiring age. Thus shall survive and be perpetuated the American Union, and when it shall be proclaimed that time shall be no more, and the curtain shall fall, and the good shall be gathered to a more perfect union, still may the destiny of our dear land recognize the conception, that

> "Perfumes, as of Eden, flowed sweetly along,
> And a voice, as of angels, awoke the glad song,
> Columbia, Columbia, to glory arise,
> The queen of the world, and the child of the skies!"

Ex. CLXXV.—*A SONG ON OUR COUNTRY AND HER FLAG.*

Written in 1861, on the Raising of the Flag on Columbia College, New York, after the Attack on Fort Sumter.

FRANCIS LIEBER.

> WE do not hate our enemy—
>   May God deal gently with us all.
> We love our land; we fight her foe;
>   We hate his cause, and that must fall.

A SONG ON OUR COUNTRY AND HER FLAG.

Our country is a goodly land;
  We'll keep her alway whole and hale;
We'll love her, live for her or die;
  To fall for her is not to fail.

Our Flag! The red shall mean the blood
  We gladly pledge; and let the white
Mean purity and solemn truth,
  Unsullied justice, sacred right.

Its blue, the sea we love to plough,
  That laves the heaven-united land,
Between the Old and Older World,
  From strand, o'er mount and stream, to strand.

The blue reflects the crowding stars,
  Bright union-emblem of the free;
Come, all of you, and let it wave—
  That floating piece of poetry.

Our fathers came and planted fields,
  And manly Law, and schools of truth;
They planted Self-Rule, which we'll guard
  By word and sword, in age, in youth.

Broad freedom came along with them
  On History's ever-widening wings.
Our blessing this, our task and toil;
  For "arduous are all noble things."

Let Emp'ror never rule this land,
  Nor fitful Crowd, nor senseless Pride.
Our Master is our self-made Law;
  To *him* we bow, and none beside.

Then sing and shout for our free land,
  For glorious FREELAND'S victory;
Pray that in turmoil and in peace
  FREELAND our land may ever be;

That faithful we be found and strong
  When History builds as corals build,
Or when she rears her granite walls—
  Her moles with crimson mortar filled.

Ex. CLXXVI.—*NEVER, OR NOW.*

OLIVER WENDELL HOLMES.

LISTEN, young heroes! Your country is calling!
    Time strikes the hour for the brave and the true;
Now, while the foremost are fighting and falling,
    Fill up the ranks that have opened for you!

You whom the fathers made free and defended,
    Stain not the scroll that emblazons their fame!
You whose fair heritage spotless descended,
    Leave not your children a birthright of shame!

Stay not for questions while Freedom stands gasping!
    Wait not till Honor lies wrapped in his pall!
Brief the lips' meeting be, swift the hands' clasping—
    "Off for the wars!" is enough for them all.

Break from the arms that would fondly caress you!
    Hark, 'tis the bugle-blast! sabres are drawn!
Mothers shall pray for you, fathers shall bless you,
    Maidens shall weep for you when you are gone!

Never, or now! cries the blood of a nation,
    Poured on the turf where the red rose shall bloom;
Now is the day and the hour of salvation—
    Never, or now! peals the trumpet of doom.

From the foul dens where your brothers are dying,
    Aliens and foes in the land of their birth,
From the rank swamps where our martyrs are lying,
    Pleading in vain for a handful of earth;

From the hot plains where they perish outnumbered,
    Furrowed and ridged by the battle-field's plough,
Comes the loud summons; too long have you slumbered—
    Hear the last angel-trump—NEVER, OR NOW!

Ex. CLXXVII.—*APPEAL TO SECESSIONISTS.*

From an Address Delivered before the Literary Societies of Amherst College, July 10th, 1861.

DANIEL S. DICKINSON.

You desire peace! Then lay down your arms and you shall have it. It was peace when you took them up—it will be peace when you lay them down. It will be peace when you abandon war and return to your accustomed pursuits. When the government of our fathers shall be again recognized, when the Constitution and the laws to which every citizen owes allegiance shall be observed and obeyed; then will the armies of the Constitution and the Union disband, by a common impulse, in obedience to a unanimous popular will. War is emphatically, and more especially is a war between brethren, a disgrace to civilization; and any war is a drain upon the life-blood of a nation, and originates in wrong. Its evils can not be written, even in human blood. It sweeps our race from earth, as if Heaven had repented the making of man. It lays its skinny hand upon society, and leaves it deformed by wretchedness and black with gore. It marches on its mission of destruction through a red sea of blood, and tinges the fruits of earth with a sanguine hue, as the mulberry reddened in sympathy with the romantic fate of the devoted lovers. It "spoils the dance of youthful blood," and writes sorrow and grief prematurely upon the glad brow of childhood. It chills the heart and hope of youth. It drinks the life-current of early manhood, and brings down the gray hairs of the aged with sorrow to the grave. It weaves the widow's weeds with the bridal wreath, and our land, like Rama, is filled with wailing and lamentation. It lights up the darkness with the flames of happy homes. It consumes, like the locusts of Egypt, every living thing in its pathway. It wrecks fortunes, brings bankruptcy and repudiation, and blasts the fields of the husbandman—it depopulates towns, and leaves cities a modern Herculaneum. It desolates the firesides, and covers the family dwelling with gloom, and an awful vacancy rests where, like the haunted mansion:

> "No human figure stirred to go or come,
>   No face looked forth from open door or casement,
>   No chimney smoked; there was no sign of home
>   From parapet to basement.

> "No dog was on the threshold, great or small,
>   No pigeon on the roof, no household creature,
> No cat demurely dozing on the wall,
>   Not one domestic feature."

It loads the people with debts to pass down from one generation to another, like the curse of original sin; upon its merciless errand of violence, it fills the land with crime and tumult and rapine, and it " gluts the grave with untimely victims and peoples the world of perdition." Yet, ruthless as is the sway, and devastating as is the course of war, it is not the greatest of evils nor the last lesson in humiliation. "Sweet are the uses of adversity." In its current of violence and blood, it may purify an atmosphere too long surcharged with discontent, and corruption, and apostasy, and treachery, and littleness, and prove how poor a remedy it is for social grievances. It may correct the dry-rot of demoralization in public station, and raise us, as a people, above the dead level of a mean and morbid ambition. It may scatter the tribe of bloated hangers-on who seek to serve their country that they may plunder and betray it; and, above all, it may arouse the popular mind to a just sense of its responsibility, until it shall select its servants with care, and hold them to a faithful discharge of their duty; until deficient morals shall be held questionable, falsehood a social fault, violation of truth a disqualification, and bribery a disgrace—until integrity shall be a recommendation, and treason and larceny crimes.

Ex. CLXXVIII.—*UNSEEN SPIRITS.*

Oh, North and South, 'twas not by chance,
  Still less by fraud or fear,
That Sumter's battle came and closed,
  Nor cost the world a tear.
'Twas not that Northern hearts were weak,
  Or Southern courage cold,
That shell and shot fell harming not
  A man on shore or hold.

It was that all their ghosts who lived
  To love the realm they made,
Came flitting so athwart the fire,
  That shot and shell were stayed.

Washington with his sad still face,
  Franklin with silver hair,
Lincoln and Putnam, Allen, Gates,
  And gallant Wayne were there.

With those who rose at Boston,
  At Philadelphia met;
Whose grave eyes saw the Union's seal
  To their first charter set.
Adams and Jay and Henry,
  Rutledge and Randolph, too—
And many a name their country's fame
  Hath sealed brave, wise and true.

An awful host—above the coast,
  About the fort they hung;
Sad faces pale, too proud to wail,
  But with sore anguish wrung.
And Faith and Truth, and Love and Ruth,
  Hovered the battle o'er,
Hindering the shot, that freight of death
  Between those brothers bore.

And thus it happed, by God's good grace,
  And those good spirits' band,
That Death forbore the leaguered place,
  The battery-guarded strand.
Thanks unto Heaven on bended knee,
  Not scoff from mocking scorn,
Befits us, that to bloodless end
  A strife like this is borne.

Ex. CLXXIX.—"*ALL OF THEM.*"

A True Story.

WITH head erect, and lips compressed,
  He throws his hammer by;
The purpose of his manly breast
  Is now to do or die.

He seeks the camp: "Put down my name:
  My boys will mind the shop;
If the rebels want my heart's best blood,
  I'll sell it drop by drop.

And now here comes my oldest boy;
  My son, what would you do?"
"Father, my brother will drive the trade;
  I've come to fight with you."

"God bless him! Well, put down his name;
  I can not send him home;
But here's the other boy, I see—
  My son, what made you come?"

"Father, I could not work alone;
  The shop may go to grass;
I've come to fight for the good old flag;
  Stand off here; let me pass."

"Yes, put him down—he's a noble boy;
  I've two that are younger still;
They'll drive the plough on the Flushing farm,
  And work with a right good will.

"My stars! and here comes one of them!
  My son, you must not go!"
"Father, when rebels are marching on,
  I cannot plough or sow."

"Well, thank God, there is one left yet;
  He will plough and sow what he can;
But he's only a boy, and can never do
  The work of a full-grown man."

With a proud, full heart the blacksmith turned,
  And walked to the other side;
For he felt a weakness he almost scorned,
  And a tear he fain would hide.

They told him then, that his youngest boy
  Was putting his name on the roll;
"It must not be," said the brave old man;
"No, no, he's the light of my soul!"

But the lad came up with a beaming face,
  Which bore neither fears nor cares;
"Father, say nothing—my name is down;
  I have let out the farm on shares!"

And now they have marched to the tented field,
  And when the wild battle shall come,
They'll strike a full blow for the Stars and Stripes,
  For God, and their country and home.

Ex. CLXXX.—*STAND BY THE FLAG!*

Letter to Kentuckians, Written from Washington, May 31, 1861.

JOSEPH HOLT.

LET us twine each thread of the glorious tissue of our country's flag about our heart strings, and looking upon our homes and catching the spirit that breathes upon us from the battle-fields of our fathers, let us resolve that, come weal or woe, we will in life and in death, now and forever, stand by the Stars and Stripes. They have floated over our cradles, let it be our prayer and our struggle that they shall float over our graves. They have been unfurled from the snows of Canada to the plains of New Orleans, to the halls of the Montezumas, and amid the solitude of every sea, and everywhere, as the luminous symbol of resistless and beneficent power, they have led the brave and the free to victory and to glory.

It has been my fortune to look upon this flag in foreign lands, and amid the gloom of an Oriental despotism, and right well do I know, by contrast, how bright are its stars and how sublime its inspirations! If this banner, the emblem for us of all that is grand in human history, and of all that is transporting in human hope, is to be sacrificed on the altars of a satanic ambition, and thus disappear forever amid the night and tempest of revolution, then will I feel—and who shall estimate the desolation of that feeling?—that the sun has indeed been stricken from the sky of our lives, and that henceforth we shall be wanderers and outcasts, with nought but the bread of sorrow and of penury for our lips, and with hands ever outstretched in feebleness and supplication, on which, in any hour, a military tyrant may rivet the fetters of a despairing bondage. May God in his infinite mercy save you and me, and the land we so much love, from the doom of such a degradation.

No contest so momentous as this has arisen in human history, for, amid all the conflicts of men and of nations, the life of no such government as ours has ever been at stake. Our fathers won our independence by the blood and sacrifice of a seven years' war, and we have maintained it against the assaults of the greatest power upon the earth; and the question now is, whether we are to perish by our own hands, and have the epitaph of suicide written upon our tomb. The ordeal through which we are passing must involve immense suffering and losses for us all, but the expenditure of not merely hundreds of millions, but of billions, will be well made, if the result shall be the preservation of our institutions.

Could my voice reach every dwelling in Kentucky, I would implore its inmates—if they would not have the rivers of their prosperity shrink away, as do unfed streams beneath the summer heats—to rouse themselves from their lethargy, and fly to the rescue of their country before it is everlastingly too late. Man should appeal to man, and neighborhood to neighborhood, until the electric fires of patriotism shall flash from heart to heart in one unbroken current throughout the land. It is a time in which the workshop, the office, the counting-house and the field may well be abandoned for the solemn duty that is upon us, for all these toils will but bring treasure, not for ourselves, but for the spoiler, if this revolution is not arrested. We are all, with our every earthly interest, embarked in mid-ocean on the same common deck. The howl of the storm is in our ears, and "the lightning's red glare is painting hell on the sky," and while the noble ship pitches and rolls under the lashings of the waves, the cry is heard that she has sprung a leak at many points, that the rushing waters are mounting rapidly in the hold. The man who, at such an hour, will not work at the pumps, is either a maniac or a monster.

Ex. CLXXXI.—*KENTUCKY.**

SOPHIA H. OLIVER.

"The first to join the patriot band,
   The last bright star to fade and die,"
Oh, first-born daughter of the land,
   Wilt thou thy sacred vow deny?
By all the lofty memories bright
   That crown with light thy glorious past,
Oh, speak again those words of might—
   "The first to come, to leave, the last!"

The land for which our fathers fought,
   The glorious heritage they gave,
The just and equal laws they wrought—
   Rise, in thy might, that land to save.
No parricidal daughter thou,
   No stain be on thy fealty cast,
Be faithful to thy boast and vow—
   "The first to come, to leave, the last!"

And, land of high, unsullied fame,
   Hast thou no grievous wrongs to right?
Thy hero, wrapped in Sumter's flame,
   And conquered in unequal fight!
Thy banner trampled in the dust—
   Hark! shouts of freemen swell the blast,
"We *will* defend our flag! we *must*
   Be first to come, to leave, the last!"

Land of my birth! how dear to me
   Has ever been thy spotless fame!
Oh, may I never, never see
   The brand of traitor on thy name!
Go—gird thee in thy armor bright;
   Be faithful to thy glorious past;
And in the battle for the right,
   Be first to come, to leave, the last!

---

* The words inscribed on the stone contributed by Kentucky to be placed in the Washington Monument, are these: "Kentucky—she was the first State to enter the Union after the adoption of the Constitution; she will be the last to leave it."

Ex. CLXXXII.—*CONSEQUENCES OF SECESSION.**

EDWARD EVERETT.

"Why should we not," it is asked, "admit the claims of the seceding States, acknowledge their independence, and put an end at once to the war?" Why should we not? I answer the question by asking another: "Why should we?" What have we to gain, what to hope, from the pursuit of that course? Peace? But we were at peace before. Why are we not at peace now? The North did not begin the war, it has been forced upon us in self-defence; and if, while they had the Constitution and the Laws, the Executive, Congress, and the Courts all controlled by themselves, the South, dissatisfied with legal protections and Constitutional remedies, has grasped the sword, can North and South hope to live in peace when the bonds of Union are broken, and amicable means of adjustment are repudiated? Peace is the very last thing which Secession, if recognized, will give us; it will give us nothing but a hollow truce,—time to prepare the means of new outrages. It is in its very nature a perpetual cause of hostility; an eternal, never-cancelled letter of marque and reprisal, an everlasting proclamation of border-war. How can peace exist, when all the causes of dissension shall be indefinitely multiplied; when unequal revenue laws shall have led to a gigantic system of smuggling; when a general stampede of slaves shall take place along the border, with no thought of rendition, and all the thousand causes of mutual irritation shall be called into action, on a frontier of fifteen hundred miles not marked by natural boundaries and not subject to a common jurisdiction or a mediating power? We did believe in peace, fondly, credulously, believed that, cemented by the mild umpirage of the Federal Union, it might dwell forever beneath the folds of the star-spangled banner, and the sacred shield of a common nationality. That was the great *arcanum* of policy; that was the State mystery into which men and angels desired to look; hidden from ages, but revealed to us:—

* This, and the two following extracts, are taken from Mr. Everett's address delivered at the Academy of Music, in New York, July 4th, 1861. As a whole, the address is a most masterly and logical statement of the origin and tendency of the Rebellion, and is equally valuable for its close reasoning and the polished elegance of its style.

> Which Kings and Prophets waited for,
> And sought, but never found:

a family of States independent of each other for local concerns, united under one government for the management of common interests and the prevention of internal feuds. There was no limit to the possible extension of such a system. It had already comprehended half of North America, and it might, in the course of time, have folded the continent in its peaceful, beneficent embrace. We fondly dreamed that, in the lapse of ages, it would have extended till half the Western hemisphere had realized the vision of universal, perpetual peace. From that dream we have been rudely startled by the array of ten thousand armed men in Charleston Harbor, and the glare of eleven batteries bursting on the torn sky of the Union, like the comet which, at this very moment, burns "in the Arctic sky, and from his horrid hair shakes pestilence and war." These batteries rained their storm of iron hail on one poor siege-worn company, because, in obedience to lawful authority, in the performance of sworn duty, the gallant Anderson resolved to keep *his* oath. Are no rights sacred but those of rebellion; no oaths binding but those taken by men already forsworn; are liberty of thought, and speech, and action nowhere to be tolerated except on the part of those by whom the laws are trampled under foot, arsenals and mints plundered, governments warred against, and their patriotic defenders assailed by ferocious and murderous mobs?

Ex. CLXXXIII.—*THE MASSACHUSETTS VOLUNTEERS.*

W. S. NEWELL.

> To the sound of martial music,
>   And the war-drum's measured beat,
> The sons of Massachusetts
>   File along the crowded street;
> And a look of solemn meaning
>   Is on every face I meet.
>
> And I see on every feature
>   The marks of honest toil;

The giant from the smithy,
    And the tiller of the soil,
Who have left the quiet hearth-stone
    For the thunders of the broil.

And their nerves are knit by labor
    At the furnace and the flume;
At the turning of the furrow,
    At the anvil and the loom,
'Mid the crash of whirling axles
    And the mill-wheel's sullen boom.

It was thus when Britain's tyrant,
    In the folly of his wrath,
Coming with his high-born prowess,
    Like the mighty man of Gath,
Found the simple son of nature
    Was the lion in his path.

Even so the heights of Bunker,
    Like the field where David stood,
Unto us have taught a lesson
    That the hand of toil is good;
And the nerves of work are better
    Than the nerves of birth and blood.

And I feel it as they pass me,
    These swarthy sons of might,—
These men of iron purpose
    To do battle for the right,—
That the hands which swung the hammer
    Will be dreadful in the fight.

And I know that God is with them,
    When, reposing in his grace,
They shall lift the scale of Justice
    To its long-deserted place,
And proclaim the law of Heaven—
    The Democracy of Race.

Ex. CLXXXIV.—*MARCHING ON.*

GEORGE W. BUNGAY.

THE day our fathers waited for is dawning on us now;
I see the mantle falling on the prophet at the plough;
I hear the trumpet ringing where the victors strike the blow—
  Our men are marching on.

Niagara shouts the chorus of the rivers to the sea,
Each wave swells like the bosom that is panting to be free,
The stars are lit in heaven for the nation's jubilee—
  Our men are marching on.

Sweet promises are written on the soft leaves of the flowers,
The birds of spring are jubilant within their leafy towers;
A rainbow has been woven in the shuttles of the showers—
  Our men are marching on.

God bless our gallant President, and grant him length of
  days;
Let all the people crown him with fame's unfading lays,
And generations yet unborn perpetuate his praise—
  Our men are marching on.

Ex. CLXXXV.—*SECESSION OF LOUISIANA CONSIDERED.*

EDWARD EVERETT.

NAPOLEON, in the vast recesses of his Titanic ambition, had cherished as a leading object of his policy the acquisition for France of a colonial empire which should balance that of England. In pursuit of this policy, he tempted Spain, by the paltry bribe of creating a kingdom of Etruria for a Bourbon prince, to give back to France the then boundless waste of the territory of Louisiana. If successful, this project would have established the French power on the mouth and on the right bank of the Mississippi, and would have opposed the most formidable barrier to the expansion of the United States. But in another moment the aspect of affairs was changed, by a stroke of policy grand, unexpected, and fruitful of consequences, perhaps without a parallel in history. The renewal of war was inevitable, and Napoleon saw that before he could take possession of Louisiana it would be wrested from him by England, who commanded the seas, and he determined at once not merely to deprive her of this magnificent conquest, but to contribute, as far as in him lay, to build up a great rival maritime power in the West. The Government of the United States, not less sagacious, seized the golden moment—a moment such as does not happen twice in a thousand years. Mr. Jefferson perceived that, unless acquired by the United States, Louisiana would in a short'time belong to France or England, and with equal wisdom and courage he determined that it should belong to neither, contemplating, however, at that time, only the acquisition of New Orleans and the adjacent territory.

But he was dealing with a man that did nothing by halves. Napoleon knew—*and we knew*—that to give up the mouth of the river was to give up its course. To the astonishment of the American envoys, they were told that he was prepared to treat with them not merely for the isle of New Orleans, but for the whole vast province which bore the name of Louisiana; whose boundaries, then unsettled, have since been carried on the North to the British line, on the West to the Pacific Ocean; a territory half as big as Europe, transferred by a stroke of the pen. Fifty-eight years have elapsed since the acquisition was made. The States of Louisiana, Arkansas, Missouri, Iowa, Minnesota, and Kansas, the territories of Nebraska, Dacotah, Jefferson, and part of Colorado, have been established within its limits, on this side of the Rocky Mountains; the State of Oregon and the Territory of Washington on their western slope; while a tide of population is steadily pouring into the region, destined, in addition to the natural increase, before the close of the century, to double the number of the States and Territories. For the entire region west of the Alleghanies and east of the Rocky Mountains, the Missouri and the Mississippi form the natural outlet to the sea. Without counting the population of the seceding States, there are ten millions of the free citizens of the country, between Pittsburg and Fort Union, who claim the course and the mouth of the Mississippi as belonging to the United States. It is theirs by a transfer of truly imperial origin and magnitude; theirs by a sixty years' undisputed title; theirs by occupation and settlement; theirs by the law of nature and of God. Louisiana, a fragment of this colonial empire, detached from its main portion and first organized as a State, undertakes to secede from the Union, and thinks that by so doing she will be allowed by the government and people of the United States to revoke this imperial transfer, to disregard this possession and occupation of sixty years, to repeal this law of nature and of God; and she fondly believes that ten millions of the free people of the Union will allow her and her seceding brethren to open and shut the portals of this mighty region at her pleasure. They *may* do so, and the swarming millions which throng the course of these noble streams and their tributaries may consent to exchange the charter which they hold from the God of Heaven for a bit of parchment signed at Montgomery or Richmond; but if I may repeat the words which I have lately used on another occasion, it will be when the Alleghanies and the Rocky Mountains, which form the eastern and western walls of the imperial valley, shall sink to the level of the sea, and the Mississippi and the Missouri shall flow back to their fountains.

Ex. CLXXXVI.—*SWORD AND PLOUGH.*

CHARLES DAWSON SHANLEY.

THE Sword came down to the red-brown field,
When the Plough to the furrow heaved and keeled;
And it looked so proud in its jingling gear,—
Said the Plough to the Sword, "What brings you here?"

Said the Sword, "Long ago, ere I was born,
They doubled my grandsire up, one morn,
To forge a share for you; and now
They want him back," said the Sword to the Plough.

The red-brown field glowed a deeper red,
As the gleam of war o'er the landscape sped;
The sabres flashed, the cannon roared,
And side by side fought the Plough and the Sword.

Ex. CLXXXVII.—*THE SOUTHERN CONFEDERACY, IF RECOG-
NIZED, BECOMES A FOREIGN POWER.*

EDWARD EVERETT.

CONSIDER the monstrous nature and reach of the pretensions in which we are expected to acquiesce; which are nothing less than that the United States should allow a *foreign power*, by surprise, treachery and violence, to possess itself of one half of their territory and all the public property and public establishments contained in it; for if the Southern Confederacy is recognized it becomes a foreign power, established along a curiously dove-tailed frontier of 1,500 miles, commanding some of the most important commercial and military positions and lines of communication for travel and trade; half the sea-coast of the Union; the navigation of the Gulf of Mexico, and, above all, the great arterial inlet into the heart of the continent, through which its very lifeblood pours its imperial tides.

I say we are coolly summoned to surrender all this to a foreign power. Would we surrender it to England, to France, to Spain? Not an inch of it; why, then, to the Southern Confederacy? Would any other government on earth, unless compelled by the direst necessity, make such a surrender? Does not France keep an army of 100,000 men in Algeria to prevent a few wandering tribes of Arabs, a recent conquest, from asserting their independence? Did not England strain her resources to the utmost tension to prevent the native kingdoms of Central India, (civilized states two thousand years ago, while painted chieftains ruled the savage clans of ancient Britain,) from re-establishing their sovereignty? and shall we be expected, without a struggle, to abandon a great integral part of the United States to a foreign power?

Let it be remembered, too, that in granting to the seceding States, jointly and severally, the right to leave the Union, we concede to them the right of resuming, if they please, their former allegiance to England, France and Spain. It rests with them, with any one of them, if the right of secession is admitted, again to plant a European government side by side with that of the United States on the soil of America; and it is by no means the most improbable upshot of this ill-starred rebellion, if allowed to prosper. Whether they desire it or not, the moment the seceders lose the protection of the United States they hold their independence at the mercy of the powerful governments of Europe. If the navy of the North should withdraw its protection, there is not a Southern State on the Atlantic or the Gulf, which might not be recolonized by Europe in six months after the outbreak of a foreign war.

Such, fellow-citizens, as I contemplate them, are the great issues before the country; nothing less, in a word, than whether the work of our noble fathers of the Revolutionary and Constitutional age shall perish or endure; whether this great experiment in national polity, which binds a family of free Republics in one united government—the most hopeful plan for combining the homebred blessings of a small state with the stability and power of a great empire—shall be treacherously and shamefully stricken down in the moment of its most successful operation, or whether it shall be bravely, patriotically, triumphantly maintained. We wage no war of conquest and subjugation; we aim at nothing but to protect our loyal fellow-citizens, who, against fearful odds, are fighting the battles of the Union in the disaffected States, and to re-establish, not for ourselves alone, but for our deluded fellow countrymen, the mild sway of the Constitution and the laws. The result can not be doubted. Twenty millions of freemen, forgetting their divisions, are rallying as one man in support of the righteous cause—their willing hearts and their strong hands—their fortunes and their lives, are laid upon the altar of the country. We contend for the great inheritance of constitutional freedom transmitted from our Revolutionary fathers. We engage in the struggle forced upon us with sorrow, as against our misguided brethren, but with high heart and faith, as we war for that Union which our Washington commended to our dearest affections. The sympathy of the civilized world is on our side, and will join us in prayers to Heaven for the success of our arms.

Ex. CLXXXVIII.—*THE WHOLE STORY TOLD IN RHYME.*

JOHN BULL he met our Jonathan;
 "Ah! Jonathan," said he, sir,
" Pray tell me now, what's all this row
 I hear across the sea, sir?

You're kicking up a pretty fuss,
   Pray tell me what it's for, sir;
Let me advise—just compromise!
   A horrid thing is war, sir.

"I shall want cotton, Jonathan,
   Likewise Virginia's weed, sir;
And really, now, I can't allow
   This quarrel to proceed, sir."
"Do tell!" said Brother Jonathan;
   "Now don't you get excited;
At home I rule—so just keep cool;
   You'll see this thing all righted.

"My Southern boys for years have held,
   The Presidential rein, sir;
Until to-day, they've held a sway
   They never can regain, sir.
And when they can not rule, they kick,
   And hate with all their might, sir;
For love of Union's second to
   Their fondness for State rights, sir.

"We only ask them to obey
   The same laws that we do, sir,
Their fathers helped our own to make—
   They were good men and true, sir.
We ask no more, we'll take no less,
   Though every single drop, sir,
Of Northern blood the land shall flood;
   Till then it can not stop, sir.

"I want but justice, bully John,
   Respect, and all my due, sir;
And when I have them, Johnny Bull,
   You shall have cotton too, sir.
But not till then—that's certain sure;
   So take the matter easy;
And when the war is over, John,
   I'll do my best to please ye."

Ex. CLXXXIX.—*ARMY HYMN.*

OLIVER WENDELL HOLMES.

O LORD of Hosts! Almighty King!
Behold the sacrifice we bring!
To every arm Thy strength impart,
Thy Spirit shed through every heart!

Wake in our breast the living fires,
The holy faith that warmed our sires;
Thy hand hath made our Nation free;
To die for her is serving Thee.

Be Thou a pillared flame, to show
The midnight snare, the silent foe;
And when the battle thunders loud,
Still guide us in its moving cloud.

God of all Nations! Sovereign Lord!
In Thy dread name we draw the sword;
We lift the starry flag on high,
That fills with light our stormy sky.

From treason's rent, from murder's stain,
Guard Thou its folds till Peace shall reign;
Till fort and field, till shore and sea,
Join our loud anthem, PRAISE TO THEE!

Ex. CXC.—*A WAR HYMN.*

THEODORE TILTON.

THOU who ordainest, for the land's salvation,
Famine and fire, and sword and lamentation,
Now unto Thee we lift our supplication—
    God save the nation!

By the great sign, foretold, of thy appearing—
Coming in clouds, while mortal men stand fearing—
Show us, amid the smoke of battle clearing
    Thy chariot nearing!

By the brave blood that floweth like a river,
Hurl thou a thunderbolt from out thy quiver!
Break thou the strong gates! Every fetter shiver!
    Smite and deliver!

Slay thou our foes, or turn them to derision,
Till, through the blood-red Valley of Decision,
Peace on our fields shine, like a prophet's vision,
    Green and Elysian!

Ex. CXCI.—*ON BOARD THE CUMBERLAND, MARCH 7th,* 1862.

GEORGE H. BOKER.

"STAND to your guns, men!" Morris cried.
  Small need to pass the word;
Our men at quarters ranged themselves
  Before the drum was heard.

And then began the sailors' jests:
  "What thing is that, I say?"
"A 'long-shore meeting-house adrift
  Is standing down the bay!"

A frown came over Morris' face;
  The strange, dark craft he knew;
"That is the iron Merrimac,
  Manned by a rebel crew.

"So shot your guns, and point them straight;
  Before this day goes by,
We'll try of what her metal's made."
  A cheer was the reply.

Meanwhile the shapeless iron mass
  Came moving o'er the wave,
As gloomy as a passing hearse,
  As silent as the grave.

She reached our range. Our broadside rang,
  Our heavy pivots roared;
And shot and shell, a fire of hell,
  Against her sides we poured.

God's mercy! From her sloping roof
   The iron tempest glanced,
As hail bounds from a cottage thatch,
   And round her leaped and danced.

Or when against her dusky hull
   We struck a fair, full blow,
The mighty, solid, iron globes
   Were crumbled up like snow.

On, on, with fast increasing speed
   The silent monster came,
Though all our starboard battery
   Was one long line of flame.

She heeded not—no gun she fired,
   Straight on our bow she bore;
Through riving plank and crashing frame
   Her furious way she tore.

Once more she backward drew a space,
   Once more our side she rent;
Then, in the wantonness of hate,
   Her broadside through us sent.

We felt our vessel settling fast,
   We knew our time was brief;
"The pumps! The pumps!" But they who pumped,
   And fought not, wept with grief.

From captain down to powder-boy,
   No hand was idle then;
Two soldiers, but by chance aboard,
   Fought on like sailor-men.

And when a gun's crew lost a hand,
   Some bold marine stepped out,
And jerked his braided jacket off,
   And hauled the gun about.

Our forward magazine was drowned;
   And up from the sick bay
Crawled out the wounded, red with blood,
   And round us gasping lay

Yes, cheering, calling us by name,
    Struggling with failing breath,
To keep their shipmates at the post
    Where glory strove with death.

With decks afloat, and powder gone,
    The last broadside we gave
From the guns' heated iron lips
    Burst out beneath the wave.

"Up to the spar-deck! save yourselves!"
    Cried Selfridge. "Up, my men!
God grant that some of us may live
    To fight that ship again!"

We turned; we did not like to go;
    Yet staying seemed but vain,
Knee-deep in water; so we left.
    Some swore, some groaned with pain.

We reached the deck. There Randall stood;
    "Another turn, men—So!"
Calmly he aimed his pivot-gun:
    "Now, Tenny, let her go!"

It did our sore hearts good to hear
    The song our pivot sang,
As rushing on from wave to wave
    The whirring bomb-shell sprang.

Brave Randall leaped upon the gun,
    And waved his cap in sport;
"Well done! well aimed! I saw that shot
    Go through an open port!"

It was our last, our deadliest shot;
    The deck was overflown;
The poor ship staggered, lurched to port,
    And gave a living groan.

Down, down, as headlong through the waves
    Our gallant vessel rushed,
A thousand gurgling watery sounds
    Around my senses gushed.

I tried to cheer. I can not say
  Whether I swam or sank;
A blue mist closed around my eyes,
  And every thing was blank.

When I awoke, a soldier lad,
  All dripping from the sea,
With two great tears upon his cheeks,
  Was bending over me.

I tried to speak. He understood
  The wish I could not speak—
He turned me. There, thank God! the flag
  Still fluttered at the peak!

And there, while thread shall hang to thread,
  Oh, let that ensign fly!
The noblest constellation set
  Against our northern sky.

A sign that we who live, may claim
  The peerage of the brave;
A monument, that needs no scroll,
  For those beneath the wave!

Ex. CXCII.—*THE VARUNA.*

Sunk April 25th, 1862.

GEORGE H. BOKER.

WHO has not heard of the dauntless Varuna?
  Who has not heard of the deeds she has done?
Who shall not hear, while the brown Mississippi
  Rushes along from the snow to the sun?

Crippled and leaking she entered the battle,
  Sinking and burning she fought through the fray,
Crushed were her sides, and the waves ran across her,
  Ere, like a death-wounded lion at bay,
Sternly she closed in the last fatal grapple,
  Then in her triumph moved grandly away.

Five of the rebels, like satellites round her,
　　Burned in her orbit of splendor and fear,
One, like the pleiad of mystical story,
　　Shot, terror-stricken, beyond her dread sphere.

We who are waiting, with crowns for the victors,
　　Though we should offer the wealth of our store,
Load the Varuna from deck down to keelson,
　　Still would be niggard, such tribute to pour
On courage so boundless. It beggars possession,
　　It knocks for just payment at heaven's bright door!

Cherish the heroes who fought the Varuna;
　　Treat them as kings if they honor your way;
Succor and comfort the sick and the wounded;
　　Oh, for the dead let us all kneel to pray!

Ex. CXCIII.—*THANKSGIVING-EVE*, 1862.

Slow across the blue Potomac fades the dim November light,
And the darkness, like a mantle, folds the tented field from sight;
Through the shadowed wood beside me breaks the wind with quivering moan,
Floating, sighing, falling, dying, as I hold my watch alone.

Forward, backward, stern and fearless, till the moonbeam's dancing ray
Breaks in many a gleaming arrow from my bayonet's point away;
So I pace the picket lonely; but, apart from mortal sight,
Watch I'm keeping with the sleeping loved ones far away to-night.

On the morrow comes Thanksgiving, when, from households far and wide,
Round their homes the children gather—seek once more the old fireside;
Fill once more the vacant places, that they left so long ago,
Self-relying, proudly trying all life's unknown joy and woe.

On the morrow comes Thanksgiving, not as long ago it came,
Bright, without a shade of sorrow lingering on its good old name;
War has waved his crimson banner, and beneath its blood stains rest
All his glory, dim and gory, laid on many a lifeless breast.

Wife and child, and aged mother, wake at morn to bend the knee,
And around the hearth-stone glowing, supplicate their God for me;
Near my vacant chair they gather, blending tears amid their prayers—
God will hear them, and anear them will my spirit kneel with theirs.

Nor is darkness all around us; we can thank our God for might—
For the strength which he has given, still to struggle for the right;
For the soul so grandly beating in the nation's onward way,
For the spirit we inherit in this new Thanksgiving day!

Still the blue Potomac ripples like a silver thread below,
And amid the sullen darkness rises high the camp-fire's glow;
So I pace the picket lonely, while, apart from mortal sight,
Watch I'm keeping with the sleeping loved ones there at home to-night.

Ex. CXCIV.—*THE PICKET GUARD.*

"ALL quiet along the Potomac," they say,
 "Except now and then a stray picket
Is shot, as he walks on his beat, to and fro,
 By a rifleman off in the thicket.
'Tis nothing—a private or two, now and then,
 Will not count in the news of the battle;
Not an officer lost—only one of the men,
 Moaning out, all alone, the death-rattle."

All quiet along the Potomac to-night,
　　Where the soldiers lie peacefully dreaming;
Their tents in the rays of the clear autumn moon,
　　Or the light of the watchfires are gleaming.
A tremulous sigh, as the gentle night-wind
　　Through the forest-leaves softly is creeping;
While stars up above, with their glittering eyes,
　　Keep guard—for the army is sleeping.

There's only the sound of the lone sentry's tread,
　　As he tramps from the rock to the fountain,
And thinks of the two in the low trundle-bed
　　Far away in the cot on the mountain.
His musket falls slack—his face, dark and grim,
　　Grows gentle with memories tender,
As he mutters a prayer for the children asleep—
　　For their mother,—may Heaven defend her!

The moon seems to shine just as brightly as then,
　　That night, when the love yet unspoken
Leaped up to his lips—when low-murmured vows
　　Were pledged to be ever unbroken.
Then drawing his sleeve roughly over his eyes,
　　He dashes off tears that are welling,
And gathers his gun closer up to its place
　　As if to keep down the heart-swelling.

He passes the fountain, the blasted pine-tree—
　　The footstep is lagging and weary;
Yet onward he goes, through the broad belt of light,
　　Toward the shades of the forest so dreary.
Hark! was it night-wind that rustled the leaves?
　　Was it moonlight so wondrously flashing?
It looked like a rifle—"Ah! Mary, good by!"
　　And the life-blood is ebbing and plashing.

All quiet along the Potomac to-night,
　　No sound save the rush of the river;
While soft falls the dew on the face of the dead—
　　The picket's off duty forever.

Ex. CXCV.—*NO PARTY NOW—ALL FOR OUR COUNTRY.*

From an Address read at the Inaugural Meeting of the Loyal National League, in Union Square, New York, on the 11th of April, 1863.

FRANCIS LIEBER.

It is just and wise that men engaged in a great and arduous cause should profess anew, from time to time, their faith, and pledge themselves to one another, to stand by their cause to the last extremity, even at the sacrifice of all they have and all that God has given them—their wealth, their blood, and their children's blood. We solemnly pledge all this to our cause, for it is the cause of our country and her noble history, of freedom, and justice, and truth—it is the cause of all we hold dearest on this earth: we profess and pledge this—plainly, broadly, openly in the cheering time of success, and most fervently in the day of trial and reverses.

We recollect how, two years ago, when reckless arrogance attacked Fort Sumter, the response to that boom of treasonable cannon was read, in our city, in the flag of our country—waving from every steeple and school-house, from City Hall and Court House, from every shop window and market stall, and fluttering in the hand of every child, and on the head-gear of every horse in the busy street. Two years have passed; uncounted sacrifices have been made—sacrifices of wealth, of blood, and limb, and life—of friendship and brotherhood, of endeared and hallowed pursuits and sacred ties—and still the civil war is raging in bitterness and heart-burning—still we make the same profession, and still we pledge ourselves firmly to hold on to our cause, and persevere in the struggle into which unrighteous men, bewildered by pride, and stimulated by bitter hatred, have plunged us.

We profess ourselves to be loyal citizens of these United States; and by loyalty we mean a candid and loving devotion to the object to which a loyal man—a loyal husband, a loyal friend, a loyal citizen—devotes himself. We eschew the attenuated arguments derived by trifling scholars from meagre etymology. We take the core and substance of this weighty word, and pledge ourselves that we will loyally—not merely outwardly and formally, according to the letter, but frankly, fervently and according to the spirit—adhere to our country, to her institutions, to freedom, and her power, and to that great institution called the government of our country, founded by our fathers, and loved by their sons, and by all right-minded men, who have become citizens of this land by choice and not by birth—who have wedded this country in the maturity of their age as verily their own. We pledge ourselves as National men devoted to the Nationality of this great people. No government can wholly dispense with loyalty, except the fiercest despotism ruling by naked intimidation; but a republic stands in greater need of it than any other government, and most of all a republic beset by open rebellion and insidious treason. Loyalty is pre-eminently a civic virtue in a free country. It is patriotism cast in the graceful mould of candid devotion to the harmless government of an unshackled nation.

In pledging ourselves thus, we know of no party. Parties are unavoidable in free countries, and may be useful if they acknowledge the country far above themselves, and remain within the sanctity of the fundamental law which protects the enjoyment of liberty prepared for, all within its sacred domain. But Party has no meaning in far the greater number of the highest and the common relations of human life. When we are ailing, we do not take medicine by party prescription. We do not build ships by party measurement; we do not pray for our daily bread by party distinctions; we do not take our chosen ones to our bosoms by party demarcations, nor do we eat or drink, sleep or wake, as partisans. We do not enjoy the flowers of spring, nor do we harvest the grain, by party lines. We do not incur punishments for infractions of the commandments according to party creeds. We do not pursue truth, or cultivate science, by party dogmas; and we do not, we must not, love and defend our country and our liberty, dear to us as part and portion of our very selves, according to party rules. Woe to him who does. When a house is on fire, and a mother with her child cries for help at the window above, shall the firemen at the engine be allowed to trifle away the precious time in party bickerings, or is then the only word—"Water! pump away; up with the ladder!"

Let us not be like the Byzantines, those wretches who quarrelled about contemptible party refinements, theological though they were, while the truculent Mussulman was steadily drawing nearer—nay, some of whom would even go to the lord of the crescent, and with a craven heart would beg for a pittance of the spoil, so that they would be spared, and could vent their party spleen against their kin in blood, and fellows in religion.

We know of no party in our present troubles; the word is here an empty sound. The only line which divides the people of the North, runs between the mass of loyal men who stand by their country, no matter to what place of political meeting they were used to resort, or with what accent they utter the language of the land, or what religion they profess, or what sentiments they may have uttered in the excitement of former discussions, on the one hand, and those on the other hand, who keep outside of that line— traitors to their country in the hour of need,—or those who allow themselves to be misled by shallow names, and by reminiscences which cling around those names from by-gone days, finding no application in a time which asks for things more sterling than names, theories, or platforms.

Ex. CXCVI.—*THE FULFILMENT OF DESTINY.*

Speech delivered in New York, April 11th, 1863.

ROSCOE CONKLING.

IT seems to be a maxim in the economy of Providence, that the trials of a nation are in the ratio of its destinies. If it be poor and powerless,—if it have no empire and hold no position envied by the world,—it may escape the blasts of war, and languish for long intervals in unmolested calmness. But if it be rich and powerful, if it claim as its own one-tenth of the globe, if in the lifetime of a single man it grow to be the foremost power in all the earth,—it must accept perils and struggles as the price of its greatness and success.

If, besides being powerful, a people have set up institutions in which no trace of aristocracy is tolerated, it has voluntarily elected to make its own soil the theatre of a contest which has been waging since time began between oppression and liberty. It is the mission and fore-ordained destiny of a people assuming to found and uphold a democratic government, to wrestle and grapple with the foes of Freedom within and without; and we had no right to expect to escape it.

Why should we? Why should we hope to elude the evil passions and instincts which have led men the world over to seek the destruction of equal rights and the aggrandizement of the few at the expense of the many. We knew that nowhere had men relinquished superior and exclusive privileges without a contest. Why should they do it here —here in the New World, the place reserved for republican government to vindicate itself forever, or to wither from the world?

Time and civilization and government had their morning not in the West but in the East. Dawn flushed, and yet centuries rolled by before light broke upon the Western Continent. Why was this? Why was half the globe kept hidden away behind a trackless waste of waters till the other half had been dug over and over to bury its dead? Why were progress and barbarism mewed up so long in the Old World, to solve in blood the problems of humanity?

Perhaps the New World was reserved till mankind should be fitted for a higher and better dispensation. Perhaps it was designed to withhold this inheritance from man until the race had been tried and instructed and exalted by the wisdom and the folly, the virtues and the vices, of wasted ages.

If this was the design, we can understand our mission and accept our responsibilities. If it is the mission of the American people to make their continent a garden for the growth of a new civilization, higher and better and truer than the world has ever known, we may understand the logic which permits blood to stain our land. If we maintain successfully that man needs no mortal master but himself, we bring forth a great new truth, and no great truth was ever yet born into the world without great pangs.

It cost great pangs to plant the germ of free government here, and the manner in which the experiment began might well convince the mind of faith that Providence had charge over it. The task was undertaken by a group of men whom no previous age could have produced. They were the victims of all the bad systems of government then extant, and they were called to devise a new system just when the world was ablaze with political intelligence. All the past was before them, and the French Revolution was just delivering its terrible message to mankind. Two forms of government had already been tried here. The Colonial system had been tested and thrown off. The Confederate system had been fully tried, and found fit to live only through the Revolution it supported. The Fathers of the Republic, in their almost inspiration, saw clearly that a government to be enduring and free must be a Union, not of States but of the people, and they fashioned their work accordingly.

The Constitution, as our fathers made it, is the ark of our safety, and "except we abide in the ship we can not be saved." Let us cling to the ship which our fathers built and launched in darkness and tempests upon the tide of time; let us take heed lest she drift upon the rocks while we wrangle among ourselves; let us feel that our crowning infamy would be to lose the vessel from brawls among the crew. Rather than that this should happen, let her go down in the shock; rather let the harpies of Europe pluck the eagle of the sea; rather than pull down her colors ourselves,

> "Nail to the mast her holy flag,
> Stretch every threadbare sail,
> And give her to the god of storms,
> The lightning and the gale."

Ex. CXCVII.—*THE HEART OF THE WAR.*

DR. J. G. HOLLAND.

PEACE in the clover-scented air,
  And stars within the dome;
And underneath, in dim repose,
  A plain, New England home.
Within, a murmur of low tones
  And sighs from hearts oppressed,
Merging in prayer, at last, that brings
  The balm of silent rest.

"I've closed a hard day's work, Marty,—
  The evening chores are done;
And you are weary with the house,
  And with the little one.
But he is sleeping sweetly now,
  With all our pretty brood;
So come and sit upon my knee,
  And it will do me good.

PATRIOTIC ELOQUENCE.

Oh, Marty! I must tell you all
   The trouble in my heart,
And you must do the best you can
   To take and bear your part.
You've seen the shadow on my face,
   You've felt it day and night;
For it has filled our little home,
   And banished all its light.

I did not mean it should be so,
   And yet I might have known
That hearts that live as close as ours
   Can never keep their own.
But we are fallen on evil times,
   And, do whate'er I may,
My heart grows sad about the war,
   And sadder every day.

I think about it when I work,
   And when I try to rest,
And never more than when your head
   Is pillowed on my breast;
For then I see the camp-fires blaze,
   And sleeping men around,
Who turn their faces toward their homes,
   And dream upon the ground.

I think about the dear, brave boys,
   My mates in other years,
Who pine for home and those they love,
   Till I am choked with tears.
With shouts and cheers they marched away
   On glory's shining track,
But, ah! how long, how long they stay!
   How few of them come back!

One sleeps beside the Tennessee,
   And one beside the James,
And one fought on a gallant ship
   And perished in its flames.
And some, struck down by foul disease,
   Are breathing out their life;
And others, maimed by cruel wounds,
   Have left the deadly strife.

Ah, Marty! Marty! only think
  Of all the boys have done
And suffered in this weary war!
  Brave heroes, every one!
Oh, often, often in the night,
  I hear their voices call:
'*Come on and help us! Is it right
  That we should bear it all?*'

And when I kneel and try to pray,
  My thoughts are never free,
But cling to those who toil and fight
  And die for you and me.
And when I pray for victory,
  It seems almost a sin
To fold my hands and ask for what
  I will not help to win.

Oh! do not cling to me and cry,
  For it will break my heart;
I'm sure you'd rather have me die
  Than not to bear my part.
You think that some should stay at home
  To care for those away;
But still I'm helpless to decide
  If I should go or stay.

For, Marty, all the soldiers love,
  And all are loved again;
And I am loved, and love, perhaps
  No more than other men.
I can not tell—I do not know—
  Which way my duty lies,
Or where the Lord would have me build
  My fire of sacrifice.

I feel—I know—I am not mean;
  And though I seem to boast,
I'm sure that I would give my life
  To those who need it most.
Perhaps the Spirit will reveal
  That which is fair and right;
So, Marty, let us humbly kneel
  And pray to Heaven for light."

Peace in the clover-scented air,
And stars within the dome;
And underneath, in dim repose,
A plain, New England home.
Within, a widow in her weeds,
From whom all joy is flown,
Who kneels among her sleeping babes,
And weeps and prays alone!

Ex. CXCVIII.—*ADDRESS AT THE CONSECRATION OF THE SOLDIER'S CEMETERY, AT GETTYSBURG, NOVEMBER,* 1863.

ABRAHAM LINCOLN.

FOURSCORE and seven years ago, our fathers brought forth upon this continent a new nation, conceived in Liberty, and dedicated to the proposition that all men are created equal. Now we are engaged in a great civil war, testing whether that nation, or any nation so conceived and so dedicated, can long endure. We are met on a great battle-field of that war. We are met to dedicate a portion of it as the final resting-place of those who here gave their lives that the nation might live. It is altogether fitting and proper that we should do this.

But, in a larger sense, we can not dedicate, we can not consecrate, we can not hallow this ground. The brave men, living and dead, who struggled here, have consecrated it far above our power to add or detract. The world will little note, nor long remember, what we say here; but it can never forget what they did here. It is for us, the living, rather to be dedicated here to the unfinished work that they have thus far so nobly carried on. It is rather for us to be here dedicated to the great task remaining before us,—that from these honored dead we take increased devotion to the cause for which they here gave the last full measure of devotion; that we here highly resolve that the dead shall not have died in vain; that the nation shall, under God, have a new birth of freedom; and that the government of the people, by the people, and for the people, shall not perish from the earth.

Ex. CXCIX.—*DIRGE FOR A SOLDIER.*

GEORGE H. BOKER.

Close his eyes, his work is done!
  What to him is friend or foeman,
Rise of moon, or set of sun,
  Hand of man, or kiss of woman?
    Lay him low, lay him low,
    In the clover or the snow!
    What cares he? he can not know.
      Lay him low!

As man may, he fought his fight,
  Proved his truth by his endeavor;
Let him sleep in solemn night,
  Sleep forever and forever.
    Lay him low, lay him low,
    In the clover or the snow!
    What cares he? he can not know!
      Lay him low!

Fold him in his country's stars,
  Roll the drum and fire the volley!
What to him are all our wars,
  What but death bemocking folly!
    Lay him low, lay him low,
    In the clover or the snow,
    What cares he? he can not know!
      Lay him low!

Leave him to God's watching eye,
  Trust him to the hand that made him;
Mortal love weeps idly by;
  God alone has power to aid him.
    Lay him low, lay him low,
    In the clover or the snow!
    What cares he? he can not know!
      Lay him low!

Ex. CC.—*AFTER THE BATTLE.*

The drums are all muffled, the bugles are still;
There's a pause in the valley, a halt on the hill;
And bearers of standards swerve back with a thrill
    Where sheaves of the dead bar the way;
For a great field is reaped, Heaven's garners to fill,
    And stern Death holds his harvest to-day.

There's a voice in the wind like a spirit's low cry;
'Tis the muster-roll sounding,—and who shall reply
For those whose wan faces glare white to the sky,
    With eyes fixed so steadfast and dimly,
As they wait the last trump, which they may not defy!
    Whose hands clutch the sword-hilt so grimly.

The brave heads late lifted are solemnly bowed,
As the riderless chargers stand quivering and cowed,—
As the burial requiem is chanted aloud,
    The groans of the death-stricken drowning,
While Victory looks on like a queen pale and proud
    Who awaits till the morning her crowning.

There is no mocking blazon, as clay sinks to clay;
The vain pomps of peace-time are all swept away
In the terrible face of the dread battle-day;
    Nor coffins nor shroudings are here;
Only relics that lay where thickest the fray,—
    A rent casque and a headless spear.

Far away, tramp on tramp, sounds the march of the foe,
Like a storm-wave retreating, spent, fitful and slow;
With sound like their spirits that faint as they go
    By the red-glowing river, whose waters
Shall darken with sorrow the land where they flow
    To the eyes of her desolate daughters.

They are fled—they are gone; but oh! not as they came;
In the pride of those numbers they staked on the game,
Never more shall they stand in the vanguard of fame,
    Never lift the stained sword which they drew;
Never more shall they boast of a glorious name,
    Never march with the leal and the true.

Where the wreck of our legions lay stranded and torn,
They stole on our ranks in the mist of the morn;
Like the giant of Gaza, their strength it was shorn
 Ere those mists have rolled up to the sky;
From the flash of the steel a new day-break seemed born,
 As we sprang up to conquer or die.

The tumult is silenced; the death-lots are cast,
And the heroes of battle are slumbering their last:
Do you dream of yon pale form that rode on the blast?
 Would ye see it once more, oh ye brave!
Yes—the broad road to honor is red where ye passed,
 And of glory ye asked—but a grave!

Ex. CCI.—*A THANKSGIVING HYMN.*

PARK BENJAMIN.

Oh, God of Battles! by whose hand,
 Uplifted to protect the right,
Are led the armies of our land
 To be triumphant in the fight;
 Without whose smile, the solemn night
Which now in shadow veils the sky
 Would never yield to morning light,
Bend down, and hear thy people's cry.

Bend from thy heaven of heavens, and see
 A nation which had grown so great
That, drawing off their heart from Thee,
 They worshipped fortune, fame and fate,
 And called upon thy name too late.
Thy righteous anger we deplore;
 Oh, look upon their hapless state
And be our sure defence once more.

Be thou, who wast our father's God,
 Our own reliance, strength and stay;
And let the sacred path they trod
 Still be their children's chosen way,

Illumined by that glorious ray
Which guided through the desert drear,
    A fire at night, a cloud by day,
For many a sad, despairing year.

Oh thou, whose smiling face appears
    At last, behind war's awful frown;
The tribute of our grateful tears,
    Like rain in Summer falling down,
    Accept, and let thy mercy crown
This contest, holy in thy sight;
    And thine be all the vast renown,
And ours the victory of Right.

Ex. CCII.—*I HAVE A COUNTRY.*

"I have a country," cried a boy, starting up. "My father is fighting for it, and my brother has died for it."

I HAVE a country! who with coward tongue
    And treacherous heart has said it is not so?
I have a country, and her flag is flung,
    Starry and bright on all the winds that blow.

I have a country! From the shores of Maine,
    Stormy and bleak, to the Pacific sea;
The granite mountains and the fertile plains,
    The mighty rivers, all belong to me.

To me alike, the sturdy northern pines
    Which toss their branches in the winds forlorn,
The feathery palm trees and the clustering vines,
    The fields of cotton and the groves of corn.

I have a country, for the brave have died
    Upon a thousand fields to make them free;
The land is mine, their blood has sanctified—
    Mine, North and South, and mine from sea to sea.

And 'neath her banner still the battles rage,
    And armies wrestle in the cannon's breath;

For here is waged the conflict of the age,
Freedom and slavery grappling unto death.

God help my country in this hour of woe,
And save her, though baptized in fire and blood;
With thy right arm hurl back the haughty foe,
Nor suffer evil to destroy the good.

Ex. CCIII.—*SECOND INAUGURAL ADDRESS OF PRESIDENT LINCOLN, MARCH 4, 1865.*

FELLOW-COUNTRYMEN: At this second appearing to take the oath of the Presidential office, there is less occasion for an extended address than there was at the first. Then, a statement somewhat in detail of a course to be pursued seemed very fitting and proper. Now, at the expiration of four years, during which public declarations have constantly been called forth on every point and phase of the great contest which still absorbs the attention and engrosses the energies of the nation, little that is new could be presented.

The progress of our arms, upon which all else chiefly depends, is as well known to the public as to myself; and it is, I trust, reasonably satisfactory and encouraging to all. With high hope for the future, no prediction in regard to it is ventured. On the occasion corresponding to this, four years ago, all thoughts were anxiously directed to an impending civil war. All dreaded it, all sought to avoid it. While the inaugural address was being delivered from this place, devoted altogether to saving the Union without war, insurgent agents were in the city, seeking to destroy it without war; seeking to dissolve the Union and divide the effects by negotiation. Both parties deprecated war; but one of them would make war rather than let the nation survive, and the other would accept war rather than let it perish: and the war came.

One-eighth of the whole population were colored slaves, not distributed generally over the Union, but located in the southern part of it. These slaves constituted a peculiar and powerful interest. All knew that this interest was somehow the cause of the war. To strengthen, perpetuate and extend this interest, was the object for which the insurgents would rend this Union by war, while government claimed no right to do more than to restrict the territorial enlargement of it. Neither party expected the magnitude nor the duration which it has already attained. Neither anticipated that the cause of the conflict might cease, even before the conflict itself should cease. Each looked for an easier triumph, and a result less fundamental and astonishing. Both read the same Bible and pray to the same God, and each invokes his aid against the other. It may seem strange that any man should dare to ask a just God's assistance in wringing his bread from the sweat of other men's faces. But let us judge not, that we be not judged. The prayer of both should not be answered. That of neither has been answered fully. The Almighty has his own purposes. "Woe unto the world because of offences, for it must needs be that offences come; but woe to that man by whom the offence cometh." If we shall suppose that American slavery is one of these offences, which, in the providence of God, must needs come, but which, having continued through his appointed time, he now wills to remove, and that he gives to both North and South this terrible war as the woe due to those by whom the offence came, shall we discern therein any departure from those divine attributes which the believers in a living God always ascribe to him?

Fondly do we hope, fervently do we pray, that this mighty scourge of war may speedily pass away. Yet if God wills that it continue until all the wealth piled by the bondman's two hundred and fifty years of unrequited toil shall be sunk, and until every drop of blood drawn with the lash shall be paid by another drawn with the sword; as was said three thousand years ago, so still it must be said that the judgments of the Lord are true and righteous altogether.

With malice toward none, with charity for all, with firmness in the right as God gives us to see the right, let us strive on to finish the work we are in; to bind up the nation's wounds; to care for him who shall have borne the battle, and for his widow and his orphans; to do all which may achieve and cherish a just and a lasting peace among ourselves, and with all nations.

Ex. CCIV.—*RESTORATION OF THE FLAG TO FORT SUMTER, APRIL 14, 1865.*

HENRY WARD BEECHER.

On this solemn and joyful day we again lift to the breeze our fathers' flag, now again the banner of the *United States*, with the fervent prayer that God will crown it with honor, protect it from treason, and send it down to our children with all the blessings of civilization, liberty and religion. Terrible in battle, may it be beneficent in peace! Happily, no bird or beast of prey has been inscribed upon it. The stars that redeem the night from darkness, and the beams of red light that beautify the morning, have been inscribed upon its folds. As long as the sun endures, or the stars, may it wave over a union neither enslaved nor enslaving!

We raise our fathers' banner that it may bring back better blessings than those of the old; that it may cast out the devil of discord; that it may restore lawful government, and a prosperity purer and more enduring than that which it protected before; that it may win parted friends from their alienation; that it may inspire hope and inaugurate universal liberty; that it may say to the sword, "*Return to thy sheath,*" and to the plough and sickle, "*Go forth ;*" that it may heal all jealousies, unite all policies, inspire a new national life, compact our strength, purify our principles, ennoble our national ambitions, and make this people great and strong, not for aggression and quarrelsomeness, but for the *peace of the world*, giving to us the glorious prerogative of leading all nations to juster laws, to more humane policies, to sincerer friendship, to national instituted liberty, and to universal Christian brotherhood.

Reverently, piously, in hopeful patriotism, we spread this banner to the sky, as of old the bow was planted on the cloud, and, with solemn fervor, beseech God to look upon it and make it the memorial of an everlasting covenant and decree, that never again on this fair land shall a deluge of blood prevail.

From this pulpit of broken stone we speak forth our earnest greeting to all our land.

We offer to the President of these United States our solemn congratulations that God has sustained his life and health under the unparalleled burdens and sufferings of four bloody years, and permitted him to behold this auspicious consummation of that national unity for which he has waited with so much patience and fortitude, and for which he has labored with so much disinterested wisdom.

To the members of the Government associated with him in the administration of perilous affairs in critical times; to the Senators and Representatives of the United States, who have eagerly fashioned the instruments by which the popular will might express and enforce itself, we tender our grateful thanks.

To the officers and men of the army and navy, who have so faithfully, skilfully and gloriously upheld their country's authority, by suffering, labor, and sublime courage, we offer a heart-tribute beyond the compass of words.

Upon those true and faithful citizens, men and women, who have borne up with unflinching hope in the darkest hour, and covered the land with their labors of love and charity, we invoke the divinest blessing of Him whom they have so truly imitated.

But chiefly to Thee, God of our fathers, we render thanksgiving and praise for that wondrous providence that has brought forth from such a harvest of war the seed of so much liberty and peace.

We invoke peace upon the North. Peace be to the West. Peace be upon the South. In the name of God we lift up our banner, and dedicate it to peace, union and liberty, now and forevermore. Amen.

Ex. CCV.—*ABRAHAM LINCOLN.*

April 15, 1865.

REV. J. P. THOMPSON.

It is said of the late President by one who was near him steadily and with him often for more than four years, that "his abiding confidence in God and in the final triumph of truth and righteousness through Him and for His sake, was His noblest virtue, his grandest principle, the secret alike of his strength, his patience and his success."

Thus trained of God for his great work, and called of God in the fulness of time, how grandly did Abraham Lincoln meet his responsibilities and round up his life. How he grew under pressure. How often did his patient heroism in the earlier years of the war serve us in the stead of victories. He carried our mighty sorrows, while he never knew rest, nor the enjoyments of office. How wisely did his cautious, sagacious, comprehensive judgment deliver us from the perils of haste. How clearly did he discern the guiding hand and the unfolding will of God. How did he tower above the storm in his unselfish patriotism, resolved to save the unity of the nation. And when the day of duty and of opportunity came, how firmly did he deal the last great blow for liberty, striking the shackles from three million slaves; while "upon this, sincerely believed to be an act of *justice*, warranted by the Constitution, (upon military necessity,) he invoked the considerate judgment of mankind, and the gracious favor of Almighty God."

Rightly did he regard this Proclamation as the central act of his administration, and the central fact of the nineteenth century. Let it be engraved upon our walls, upon our hearts; let the scene adorn the Rotunda of the Capitol —henceforth a sacred shrine of Liberty. It needed only that the seal of martyrdom upon such a life should cause his virtues to be transfigured before us in imperishable grandeur, and his name to be emblazoned with Heaven's own light upon that topmost arch of fame which shall stand when governments and nations fall.

The historian of France has written that when Louis XIV. died, "it was not a man, it was a world that ended." But with Abraham Lincoln a new era was born that is glorified and made perpetual through his death. He has told how once he was startled and terrified at being awakened at midnight to see the stars falling and to hear that the end of the world had come. But he looked up at the Great Bear and the Pointers, and seeing them unshaken he returned to his rest. And now that he has gone so calmly to his last rest, we look up through the cloud and see the steady pointers of the sky. A star of the first magnitude has fallen from the meridian; but the pole is unchanged, and the world holds on its course. Angel hands are only shifting the curtains of the sky for the dawn. The day is brightening; let us turn from this night of sorrow and blood to welcome it with our morning hymn of hope and praise.

Ex. CCVI.—*ABRAHAM LINCOLN.*

WILLIAM CULLEN BRYANT.

Oh, slow to smite and swift to spare,
  Gentle and merciful and just!
Who, in the fear of God, didst bear
  The sword of power, a nation's trust!

In sorrow by thy bier we stand,
  Amid the awe that hushes all,
And speak the anguish of a land
  That shook with horror at thy fall.

Thy task is done; the bond are free;
  We bear thee to an honored grave,
Whose proudest monument shall be
  The broken fetters of the slave.

Pure was thy life; its bloody close
  Hath placed thee with the sons of light,
Among the noble host of those
  Who perished in the cause of Right.

Ex. CCVII.—*COMMEMORATIVE ADDRESS ON THE DEATH OF PRESIDENT LINCOLN.*

Delivered before the Athenæum Club, New York, April 18th, 1865.

PARKE GODWIN.

Mr. President:—How grand and how glorious, yet how terrible, are the times in which we are permitted to live! How profound and various the emotions that alternately depress and thrill our hearts, like these April skies—now all smiles, and now all tears. Within a week—the Holy Week, as it is called in the rubrics of our churches—we have had our triumphal entries, amid the waving of the palms of Peace; we have had our dread Friday of Crucifixion; we have had, too, in the recently renewed patriotism of the nation, a resurrection of a new and better life!

It seems but a day or two since we listened to the music of the glad and festive parade; we saw the banners of our pride waving with beauty in every air, their stars bright as the stars of the morning, and their rays of white and red, like the beams of the rainbow, telling that the tempest was past. We pressed hands and hurrahed, and grew almost delirious with the joy that Peace had come, that Unity was secured, that Liberty and Justice, like the cherubim of the Ark, would stretch their wings over the altars of our country, and stand forever as the guardian angels of her sanctity and glory.

But now these exultant strains are changed into the dull and heavy toll of bells; those flags are folded and draped in the emblems of mourning; and our hearts, giving forth no more the cheering shouts of Victory, are despondent and full of sadness.

The great Captain of our cause—the Commander-in-chief of our armies and navies—the President of our civic councils—the centre and director of movements—this true son of the People—once the poor flat-boatman—the village-lawyer that was—the raw, uncouth, yet unsophisticated child of our American society and institutions, whom that society and those institutions had lifted out of his low estate to the foremost dignity of the world—ABRAHAM LINCOLN—smitten by the basest hand ever upraised against human innocence, is gone, gone, gone! He who had borne the heaviest of the brunt in our four long years of war—whose pulse beat livelier, whose eyes danced brighter than any other's, when

——" The storm drew off
In scattered thunders groaning round the hills,"—

in the supreme hour of his joy and glory was struck down. That genial, kindly heart has ceased to beat; that noble brain has oozed from its mysterious beds; that manly form lies stiff in Death's icy fetters, and all of him that was mortal has sunk "to the portion of weeds and outworn faces."

Yet we sorrow not as those who are without hope. Our Chief has gone, but our cause remains; dearer to our hearts because he has now become its martyr; consecrated by his sacrifice; more widely accepted by all parties; and fragrant and lovely forevermore in the memories of all the great and the good of all lands and for all time. The frenzied hand which slew the head of the government, in the mad hope of paralyzing its functions, only drew the hearts of the people together more closely to strengthen and sustain its power. Oh, foolish and wicked dream, oh, insanity of fanaticism, oh, blindness of black hate—to think that this majestic temple of human liberty, with its clustered columns of free and prosperous states, and whose base is as broad as the continent—could be shaken to pieces by striking off the ornaments of its capital! No! this Nation lives, not in one man nor in a hundred men, however able, however eminent, however endeared to us; but in the affections, the virtues, the energies and the will of the whole American people. Our good ship of State, which the tempests assail with their wild fury, which the angry surges lift in their arms, that they may drop her into the yawning gulf, while the treacherous hidden rocks below grind and torture, yet sails on securely to her destined port; and when the very Prince of the power of the air smites her captain at the helm, and the first mate in his berth: she still sails on securely, for her crew is still there; they know her bearings, and will steer right on by the compass of Eternal Justice, and under the celestial light of Liberty.

Ex. CCVIII.—*ABRAHAM LINCOLN.*

With earnest heart, unshrinkingly upholding
    The awful cause God raised him to protect:
With patient heart, the mighty scheme unfolding,
    Looking to Him to counsel and direct.

Steadfast and calm, through hopes deferred, defeated;
    Saddened by many cares, oppressed by none,
Thank God! he lived to see that work completed,
    Then passed away from earth—his work was done.

Not so it seemeth to our darkened vision—
    Still do the shadows veil the dawning light;
But hope like his failed never of fruition,
    Since God is on the throne and judgeth right.

Pure, humble heart, unstained by selfish quarrel,
    Amid the strife of party ever calm,
He gladly twined our heroes' brows with laurel,
    Then bowed his own to wear the martyr's palm.

Kind, tender heart, through all its pulses thrilling
    With pity for a captive brother's woe!
No rest for him, while steadfastly fulfilling
    God's solemn mandate, "Let my people go."

No rest for him, who felt each slave's oppression,
    Who knew their blood for blood must loudly call;
No rest till he effaced the foul transgression;
    Then gave his own, the dearest blood of all.

And now, around his bier a weeping nation
    Their ardent love and gratitude express;
Not with a mournful dirge of lamentation,
    But with a solemn, thrilling tenderness.

His was the courage and the strength that bore them
    Through the lone wilderness and sea of blood;
Who, when the promised land stretched fair before them,
    Upon the towering summit meekly stood;

Saw them, ere long, that peaceful land possessing,
    Above all nations prosperous and blest,—
Then, lifting up his voice in solemn blessing,
    He passed unto his everlasting rest.

And on each heart his words of benediction,
    With sad, prophetic meaning, now must fall:
"Patience and faith in every dark affliction—
    Malice to none, but charity for all."

Mourn then, but not for him; he died victorious;
    A memory more cherished none could crave;
God took his spirit to a rest most glorious;
    We lay his body in an honored grave.

Ex. CCIX.—*FUTURE OF THE FREEDMEN.**

ANDREW JOHNSON.

WHILE I have no doubt that now, after the close of the war, it is not competent for the General Government to

---

* From the first annual message from President Johnson to Congress, Dec. 4, 1865.

extend the elective franchise in the several States, it is equally clear that good faith requires the security of the freedmen in their liberty and their property, their right to labor, and their right to claim the just return of their labor. I can not too strongly urge a dispassionate treatment of this subject which should be carefully kept aloof from all party strife. We must equally avoid hasty assumptions of any natural impossibility for the two races to live side by side in a state of mutual benefit and good will. The experiment involves us in no inconsistency; let us, then, go on and make that experiment in good faith, and not be too easily disheartened. The country is in need of labor, and the freedmen are in need of employment, culture, and protection. While their right of voluntary migration and expatriation is not to be questioned, I would not advise their forced removal and colonization. Let us rather encourage them to honorable and useful industry, where it may be beneficial to themselves and to the country; and, instead of hasty anticipations of the certainty of failure, let there be nothing wanting to the fair trial of the experiment. The change in their condition is the substitution of labor by contract for the status of slavery. The freedman can not fairly be accused of unwillingness to work, so long as a doubt remains about his freedom of choice in his pursuits, and the certainty of his recovering his stipulated wages. In this the interest of the employer and the employed coincide. The employer desires in his workmen spirit and alacrity, and these can be permanently secured in no other way. And if the one ought to be able to enforce the contract, so ought the other. The public interest will be best promoted, if the several States will provide adequate protection and remedies for the freedmen. Until this is in some way accomplished, there is no chance for the advantageous use of their labor; and the blame of ill-success will not rest on them.

I know that sincere philanthropy is earnest for the immediate realization of its remotest aims; but time is always an element in reform. It is one of the greatest acts on record to have brought four millions of people into freedom. The career of free industry must be fairly opened to them; and then their future prosperity and condition must, after all, rest mainly on themselves. If they fail, and so perish away, let us be careful that the failure shall not be attributable to any denial of justice. In all that relates to the destiny of the freedmen, we need not be too anxious to read the future;

many incidents which, from a speculative point of view, might raise alarm will quietly settle themselves.

Now that slavery is at an end, or near its end, the greatness of its evil, in the point of view of public economy, becomes more and more apparent. Slavery was essentially a monopoly of labor, and as such locked the States where it prevailed against the incoming of free industry. Where labor was the property of the capitalist, the white man was excluded from employment, or had but the second best chance of finding it; and the foreign emigrant turned away from the region where his condition would be so precarious. With the destruction of the monopoly, free labor will hasten from all parts of the civilized world to assist in developing various and immeasurable resources which have hitherto lain dormant. The eight or nine States nearest the Gulf of Mexico have a soil of exuberant fertility, a climate friendly to long life, and can sustain a denser population than is found as yet in any part of our country. And the future influx of population to them will be mainly from the North, or from the most cultivated nations in Europe. From the sufferings that have attended them during our late struggle, let us look away to the future which is sure to be laden for them with greater prosperity than has ever before been known. The removal of the monopoly of slave labor is a pledge that those regions will be peopled by a numerous and enterprising population, which will vie with any in the Union in compactness, inventive genius, wealth and industry.

Our government springs from and was made for the people—not the people for the government. To them it owes allegiance; from them it must derive its courage, strength and wisdom. But while the government is thus bound to defer to the people, from whom it derives its existence, it should, from the very consideration of its origin, be strong in its power of resistance to the establishment of inequalities. Monopolies, perpetuities and class legislation are contrary to the genius of free government, and ought not to be allowed. Here, there is no room for favored classes or monopolies; the principle of our government is that of equal laws and freedom of industry. Wherever monopoly attains a foothold, it is sure to be a source of danger, discord and trouble. We shall but fulfil our duties as legislators by according "equal and exact justice to all men," special privileges to none. The government is subordinate to the people; but, as the agent and the representative of the people, it must be held superior to monopolies, which, in themselves, ought never to be granted, and which, where they exist, must be subordinate and yield to the government.

Ex. CCX.—*NATURE AND DESTINY OF OUR GOVERNMENT.**

ANDREW JOHNSON.

WHEN, on the organization of our government, under the Constitution, the President of the United States delivered his inaugural address to the two Houses of Congress, he said to them, and through them to the country and to mankind, that "the preservation of the sacred fire of liberty and the destiny of the republican form of government are justly considered as deeply, perhaps as finally, staked on the experiment intrusted to the American people." And the House of Representatives answered WASHINGTON, by the voice of MADISON: "We adore the invisible hand which has led the American people, through so many difficulties, to cherish a conscious responsibility for the destiny of republican liberty." More than seventy-six years have glided away since these words were spoken; the United States have passed through severer trials than were foreseen; and now, at this new epoch in our existence as one nation, with our Union purified by sorrows, and strengthened by conflict, and established by the virtue of the people, the greatness of the occasion invites us once more to repeat, with solemnity, the pledges of our fathers to hold ourselves answerable before our fellow men for the success of the republican form of government. Experience has proved its sufficiency in peace and in war; it has vindicated its authority through dangers, and afflictions, and sudden and terrible emergencies, which would have crushed any system that had been less firmly fixed in the hearts of the people. At the inauguration of WASHINGTON the foreign relations of the country were few, and its trade was repressed by hostile regulations; now all the civilized nations of the globe welcome our commerce, and their governments profess toward us amity. Then our country felt its way hesitatingly along an untried path, with States so little bound together by rapid means of communication as to be hardly known to one an-

* Conclusion of the Inaugural Address

other, and with historic traditions extending over very few years; now intercourse between the States is swift and intimate; the experience of centuries has been crowded into a few generations, and has created an intense, indestructible nationality. Then our jurisdiction did not reach beyond the inconvenient boundaries of the territory which had achieved independence; now, through cessions of lands, first colonized by Spain and France, the country has acquired a more complex character, and has for its natural limits the chain of Lakes, the Gulf of Mexico, and on the east and the west the two great oceans. Other nations were wasted by civil wars for ages before they could establish for themselves the necessary degree of unity; the latent conviction, that our form of government is the best ever known to the world, has enabled us to emerge from civil war within four years, with a complete vindication of the constitutional authority of the General Government, and with our local liberties and State institutions unimpaired. The throngs of emigrants that crowd to our shores are witnesses of the confidence of all peoples in our permanence. Here is the great land of free labor, where industry is blessed with unexampled rewards, and the bread of the workingman is sweetened by the consciousness that the cause of the country "is his own cause, his own safety, his own dignity." Here every one enjoys the free use of his faculties and the choice of activity as a natural right. Here, under the combined influence of a fruitful soil, genial climes and happy institutions, population has increased fifteen-fold within a century. Here, through the easy development of boundless resources, wealth has increased with twofold greater rapidity than numbers, so that we have become secure against the financial vicissitudes of other countries, and, alike in business and opinion, are self-centred and truly independent. Here more and more care is given to provide education for every one born on our soil. Here religion, released from political connection with the civil government, refuses to subserve the craft of statesmen, and becomes, in its independence, the spiritual life of the people. Here toleration is extended to every opinion, in the quiet certainty that truth needs only a fair field to secure the victory. Here the human mind goes forth unshackled in the pursuit of science, to collect stores of knowledge and acquire an ever-increasing mastery over the forces of nature. Here the national domain is offered and held in millions of separate freeholds, so that our fellow-citizens, beyond the occupants of any other parts of the earth, constitute in reality a people. Here exists the democratic form of government; and that form of government, by the confession of European statesmen, "gives a power of which no other form is capable, because it incorporates every man with the State, and arouses everything that belongs to the soul."

Where, in past history, does a parallel exist to the public happiness which is within the reach of the people of the United States? Where, in any part of the globe, can institutions be found so suited to their habits or so entitled to their love as their own free constitution? Every one of them, then, in whatever part of the land he has his home, must wish its perpetuity. Who of them will not now acknowledge, in the words of WASHINGTON, that "every step by which the people of the United States have advanced to the character of an independent nation, seems to have been distinguished by some token of Providential agency?" Who will not join with me in the prayer, that the invisible hand which has led us through the clouds that gloomed around our path, will so guide us onward to a perfect restoration of fraternal affection, that we of this day may be able to transmit our great inheritance, of State Governments in all their rights, of the General Government in its whole constitutional vigor, to our posterity, and they to theirs through countless generations?

Ex. CCXI.—*DIALOGUE—THE OLD CONTINENTAL.*

Characters—CAPTAIN, a veteran soldier of the Revolution. NATHAN, a school-boy.

Nathan. Good morning, Captain. How do you stand the hot weather?

Captain. Lord bless you, boy, it's a cold bath to what we had at Monmouth. Did I ever tell you about that 'ere battle?

N. I have always understood that it was dreadful hot that day!

Capt. Lord bless you, boy, it makes my crutch sweat to think on't—and if I didn't hate long stories, I'd tell you things about that 'ere battle sich as you would'nt believe, you rogue, if I did'nt tell you. It beats all natur how hot it was.

N. I wonder you didn't all die of heat and fatigue.

Capt. Why, so we should, if the reg'lars had all died first; but you see they never liked the Jarseys, and wouldn't lay their bones there. Now, if I didn't hate long stories, I'd tell you all about that 'ere business, for you see they don't do things so nowadays.

N. How so? Do not people die as they used to?

Capt. Lord bless you, no. It beat all natur to see how long the reg'lars would kick after we killed them.

N. What! Kick after they were killed! That does beat all natur, as you say.

Capt. Come, boy, no splitting hairs with an old continental, for you see, if I didn't hate long stories, I'd tell you things about that 'ere battle that you'd never believe. Why, Lord bless you, when Gin'ral Washington telled us we might give it to'em, we gin it to'em, I tell you.

N. You gave what to them?

Capt. Cold lead, you rogue. Why, bless you, we fired twice to their once, you see; and if I did'nt hate long stories, I'd tell you how we did it. You must know, the reg'lars wore their close-bodied red coats, because they thought we were afeard on'em, but we didn't wear any coats, because, you see, we hadn't any.

N. How happened you to be without coats?

Capt. Why, Lord bless you, they would wear out, and the States couldn't buy us any more, you see, and so we marched the lighter, and worked the freer for it. Now, if I didn't hate long stories, I'd tell you what the gin'ral said to me next day when I had a touch of the rheumatiz from lying on the field without a blanket all night. You must know, it was raining hard just then, and we were pushing on like all natur arter the reg'lars.

N. What did the general say to you?

Capt. Not a syllable says he, but off comes his coat and he throws it over my shoulders: "There, captain," says he, "wear that, for we can't spare you yet." Now, don't that beat all natur, hey?

N. So you wore the general's coat, did you?

Capt. Lord bless your simple heart, no. I didn't feel sick arter that, I tell you. "No, gin'ral," says I, "they can spare me better than they can you, just now, and so I'll take the will for the deed," says I.

N. You will never forget his kindness, captain.

Capt. Not I, boy! I never feel a twinge of the rheumatiz but what I say, God bless the gin'ral. Now, you see, I hate long stories, or I'd tell you how I gin it to a reg'lar that tried to shoot the gin'ral at Monmouth. You know we were at close quarters, and the gin'ral was right between the two fires.

N. I wonder he was not shot.

Capt. Lord bless your ignorant soul, nobody could kill the gin'ral; but, you see, a sneaking reg'lar didn't know this, and so he levelled his musket at him, and, you see, I seed what he was arter, and I gin the gin'ral's horse a slap on the haunches, and it beats all natur how he sprung, and the gin'ral all the while as straight as a gun-barrel.

N. And you saved the general's life.

Capt. Didn't I tell you nobody could kill the gin'ral! but you see, his horse was in the wake of my gun, and I wanted to get the start of that cowardly reg'lar.

N. Did you hit him?

Capt. Lord bless your simple soul, does the thunder hit where it strikes! though the fellow made me blink a little, for he carried away part of this ear. See there? [*Showing his ear.*] Now don't that beat all natur?

N. I think it does. But tell me how it is that you took all these things so calmly? What made you so contented under your privations and hardships?

Capt. Oh, bless your young soul, we got used to it. Besides, you see, the gin'ral never flinched nor grumbled.

N. Yes, but you served without being paid.

Capt. So did the gin'ral, and the States, you know, were poor as all natur.

N. But you had families to support.

Capt. Ay, ay, but the gin'ral he always told us that God and our country would take care of them, you see. Now, if I didn't hate long stories, I'd tell you how it turned out just as he said, for he beat all natur for guessing right.

N. Then you feel happy, and satisfied with what you have done for your country, and what she has done for you?

Capt. Why, Lord bless you, if I hadn't left one of my legs at Monmouth, I wouldn't have touched a stiver of the States' money, and as it is, I am so old that I shall not need it long. You must know, I long to see the gin'ral agin, for if he don't hate long stories as bad as I do, I shall tell him all about America, you see, for it beats all natur how things have changed since he left us.

Ex. CCXII.—*DIALOGUE—THE YANKEE MARKSMAN.*

WILLIAM BENTLEY FOWLE.

Characters — LORD PERCY, with his regiment, firing at a target on Boston Common. JONATHAN, an awkward-looking country boy, who has outgrown his jacket and trowsers. Time 177–.

Percy. Now, my boys, for a trial of your skill! Imagine the mark to be a Yankee; and here is a guinea for whoever hits his heart.

[*Jonathan draws near to see the trial: and when the first soldier fires, and misses, he slaps his hand on his thigh, and laughs immoderately. Lord Percy notices him. When the second soldier fires, and misses, Jonathan throws up his old hat, and laughs again*].

Percy [*savagely*]. Why do you laugh, fellow?

Jon. To think how safe the Yankees are, if you must know.

Percy. Why, do you think *you* could shoot better?

Jon. I don't know; I could try.

Percy. Give him a gun, soldier, and you may return the fellow's laugh.

Jon. [*Takes the gun and looks at every part of it carefully.*] It won't *bust*, will it? Father's don't shine like this, but I guess it's a better gun.

Percy. Why do you guess so?

Jon. 'Cause I know what that'll deu, and I have some doubts about this 'ere. But look a-here! You called that-air mark a Yankee, an I won't fire at a Yankee.

Percy. Well, call it a British regular if you please; only fire.

Jon. Well, a reg'lar it is then. Now for freedom, as father says. [*Raises the gun and fires.*] There, I guess that-air red-coat has got a hole into it! [*Turning to soldiers.*] Why don't you laugh at me now, as that-air fellow said you might? [*pointing to Percy.*]

Percy. You awkward fellow, that was an accident. Do you think you could hit the mark again?

Jon. He! I don't know; I could try.

Percy. Give him another gun, soldiers; and take care that the clown does not shoot you. I should not fear to stand before the mark myself.

Jon. I guess you'd better not.

Percy. Why! Do you think you could hit me?

Jon. I don't know; I could try.

Percy. Fire away, then.

[*Jonathan fires again and hits the mark.*]

Jon. Ha, ha, ha! How father would laugh to see me shooting at half-gunshot!

Percy. Why, you rascal! do you think you could hit the mark at twice that distance?

Jon. He! I don't know; I'm not afeard to try.

Percy. Give him another gun, soldiers, and place the mark farther off.

[*Jonathan fires again and hits as before.*]

Jon. There, I guess that-air reg'lar is as dead as the pirate that father says the judge hangs till he is dead, dead, dead—three times dead, and that is one more death than Scripture tells on.

Percy. There, fellow, is a guinea for you.

Jon. Is it a good one? [*ringing it.*]

Percy. Good? Yes. Now begone.

Jon. I should like to stay and see them fellows kill some more Yankees.

Percy [*aside*]. The fellow is more rogue than fool. [*To Jonathan.*] Sirrah, what is your name?

Jon. Jonathan.

Percy. Jonathan what?

Jon. Yes, Jonathan Wot. I was named arter father.

Percy. Do you think your father can shoot as well as you can?

Jon. I don't know, but I guess he wouldn't be afeard to try.

Percy. Where did you learn to shoot?

Jon. Oh, father larnt me, when I wasn't knee high to a woodchuck.

Percy. Why did he teach you so young?

Jon. 'Cause he said I might have to shoot red-coats one of these days.

Percy. Ah! Pray, my boy, can all the farmers in your town shoot as well as you do?

Jon. I guess they can, and better teu.

Percy. Would they like to shoot at red-coats, as you call them?

Jon. I've heerd them say they'd like to try.

Percy. Come, my good fellow, while you are well off,

you had better join us and fight for your king; for we shall hang every Yankee we catch.

Jon. I guess you won't ketch any.

Percy. Well, we can *try*, as you say, and since we have caught you, we will hang you for a traitor.

Jon. No you won't. You paid me yourself for killing them three red-coats; so I guess you won't hang me for *that*.

Percy. No, my good fellow, I like you too well. I am sorry that my duty to my king obliges me to injure men who show in every thought and action that they are true Englishmen. You may go free; but the next time you see my troops firing at a mark for exercise, you must not be so uncivil as to laugh at them if they miss. What say you?

Jon. I don't know whether I can help it.

Percy. Well, you can *try*, can't you?

Jon. I s'pose I can; for Deacon Simple tried to milk his geese, but his wife didn't make no more butter for his trying, I guess.

Percy. Begone! or I shall have to put you under guard. Officer, give him a pass to Charlestown; but never let him come among our troops again. His example is a bad one.

Ex. CCXIII.—*DIALOGUE—IMPRESSMENT OF AN AMERICAN SEAMAN.*

EPES SARGENT.

Characters—CAPT. MARTINET, LIEUT. PERLEY.

Capt. Martinet. Well, Lieutenant, how does the prisoner bear his sentence?

Lieut. Perley. Stiffly and stubbornly, sir. He sticks to the assertion that he is a Yankee.

Capt. M. Yankee or Yahoo, he will have to swing at the yard-arm for mutiny in striking his commanding officer. The rascal hit me full in the face.

Lieut. P. Will it not be rather awkward, sir, if it should turn out that he is an American?

Capt. M. Of course, he is an American; a regular down-easter. You can tell it by his talking through his nose. But what do I care for that?

Lieut. P. We are on the verge of a war with the United States; this may help it on.

Capt. M. Let it come. What are we to do? We must have seamen. The law tells us we may take them by impressment. The Yankee ships are manned more than half by British seamen. We must board the Yankee ships to get the men we want. If, now and then, we impress a Yankee instead of a British subject, is that any reason why we should suffer the Yankee to break the first law of the service and strike his commander? No! Get ready the yard-arm, Lieutenant. The fellow must swing for it.

Lieut. P. Ay, ay, sir. I will see that everything is ready.

Capt. M. Send the prisoner to me.

Lieut. P. Ay, ay, sir. [*Exit.*]

Capt. M. British subject or not, he put his dirty fist in my face. He has been tried by a court-martial and convicted, and it shall not be my fault if he is not punished.

[*Enter* HIRAM, *with his arms pinioned.*]

Hiram. I was told you wished to see me.

Capt. M. Well, prisoner, what have you to say for yourself? You have had a fair trial, and been convicted of mutiny. The penalty is death by hanging at the yard-arm. The ceremony is fixed for this afternoon. Have you any objection to make?

Hiram. Objection? Yes, the objection that the murderer's victim makes to the murderer's blow. You know in your heart it will be murder.

Capt. M. What do you mean?

Hiram. I mean that I am not a British subject, and you know it. What right had you to take me out of an American vessel?

Capt. M. The right that British law and British power give us to seize and impress a British seaman wherever we can find one, on the high seas or elsewhere.

Hiram. But I am not a British seaman. I am a native-born American. Defend your claim to touch me, if you can.

Capt. M. We find we can not distinguish between English and Americans. If we took the word of every sailor who claims to be an American, we couldn't get enough for our ships. So it is a case of necessity, you see. Your true way was to keep quiet, and not turn mutineer.

Hiram. What if you were seized by an American press-gang, and placed on board an American ship; and what if, in trying to escape, you should strike an officer, and be sentenced to death—would not those who took your life for the act be rightly called murderers?

Capt. M. Prisoner, I do not choose to argue with you. If you have fallen under our laws——

Hiram. *Fallen* under your laws? I was forced—forced from my own ship on the high seas. Your plea is the pirate's plea.

Capt. M. Prisoner, the subordinate who strikes me must die, either by my own hand or that of the law.

Hiram. I understand you now. You are more anxious to revenge your personal dignity than to punish a public wrong. But do not be too sure. There is many a slip between the cup and the lip. The diversion you have promised yourself for this afternoon will not come off.

Capt. M. If I live, you shall be strung up at the yard-arm this day!

Hiram. You think so; but you will be disappointed.

Capt. M. What is to prevent it, here on my own ship, with my own crew?

Hiram. As I left the deck just now, I saw a little sail-boat coming this way. Jotham was at the helm.

Capt. M. And who is Jotham?

Hiram. You know him; Captain Jotham Luff, of the American brig Nancy; *my* captain, from whom your press-gang forced me.

Capt. M. I told that impudent fellow not to come near me again. What will he do?

Hiram. I don't know. I only know he'll do something. He would never dare to go back to Marblehead and say that he had left me to be strung up at the yard-arm of a British frigate. The women would tar and feather him, and drag him in a cart, as they did old Floyd Ireson.

Capt. M. The execution shall take place at once.

Hiram. You are too late. I hear Captain Jotham's step on the deck. Here he comes.

[*Enter* CAPTAIN JOTHAM LUFF.]

Jotham. How are you, Captain? Middling, well, I hope. Well, Hiram, my boy, they have trussed you up like a turkey for the spit. [*Takes out jack-knife, cuts cords, and frees* HIRAM.] There, Captain, it looked so uncomfortable, I couldn't help it.

Capt. M. [*shaking his fist*]. You impudent Yankee! I'll have you keel-hauled, you——

Jotham. Come, now, don't blaze away in that style! Where's the harm? You aren't afraid, are you, of Hiram and me?

Capt. M. What's the object of this visit?

Jotham. To take Hiram back with me.

Capt. M. I told you, yesterday, that no power on earth could save him from being hung. So leave this ship, or I will call those who will put you into your boat by force.

Jotham. I reckon you'll do no such thing. I reckon you'll hear what I have to say, and then do what I tell you to. Sit down, and make yourself at home. [*Sits.*] Sit down, Hiram. [*Hiram sits.*]

Capt. M. [*standing*]. Well, there's no impudence like that of a Yankee.

Jotham [*whittling the stick that* HIRAM *was pinioned by*]. You must know, Captain, that when I left you yesterday, I was almost as mad as you are now—pretty badly roiled up. When I got on board my brig, whom should I find there but two lords—Lord Pembroke and Lord Annesly—who had been out in a sail-boat, and had stopped to take a look at my vessel! Perhaps you know them.

Capt. M. Yes, one of them is my nephew.

Jotham. Well, it occurred to me at once that two lords were about a fair exchange for an American sailor; so I impressed them.

Capt. M. Impressed them! What do you mean?

Jotham [*rising*]. Don't you know what *impressment* is? When you force a man into your service against his will, that's impressment. Do you think we Americans are going to stand that? Never! War, first, to the hilt. We are ready for you; the whole country is eager to wipe out the disgrace; and war will come. Let it come.

Capt. M. What have you done to their lordships?

Jotham. Treated them precisely as you have been treating Hiram here.

Capt. M. Rascal! Scoundrel!

Jotham. Keep cool! It's a fact. I put a stick through their elbows, and trussed them up just as you had Hiram; kept them on bread and water; and this afternoon, if I don't prevent it, they will both be hung at the yard-arm of the Nancy.

Capt. M. Hung! Your proof of this?

Jotham [*producing a letter*]. There's the proof, in a letter from their lordships. Read it. You know the handwriting?

Capt. M. [*reading aloud*]. "The Yankee will do what he threatens. Be sure of that. His vessel is a fast sailer, and can not be overtaken. Grant all he asks, if you would save our lives. Yours, Annesley, Pembroke." Villain! Do you mean to say you would hang two noblemen within sight of the English coast?

Jotham. I *do* mean to say just that. Touch a hair of that lad's head, and before sundown they shall die like dogs.

Capt. M. What if I seize your person as a security for their lives? You didn't think of that—eh?

Jotham. O! but I did! That was my risk. I left their lordships in the hands of my mate, Persevere Peabody, who has orders to hang them, in case I don't send him a signal from your vessel before five o'clock not to do it. [*Shows his watch.*] It's after four, already, Captain.

Capt. M. Your mate will not dare to touch a hair of their heads!

Jotham. O! you don't know Persevere Peabody. Says he, as I was leaving: "Captain Jotham," says he, "I never hung a lord in all my life; but never fear; I'll do it in a style that shall be an eternal credit to the American eagle." And, will you believe it?—the rogue, when he thought I wasn't looking, put the clock half an hour ahead, that he might have an excuse for finishing the job the sooner. The critter set the steward to work on some old black silk neckerchiefs. Says I, "What's all this for, Persevere?" Says he, "Their lordships will need black caps to be hung in. I mean to do everything regular, Captain." Oh, he is a terrible fellow, is Persevere Peabody.

Capt. M. [*alarmed*]. Did you say he put the clock half an hour ahead? Then he may be about it now.

Jotham. That's a fact.

Capt. M. What's your signal for stopping this barbarity?

Jotham. That's my secret. I'm not such a simpleton as to tell you that before I have made all right.

Capt. M. Name your terms quickly.

Jotham. First, Hiram's release, and a safe return for him and me to our vessel.

Capt. M. Never! I'll never consent.

Jotham. Yes, you will. Second, ten guineas to Hiram, by way of damages.

Capt. M. I'll sink my ship first!

Jotham. No, you'll not. Third, and last, a hundred

guineas for me, for losses by detention of my brig in waiting for Hiram.

Capt. M. Do your worst! I'll never agree to such terms.

Jotham. Yes, you will.

Capt. M. Not till I am struck idiotic.

Jotham. Yes, you will.

Hiram. Never mind the ten guineas, Captain Jotham.

Jotham. Hold your tongue, Hiram; I'll not bate a farthing.

[*Re-enter* LIEUT. PERLEY.]

Lieut. P. The Yankee ship in the offing, sir, is firing minute-guns.

Jotham. All right.

Capt. M. What does it mean?

Jotham. It means that Captain Persevere Peabody is making all ready to hang the two lords we impressed yesterday.

Capt. M. Stop him at once, or I'll have you put to the torture.

Jotham. You have my terms, Captain. I can't budge, let the British lion roar ever so loud.

Capt. M. What shall I do, Perley?

Lieut. P. The Yankee has proved too clever for us. My advice to you is to knock under at once.

Capt. M. Confound the extortionate, tobacco-chewing, psalm-singing trickster!

Lieut. P. Should any harm come to their lordships, you will be severely censured.

Capt. M. Too true. [*To Jotham.*] Look you, sir, 1 accept your terms.

Jotham. A safe return for Hiram and me; ten guineas for Hiram; a hundred guineas for me.

Capt. M. Yes, yes, yes.

Jotham. You hear, Lieutenant?

Capt. M. The pledge is given. There is no escape from it. The word of a British officer is as good as his bond.

Jotham. Then take the American flag out of my boat and run it up to your fore peak. Persevere Peabody will be disappointed, but he'll not dare to disobey.

Lieut. P. I'll have it done. [*Exit.*]

Jotham. Now, Captain, you'll sleep better, and feel better all the rest of your life, to think you've been saved from putting a fellow-creature to death. What would have been your reflections——

Capt. M. Stop your palaver, and come and get your money. [*Exit.*]

Jotham. Well, Hiram, it will not turn out a bad speculation, after all.

Hiram. Better than my last whaling voyage, Captain.

Jotham. Hurrah for our side! Hurrah for free trade and sailors' rights!

Hiram. Just my sentiments, Captain. Hurrah!

Ex. CCXIV.—*DIALOGUE—JOHN BULL AND SON.*

WILLIAM BENTLEY FOWLE.

Characters—JOHN BULL AND JONATHAN.

John [*seated*]. Jonathan!

Jonathan. What do you want, sir?

John. Come here, sirrah. Is it true, as they tell me, that you have set up for yourself over the water?

Jona. I'll take my oath on't, father.

John. What do you mean by doing so, you young rogue?

Jona. I mean to be free, sir.

John. Free, you young rogue, were you not free enough before.

Jona. Not quite, sir. I wanted an almighty swing, and your lot was too small.

John. Too small, you villain! It commands the world.

Jona. I could put it into one of my ponds without obstructing navigation. We do things on a large scale there, sir.

John. Was there ever such impudence? What do you do, fellow, that we do not?

Jona. We hatch cities, father, as fast as you do broods of chickens, and every year we set off two or three kingdoms, or States, as we call them.

John. What do you make them of?

Jona. Out of strips of my garden, sir.

John. Why, how big is your garden?

Jona. It reaches from sunrise to sundown one way, and from one end to t'other end the other way.

John. Do you pretend to say your garden is large enough to allow of your cutting kingdoms out of it?

Jona. To be sure I do. I have set off thirty-odd kingdoms, some of them ten times as big as your old homestead, and have staked out a dozen more; and, having more land still than I know what to do with, I have concluded to invite all creation to come over and take a lot " free-gratis-for-nothing," just to get it off my hands.

John. The deuce is in you. Why, Jonathan, my folks are all running away from me. Three or four millions of Irish bog-trotters decamped all at once, and the Lord knows where they are gone.

Jona. So do I, father. They have all squatted on one of my potato-patches.

John. You ungrateful dog, what do you mean by stealing my hands?

Jona. They said you couldn't support them, sir, and I thought it my duty to help the old man, as they call you.

John. Well, Jonathan, what are you going to do with yourself when you grow up?

Jona. Good gracious, father, what do you mean by growing up? I could whip two of you, now.

John. You lie, you rascal!

Jona. I never mean to try, father, but in answer to your question, what I mean to do, I say, I mean to govern all creation, one of these days.

John. What do you mean? Do you expect to lord it over me?

Jona. I guess you'll be glad, one of these days, to have me give you a lift.

John. What language do your boys talk, Jonathan?

Jona. English, sir, better than you speak it here. One of them has just made a dictionary for you, in order to keep you right.

John. The young scape-grace! Well, Jonty, how do your boys, on the whole, feel towards the old homestead?

Jona. They are proud of it, sir, and will never see the old man want, or the farm pass into the hands of strangers.

John. Give me your hand, Jonty. They told me you were a great lubber that didn't care for me.

Jona. They lied, father, and if you will tell me who said so, I will make him eat his words without picking out the bones.

John. Come, come, you young rogue, you almost beat

your old father at boasting, but I guess you'll turn out a clever boy, after all, and, one of these days, when my gout is easy, I may walk over and make you a call.

Jona. Do, sir. You shall never miss a welcome from Jonathan, while there is any roast beef or plum pudding to be had this side of t'other end of any distance. [*Jonathan goes out.*]

John. He's my boy, after all. Old John Bull will never die while Jonathan lives.

———◆———

Ex. CCXV.—*DIALOGUE BETWEEN MR. DOLE, INDIAN COMMISSIONER, AND OPOTHLEYOHOLO AND LAGARASH, INDIAN CHIEFS*—1862.

REBELLION RECORD.

Indian Chief. We are glad to see you. We want help. Our people have been driven from home, and are suffering.

Mr. Dole. The Government did not expect the Indians to enter this contest at all. Now that the rebel portion of them have entered the field, the Great Father will march his troops into your country. The country appreciates your services. We honor you. You are in our hearts. One party tells us that John Ross is for the Union, and one that he is not.

Chief. Both are probably right. Ross made a sham treaty with Albert Pike, to save trouble. Ross is like a man lying on his face, watching an opportunity to turn over. When the Northern troops come within the ring, he will turn over.

Mr. Dole. You did not, and our people remember you. But we hope you will show no revenge.

Chief. The rebel Indians are like a cross, bad dog. The best way to end the breed is to kill the dog.

Mr. Dole. Only the leaders and plotters of treason should suffer.

Chief. That's just what I think. Burn over a bad field of grass, and it will spring up again. It must be torn up by the roots, even if some good blades suffer. I hope the government money will be paid us.

Mr. Dole. We can not pay you until we know who among you are Union and who are rebel.

Chief. Those left back there are not loyal. They turned against the Government with their eyes open. If we gain our land we should have it and they nothing. We have talked it over among ourselves, and concluded not to do any thing for them.

Mr. Dole. We can not pay you until your chiefs are together, and a council held.

Chief. All those left back there are Secesh.

Mr. Dole. I have not power to use the money except in a legal and regular way. We will take care of you, and the delay in paying you will be as brief as possible.

Chief. The Creeks have one thousand five hundred warriors who want to fight for the Union. The Seminoles have two hundred and fifty, and they will all fight for the Great Father.

Mr. Dole. The Great Father has decided to accept your services to put down this rebellion, in case it is your pleasure to give them. You will not be expected to fight white men unless they are arrayed against loyal Indians. We should not have called upon you at all had not your own brothers been driven from their homes. You go to their assistance, not ours.

Chief. We came down from our nation to find out how it was, and we want to hear *the straight*. I depend on my nation; I sit with my ears open to hear what they will do.

Mr. Dole. Unless the chiefs speak out, the warriors will refuse to do so. Will you yourselves urge your people to act?

Chief. We want to know how long the war is to be, and in what way we are to fight.

Mr. Dole. Not more than twelve months. As to the manner of fighting—you can all draw a bead at two hundred yards. *Your* way of fighting will answer our purpose.

Chief. We want to go down there on horseback.

Mr. Dole. We are going to send twenty thousand white men, on foot.

Chief. Yes, that's the way white men fight. Indians don't. When we fight, we don't fight all the time. We don't want to fight so long. I think we can end the war in one battle.

Mr. Dole. That will suit us. You are a large, noble and brave set of men. Let me hear you say that you will be brave warriors, whether others are or not.

Chief. I told you that whatever my Father wanted me to do, I would do.

Mr. Dole. When you go home, tell your warriors to get ready, and prepare to be as brave as in former times. Tell them that your brother red men have been driven from their homes, and they need your assistance. If only white men were at war, we should not call upon you.

Ex. CCXVI.—*INDIAN NAMES.*

LYDIA HUNTLEY SIGOURNEY.

Ye say they all have passed away,
  That noble race and brave,
That their light canoes have vanished
  From off the crested wave;
That 'mid the forest where they roamed
  There rings no hunter's shout:
But their name is on your waters—
  Ye may not wash it out.

'Tis where Ontario's billow
  Like Ocean's surge is curled,
Where strong Niagara's thunders wake
  The echo of the world,—
Where red Missouri bringeth
  Rich tribute from the west,
And Rappahannock sweetly sleeps
  On green Virginia's breast.

Ye say their cone-like cabins,
  That clustered o'er the vale,
Have fled away like withered leaves
  Before the autumn gale;
But their memory liveth on your hills,
  Their baptism on your shore;
Your everlasting rivers speak
  Their dialect of yore.

Old Massachusetts wears it
  Within her lordly crown,

And broad Ohio bears it
　Within her young renown;
Connecticut hath wreathed it
　Where her quiet foliage waves,
And old Kentucky breathed it hoarse
　Through all her ancient caves.

Wachusett hides its lingering voice
　Within his rocky heart,
And Alleghany graves its tone
　Throughout his lofty chart;
Monadnock on his forehead hoar
　Doth seal the sacred trust:
Your mountains build their monument,
　Though ye destroy their dust.

Ye call these red-browed brethren
　The insects of an hour,
Crushed like the noteless worm amid
　The regions of their power:
Ye drive them from their fathers' lands,
　Ye break of faith the seal:
But can ye from the court of Heaven
　Exclude their last appeal.

Ye see their unresisting tribes,
　With toilsome step and slow,
On through the trackless desert pass,
　A caravan of woe.
Think ye the Eternal ear is deaf?
　His sleepless vision dim?
Think ye the *soul's* blood may not cry
　From that far land to Him?

www.ingramcontent.com/pod-product-compliance
Lightning Source LLC
Chambersburg PA
CBHW030319240426
43673CB00040B/1215